Under the
Influence

UNDER THE INFLUENCE

THE LITERATURE OF ADDICTION

Edited by Rebecca Shannonhouse

Foreword by Pete Hamill

THE MODERN LIBRARY

NEW YORK

2003 Modern Library Paperback Edition

Compilation copyright © 2003 by Random House, Inc.
Introduction and selection introductions copyright © 2003 by Rebecca Shannonhouse
Foreword copyright © 2003 by Diedre Enterprises, Inc.

Owing to limitations of space, permission acknowledgments can be found
on pages 304–305.

LIBRARY OF CONGRESS CATALOGING-IN-PUBLICATION DATA
Under the influence: the literature of addiction/edited by Rebecca Shannonhouse;
foreword by Pete Hamill.
p. cm.
ISBN 0-375-75716-3 (pbk.)
1. Drug abuse—Literary collections. 2. Drug abuse. I. Shannonhouse, Rebecca.

PN6071.D77 U53 2003
808.8'0355—dc21   2002026341

Modern Library website address: www.modernlibrary.com

Printed in the United States of America

2   4   6   8   9   7   5   3   1

THE VIOLETS IN THE MOUNTAINS
HAVE BROKEN THE ROCKS.

– TENNESSEE WILLIAMS

INTRODUCTION

Rebecca Shannonhouse

Why do some people become addicts? Whether it's drinking, drugging, or a more contemporary diagnosis of excess like gambling or overeating, there is no simple answer. Ask a psychiatrist and you are apt to hear that addiction is a futile attempt to outrun the crushing influence of a painful, conflicted childhood. A geneticist will tell you that a biological predisposition drives a person to overindulge in agents of self-destruction. A member of the clergy may call addiction a misguided attempt to fill a gaping spiritual void.

Over a century ago the Russian novelist Leo Tolstoy examined the primary addictions of his time—drinking and smoking. In a little-known essay he suggested that these bad habits were nothing more than urgent though well-concealed attempts to "stifle the conscience." Those who become enslaved, Tolstoy wrote, lack "moral enlightenment."

Today our notion of addiction is far more forgiving. What once was viewed as a shocking moral deficiency is now increasingly seen as a tragic vulnerability. We see the courage it takes for a politician's wife to disclose her addiction to alcohol. We rally behind an actor who enters rehab to overcome his incessant urges to down pills that snuff out the ache of loneliness. We empathize with the housewife who cannot stop bingeing on Mallomars or frosty pints of Häagen-Dazs.

Now more than ever there is also an attempt to conquer the unwieldy animal we call addiction. Statisticians crunch numbers to compute the enormous financial toll of addiction. Neuroscientists use sophisticated scans to peer inside the brains of crack addicts, looking for the neurobiological link that feeds their craving for the drug. Pharmaceutical companies scramble to introduce a pill to quell the irresistible urge to drink. But the underlying question still remains: Why does one become an addict? And what does it take to derail such ravenous desires?

Literature is perhaps the most compelling way to broach these unanswered questions. More than any clinical or scientific treatise, good writing gives shape and meaning to the raw experience of addiction. Through a vast array of short stories, novels, memoirs, and essays, we have the privilege of stepping inside the perilous lives of men and women who seek solace in a substance or excessive behavior. Through these works we can begin to understand the addict's unending chase to recapture those fleeting moments of ecstasy.

In this book I have compiled what I consider to be the most important works on addiction. Most of the selections are written by great historical and contemporary authors who have weighed in on the inescapable allure of addictive behavior. Other works included in this collection are by anonymous writers and "unknowns" who beautifully capture untold stories from the front lines. The selections are, by turns, intriguing, surprising, heartbreaking, tragic, and, ultimately, the most *truthful* portrait of the life experience known as addiction.

Beginning with the first selection of this book, Thomas De Quincey's *Confessions of an English Opium-Eater,* we see that addiction can quietly edge its way into one's life. In perhaps the most famous addiction tale ever written, De Quincey divulges that his fierce drug habit arose during his college years when a friend casually suggested that he try opium to blunt his rheumatic head and face pain. Similarly, in Dorothy Parker's classic, exquisitely written short story "Big Blonde," addiction emerges as a by-product of despair. Describing how Hazel Morse's drinking unfolded, Parker writes: "She had never needed to drink, formerly. She could sit for most of a night at a table where the others were imbibing earnestly and never droop in looks or spirits. . . . But now anguish was in her. . . . Her heart felt tight and sore in her breast, and her mind turned like an electric fan."

Americans received one of their first tastes of confessional literature in Jack London's first-person drunkologue, *John Barleycorn.* In this famous autobiographical epic, London discloses that addiction can strike at almost any time in life. For him, it began at age five—the first time he got drunk. As he progressed through boyhood and into adulthood, the habit shadowed him, ultimately defining him as a man. It was this very type of preordained alcoholism that Dr. William Lee Howard warns mothers against in a 1907 essay tucked away in the pages of *Ladies' Home Journal.* After treating a young man who died from alcoholism, Dr. Howard concludes that the victim's own mother had set him on his destructive path by introducing him to drug-laced "soothing syrups" while he was still just an infant.

The American journalist Virgil G. Eaton casts a wider net of complicity in his 1888 essay "How the Opium Habit Is Acquired." In this work—a riveting example of nineteenth-century investigative journalism—Eaton presciently labels tobacco a narcotic. In muckraking for the forces behind opium addiction, Eaton points the finger at physicians who casually prescribed the drug to treat everything from headache and "sore eyes" to laryngitis and gastritis. Similarly, it is a physician who repeatedly administers shots of morphine to a housewife suffering from intractable loneliness in Margarita Spalding Gerry's stirring 1909 short story "The Enemy." For a more charitable view of a doctor's influence on an addict, O. Henry's short story "Let Me Feel Your Pulse" is included.

To demonstrate how attitudes toward drug use have evolved over the years, I have also included works that herald drugs as great cures for various forms of sickness. Among the most influential—if not vocal—proponents for cocaine use was Sigmund Freud. After experimenting with the drug himself, he proclaims in *The Cocaine Papers* that cocaine is an effective treatment for numerous conditions, including alcohol and morphine addiction and even stomach disorders. In a striking display of miscalculation, Dr. Freud fails to foresee the addictive qualities of cocaine itself: "The treatment of morphine addiction with coca does not, therefore, result merely in the exchange of one kind of addiction for another—it does not turn the morphine addict into a *coquero;* the use of coca is only temporary." In *The Doors of Perception,* another classic tale of drug experimentation, Aldous

Huxley similarly contends that mescaline has little effect on one's intellect.

To view addiction from yet another angle, I've also turned to a cast of characters who witness, rather than experience, the devastating effects of untamed compulsions. Perhaps the most knowledgeable of these observers is the bartender. A 1919 essay published here includes an anonymous New York bartender's insights about alcohol's effect on the drinker's personality. "There is one reason, and only one, why men drank," he writes. "Don't fool yourself that men drank wine because of the bouquet; that men drank beer for its color or creaminess. . . . Men drank for the alcohol in the drink and for no other reason." In John Cheever's searing short story "The Sorrows of Gin," the blight of alcoholism is seen through the eyes of a besotted suburbanite's young daughter. In Donna Steiner's breathtaking essay "Sleeping with Alcohol," the author recounts the challenge of coping with a lover who devotes more energy to her alcohol habit than her relationship.

Although the literature of addiction has historically focused on alcohol and drugs, a more contemporary view maintains that there need not be a substance for lives to be turned upside down by onerous compulsions. There are fewer writings on addiction to sex, shopping, overeating—even Web surfing. But some notable selections do exist. Originally published in *The New Yorker,* Abraham Verghese's heart-wrenching essay "The Pathology of Sex" tells of a medical student's insatiable appetite for loveless sexual encounters. In *Double Down,* Frederick and Steven Barthelme's soul-searching memoir of their gambling escapades, we see how addicts can conveniently rationalize the dangers they are courting. "One of the virtues of having gambling as your vice—as opposed to sex, drugs, or alcohol—was that the disadvantages were felt only at the bank."

Sadly, we also see that not even genuine self-knowledge can stop addiction or its disastrous consequences. At first glance, "Confessions of a Middle-Aged Ecstasy Eater" portrays drug-taking as a response to painful losses and missteps within one's most intimate relationships. But like all good addicts, this anonymous middle-aged ecstasy eater seals his self-loathing with an action that not even he can rationalize away. In Edgar Allan Poe's masterful short story "The Black Cat" the narrator also possesses a remarkably clear understanding of alcohol's influence on his life. Still, this insight does not stop him from committing acts of unspeakable depravity.

Not surprisingly, shame and remorse are the addict's constant companions. This fact is apparent in Sue William Silverman's memoir *Love Sick*. The day before she checks into a twenty-eight-day rehab for sex addiction, Silverman has sex with a married man at a nearby motel. That same evening she tries to pretend that her life is normal as she eats dinner with her husband. "I can't tell Andrew," Silverman writes. "For I believe if he sees the real me, he'll leave me. . . . Ordinary married life is too tame and mild. I want to hold on to him, but Andrew, as well as our ten-year marriage, only skims the periphery of my senses." In a 1921 essay titled "On Giving Up Smoking" even a longtime smoker who tries to put down tobacco suffers from a whirlwind of rationalizations when he cannot control his compulsion.

Unchecked, addiction becomes a way of life, as we see in William S. Burroughs's *Naked Lunch* and Linda Yablonsky's *The Story of Junk*. In excerpts from both of these novels, we encounter the harsh realities of a seasoned junkie's day-to-day life. In Terry Southern's short story "The Blood of a Wig," we see a drug addict's willingness to test the edges of his high.

Of course, some addicts grow weary of their dizzying lives and seek help for their lethal habits. Kate Braverman's short story "They Take a Photograph of You When You First Get Here" meticulously depicts the muddled, sometimes violent thinking of a drug addict in rehab. Margaret Bullitt-Jonas's elegant memoir, *Holy Hunger*, recounts how recovery from food addiction occurs within the safe haven of Overeaters Anonymous.

No anthology is ever complete. This book is intended to provide a broad representation of the historical and contemporary writings that comprise the literature of addiction. Although these nonfictional and fictional accounts vividly portray the human side of addiction, it is a story that continues to unfold. Each day, a curious teenager will smoke crack for the first time. A burnt-out teacher will eat herself into oblivion. A forgotten grandmother will look forward to little else than her afternoon martinis. For those who have sought escape through drinking or drugging, overeating or sleeping with strangers, this book authenticates the trajectory of their self-annihilation. The writings also speak to those who have witnessed a loved one's descent into addiction. Though these experiences may be painful to revisit, they are worth remembering—and retelling. Only then will all the victims of addiction be given the chance to see that they are not alone. And, even more important, that there is a way out.

UNDER THE
INFLUENCE

FROM

CONFESSIONS OF AN ENGLISH OPIUM-EATER

Thomas De Quincey

1821

At the age of nineteen, the English author Thomas De Quincey tried opium for the first time. Writing in frank, unsentimental language, he recorded his experiences with the drug in London Magazine. *Though his chronicle of opium use eventually secured his career as a respected writer, De Quincey continued to suffer long periods of loneliness and depression.* Confessions of an English Opium-Eater *details both the pleasures and the pain of one man's formidable drug habit.*

It is so long since I first took opium, that if it had been a trifling incident in my life, I might have forgotten its date: but cardinal events are not to be forgotten; and from circumstances connected with it, I remember that it must be referred to the autumn of 1804. During that season I was in London, having come thither for the first time since my entrance at college. And my introduction to opium arose in the following way. From an early age I had been accustomed to wash my head in cold water at least once a day: being suddenly seized with toothache, I attributed it to some relaxation caused by an accidental intermission of that practice, jumped out of bed, plunged my head into a basin of cold water, and with hair thus wetted went to sleep. The next morning, as I need hardly say, I awoke with excruciating rheumatic pains of the head and face, from which I had hardly any respite for about twenty days. On the twenty-first day, I think it was, and on a Sunday, that I went out into the streets; rather to run away, if possible, from my torments, than with any distinct purpose. By accident I met a college acquaintance who recommended opium. Opium! dread agent of unimaginable pleasure and pain! I had heard of it as I had of manna or of ambrosia, but no further: how unmeaning a sound was it at that time! what solemn chords does it now strike upon my heart! what heart-quaking vibrations of sad and happy remembrances! Reverting for a moment to these, I feel a mystic importance attached to the minutest circumstances connected with the place and the time, and the man (if man he was) that first laid open to me the Paradise of Opium-eaters. It was a Sunday afternoon, wet and cheerless: and a duller spectacle this earth of ours has not to show than a rainy Sunday in London. My road homewards lay through Oxford-street; and near "the *stately* Pantheon" (as Mr. Wordsworth has obligingly called it), I saw a druggist's shop. The druggist, unconscious minister of celestial pleasures!— as if in sympathy with the rainy Sunday, looked dull and stupid, just as any mortal druggist might be expected to look on a Sunday: and, when I asked for the tincture of opium, he gave it to me as any other man might do: and furthermore, out of my shilling, returned me what seemed to be real copper halfpence, taken out of a real wooden drawer. Nevertheless, in spite of such indications of humanity, he has ever since existed in my mind as the beatific vision of an immortal druggist, sent down to earth on a special mission to myself. And it confirms me in this way of considering him, that, when I next came up to London, I sought him near the stately Pantheon, and found him not: and thus to me, who knew not his name (if indeed he had one) he seemed rather to have vanished from Oxford-street than to have removed in any bodily fashion. The reader may choose to think of him as, possibly, no more than a sublunary druggist: it may be so: but my faith is better: I believe him to have evanesced, or evaporated. So unwillingly would I connect any mortal remembrances with that hour, and place, and creature, that first brought me acquainted with the celestial drug.

Arrived at my lodgings, it may be supposed that I lost not a moment in taking the quantity prescribed. I was necessarily ignorant of the whole art and mystery of opium-taking: and, what I took, I took under every disadvantage. But I took it:—and in an hour, oh! heavens! what a revulsion! what an upheaving, from its lowest depths, of the inner spirit! what an apocalypse of the world within me! That my pains had vanished, was now a trifle in my eyes:—this negative effect was swallowed up in the immensity of those positive effects which had opened before me—in the abyss of divine enjoyment thus suddenly revealed. Here was a panacea . . . for all human woes: here was the secret of happiness, about which philosophers had disputed for so many ages, at once discovered: happiness might now be bought for a penny, and carried in the waistcoat pocket: portable ecstasies might be had corked up in a pint bottle: and peace of mind could be sent down in gallons by the mail coach. But, if I talk in this way, the reader will think I am laughing: and I can assure him, that nobody will laugh long who deals much with opium: its pleasures even are of a grave and solemn complexion; and in his happiest state, the opium-eater cannot present himself in the character of *l'Allegro:* even then, he speaks and thinks as becomes *Il Penseroso.* Nevertheless, I have a very reprehensible way of jesting at times in the midst of my own misery: and, unless when I am checked by some more powerful feelings, I am afraid I shall be guilty of this indecent practice even in these annals of suffering or enjoyment. The reader must allow a little to my infirm nature in this respect: and with a few indulgences of that sort, I shall endeavour to be as grave, if not drowsy, as fits a theme like opium, so antimercurial as it really is, and so drowsy as it is falsely reputed.

And, first, one word with respect to its bodily effects: for upon all that has been hitherto written on the subject of opium, whether by travellers in Turkey (who may plead their privilege of lying as an old immemorial right), or by professors of medicine, writing *ex cathedrá,*— I have but one emphatic criticism to pronounce—Lies! lies! lies! I remember once, in passing a bookstall, to have caught these words from a page of some satiric author:—"By this time I became convinced that the London newspapers spoke truth at least twice a week, viz., on Tuesday and Saturday, and might safely be depended upon for—— the list of bankrupts." In like manner, I do by no means deny that some truths have been delivered to the world in regard to opium: thus it has been repeatedly affirmed by the learned, that opium is a dusky brown in colour; and this, take notice, I grant: secondly, that it is rather dear; which also I grant: for in my time, East-India opium has been three guineas a pound, and Turkey eight: and, thirdly, that if you eat a good deal of it, most probably you must—do what is particularly disagreeable to any man of regular habits, viz. die.[1] These weighty propositions are, all and singular, true: I cannot gainsay them: and truth ever was, and will be, commendable. But in these three theorems, I believe we have exhausted the stock of knowledge as yet accumulated by man on the subject of opium. And therefore, worthy doctors, as there seems to be room for further discoveries, stand aside, and allow me to come forward and lecture on this matter.

First, then, it is not so much affirmed as taken for granted, by all who ever mention opium, formally or incidentally, that it does, or can produce intoxication. Now, reader, assure yourself, *meo periculo,* that no quantity of opium ever did, or could intoxicate. As to the tincture of opium (commonly called laudanum) *that* might certainly intoxicate if a man could bear to take enough of it; but why? because it contains so much proof spirit, and not because it contains so much opium. But crude opium, I affirm peremptorily, is incapable of producing any state of body at all resembling that which is produced by alcohol: and not in *degree* only incapable, but even in *kind:* it is not in the quantity of its effects merely, but in the quality, that it differs altogether. The pleasure given by wine is always mounting, and tending to a crisis, after which it declines: that from opium, when once generated, is stationary for eight or ten hours: the first, to borrow a technical distinction from medicine, is a case of acute—the second, of chronic pleasure: the one is a flame, the other a steady and equable glow. But the main distinction lies in this, that whereas wine disorders the mental faculties, opium, on the contrary (if taken in a proper manner), introduces amongst them the most exquisite order, legislation, and harmony. Wine robs a man of his self-possession: opium greatly invigorates it. Wine unsettles and clouds the judgment, and gives a preternatural brightness, and a vivid exaltation to the contempts and the admirations, the loves and the hatreds, of the drinker: opium, on the contrary, communicates serenity and equipoise to all the faculties, active or passive: and with respect to the temper and moral feelings in general,

1. Of this, however, the learned appear latterly to have doubted: for in a pirated edition of Buchan's *Domestic Medicine,* which I once saw in the hands of a farmer's wife who was studying it for the benefit of her health, the doctor was made to say—"Be particularly careful never to take above five-and-twenty *ounces* of laudanum at once"; the true reading being probably five-and-twenty *drops,* which are held equal to about one grain of crude opium.

it gives simply that sort of vital warmth which is approved by the judgment, and which would probably always accompany a bodily constitution of primeval or antediluvian health. Thus, for instance, opium, like
wine, gives an expansion to the heart and the benevolent affections:
but then, with this remarkable difference, that in the sudden development of kindheartedness which accompanies inebriation, there is
always more or less of a maudlin character, which exposes it to the
contempt of the bystander. Men shake hands, swear eternal friendship,
and shed tears—no mortal knows why: and the sensual creature is
clearly uppermost. But the expansion of the beniger feelings, incident to opium, is no febrile access, but a healthy restoration to that
state which the mind would naturally recover upon the removal of any
deep-seated irritation of pain that had disturbed and quarrelled with
the impulses of a heart originally just and good. True it is, that even
wine, up to a certain point, and with certain men, rather tends to exalt
and to steady the intellect: I myself, who have never been a great wine-
drinker, used to find that half a dozen glasses of wine advantageously
affected the faculties—brightened and intensified the consciousness—
and gave to the mind a feeling of being "ponderibus librata suis": and
certainly it is most absurdly said, in popular language, of any man, that
he is *disguised* in liquor: for, on the contrary, most men are disguised by
sobriety; and it is when they are drinking (as some old gentleman says
in Athenæus), that men ἑαντοὺς ἐμφανίζουιν οἵτινες εἰσίν—display
themselves in their true complexion of character; which surely is not
disguising themselves. But still, wine constantly leads a man to the brink
of absurdity and extravagance; and, beyond a certain point, it is sure to
volatilize and to disperse the intellectual energies: whereas opium always seems to compose what had been agitated, and to concentrate
what had been distracted. In short, to sum up all in one word, a man
who is inebriated, or tending to inebriation, is, and feels that he is, in a
condition which calls up into supremacy the merely human, too often
the brutal, part of his nature: but the opium-eater (I speak of him who
is not suffering from any disease, or other remote effects of opium)
feels that the diviner part of his nature is paramount; that is, the moral
affections are in a state of cloudless serenity; and over all is the great
light of the majestic intellect.

This is the doctrine of the true church on the subject of opium: of
which church I acknowledge myself to be the only member—the alpha

and the omega: but then it is to be recollected, that I speak from the ground of a large and profound personal experience: whereas most of the unscientific authors who have at all treated of opium, and even of those who have written expressly on the materia medica, make it evident, from the horror they express of it, that their experimental knowledge of its action is none at all. I will, however, candidly acknowledge that I have met with one person who bore evidence to its intoxicating power, such as staggered my own incredulity: for he was a surgeon, and had himself taken opium largely. I happened to say to him, that his enemies (as I had heard) charged him with talking nonsense on politics, and that his friends apologized for him, by suggesting that he was constantly in a state of intoxication from opium. Now the accusation, said I, is not *primâ facie,* and of necessity, an absurd one: but the defence *is.* To my surprise, however, he insisted that both his enemies and his friends were in the right: "I will maintain," said he, "that I *do* talk nonsense; and, secondly, I will maintain that I do not talk nonsense upon principle, or with any view to profit, but solely and simply, said he, solely and simply,—solely and simply (repeating it three times over), because I am drunk with opium; and *that* daily." I replied that, as to the allegation of his enemies, as it seemed to be established upon such respectable testimony, seeing that the three parties concerned all agreed in it, it did not become me to question it; but the defence set up I must demur to. He proceeded to discuss the matter, and to lay down his reasons; but it seemed to me so impolite to pursue an argument which must have presumed a man mistaken in a point belonging to his own profession, that I did not press him even when his course of argument seemed open to objection: not to mention that a man who talks nonsense, even though "with no view to profit," is not altogether the most agreeable partner in a dispute, whether as opponent or respondent. I confess, however, that the authority of a surgeon, and one who was reputed a good one, may seem a weighty one to my prejudice: but still I must plead my experience, which was greater than his greatest by 7000 drops a day; and, though it was not possible to suppose a medical man unacquainted with the characteristic symptoms of vinous intoxication, it yet struck me that he might proceed on a logical error of using the word intoxication with too great latitude, and extending it generically to all modes of nervous excitement, instead of restricting it as the expression for a specific sort of excitement, connected with certain diagnostics. Some people have maintained, in my hearing, that they had been drunk upon green tea: and a medical student in London, for whose knowledge in his profession I have reason to feel great respect, assured me, the other day, that a patient, in recovering from an illness, had got drunk on a beef-steak.

Having dwelt so much on this first and leading error, in respect to opium, I shall notice very briefly a second and a third; which are, that the elevation of spirits produced by opium is necessarily followed by a proportionate depression, and that the natural and even immediate consequence of opium is torpor and stagnation, animal and mental. The first of these errors I shall content myself with simply denying; assuring my reader, that for ten years, during which I took opium at intervals, the day succeeding to that on which I allowed myself this luxury was always a day of unusually good spirits.

With respect to the torpor supposed to follow, or rather (if we were to credit the numerous pictures of Turkish opium-eaters) to accompany the practice of opium-eating, I deny that also. Certainly, opium is classed under the head of narcotics; and some such effect it may produce in the end: but the primary effects of opium are always, and in the highest degree, to excite and stimulate the system: this first stage of its action always lasted with me, during my noviciate, for upwards of eight hours; so that it must be the fault of the opium-eater himself if he does not so time his exhibition of the dose (to speak medically) as that the whole weight of its narcotic influence may descend upon his sleep. Turkish opium-eaters, it seems, are absurd enough to sit, like so many equestrian statues, on logs of wood as stupid as themselves. But that the reader may judge of the degree in which opium is likely to stupify the faculties of an Englishman, I shall (by way of treating the question illustratively, rather than argumentatively) describe the way in which I myself often passed an opium evening in London, during the period between 1804 and 1812. It will be seen, that at least opium did not move me to seek solitude, and much less to seek inactivity, or the torpid state of self-involution ascribed to the Turks. I give this account at the risk of being pronounced a crazy enthusiast or visionary: but I regard *that* little: I must desire my reader to bear in mind, that I was a hard student, and at severe studies for all the rest of my time: and certainly I had a right occasionally to relaxations as well as other people: these, however, I allowed myself but seldom.

The late Duke of [Norfolk] used to say, "Next Friday, by the blessing of Heaven, I purpose to be drunk": and in like manner I used to fix beforehand how often, within a given time, and when, I would commit a debauch of opium. This was seldom more than once in three weeks: for at that time I could not have ventured to call every day (as I did afterwards) for "*a glass of laudanum negus, warm, and without sugar.*" No: as I have said, I seldom drank laudanum, at that time, more than once in three weeks: this was usually on a Tuesday or a Saturday night; my reason for which was this. In those days Grassini sang at the Opera: and her voice was delightful to me beyond all that I had ever heard. I know not what may be the state of the Opera-house now, having never been within its walls for seven or eight years, but at that time it was by much the most pleasant place of public resort in London for passing an evening. Five shillings admitted one to the gallery, which was subject to far less annoyance than the pit of the theatres: the orchestra was distinguished by its sweet and melodious grandeur from all English orchestras, the composition of which, I confess, is not acceptable to my ear, from the predominance of the clangorous instruments, and the absolute tyranny of the violin. The choruses were divine to hear: and when Grassini appeared in some interlude, as she often did, and poured forth her passionate soul as Andromache, at the tomb of Hector, &c. I question whether any Turk, of all that ever entered the paradise of opium-eaters, can have had half the pleasure I had. But, indeed, I honour the Barbarians too much by supposing them capable of any pleasures approaching to the intellectual ones of an Englishman. For music is an intellectual or a sensual pleasure, according to the temperament of him who hears it. And, by the by, with the exception of the fine extravaganza on that subject in Twelfth Night, I do not recollect more than one thing said adequately on the subject of music in all literature: it is a passage in the *Religio Medici* of Sir T. Brown; and, though chiefly remarkable for its sublimity, has also a philosophic value, inasmuch as it points to the true theory of musical effects. The mistake of most people is to suppose that it is by the ear, they communicate with music, and, therefore, that they are purely passive to its effects. But this is not so: it is by the reaction of the mind upon the notices of the ear (the *matter* coming by the senses, the *form* from the mind), that the pleasure is constructed: and therefore it is that people of equally good ear differ so much in this point from one another. Now opium, by greatly increasing the activity of the mind generally, increases, of necessity, that particular mode of its activity by which we are able to construct out of the raw material of organic sound an elaborate intellectual pleasure. But, says a friend, a succession of musical sounds is to me like a collection of Arabic characters: I can attach no ideas to them! Ideas! my good sir? there is no occasion for them: all that class of ideas, which can be available in such a case, has a language of representative feelings. But this is a subject foreign to my present purposes: it is sufficient to say, that a chorus, &c. of elaborate harmony, displayed before me, as in a piece of arras work, the whole of my past life—not as if recalled by an act of memory, but as if present and incarnated in the music: no longer painful to dwell upon: but the detail of its incidents removed, or blended in some hazy abstraction; and its passions exalted, spiritualized, and sublimed. All this was to be had for five shillings. And over and above the music of the stage and the orchestra, I had all around me, in the intervals of the performance, the music of the Italian language talked by Italian women: for the gallery was usually crowded with Italians: and I listened with a pleasure such as that with which Weld the traveller lay and listened, in Canada, to the sweet laughter of Indian women; for the less you understand of a language, the more sensible you are to the melody or harshness of its sounds: for such a purpose, therefore, it was an advantage to me that I was a poor Italian scholar, reading it but little, and not speaking it at all, nor understanding a tenth part of what I heard spoken.

These were my Opera pleasures: but another pleasure I had which, as it could be had only on a Saturday night, occasionally struggled with my love of the Opera; for, at that time, Tuesday and Saturday were the regular Opera nights. On this subject I am afraid I shall be rather obscure, but, I can assure the reader, not at all more so than Marinus in his life of Proclus, or many other biographers and autobiographers of fair reputation. This pleasure, I have said, was to be had only on a Saturday night. What then was Saturday night to me more than any other night? I had no labours that I rested from; no wages to receive: what needed I to care for Saturday night, more than as it was a summons to hear Grassini? True, most logical reader: what you say is unanswerable. And yet so it was and is, that, whereas different men throw their feelings into different channels, and most are apt to show their interest in the concerns of the poor, chiefly by sympathy, expressed in some shape or other, with their distresses and sorrows, I, at that time, was disposed to express my interest by sympathising with their pleasures. The pains of poverty I had lately seen too much of; more than I wished to remember: but the pleasures of the poor, their consolations of spirit, and their reposes from bodily toil, can never become oppressive to contemplate. Now Saturday night is the season for the chief, regular, and periodic return of rest to the poor: in this point the most hostile sects unite, and acknowledge a common link of brotherhood: almost all Christendom rests from its labours. It is a rest introductory to another rest: and divided by a whole day and two nights from the renewal of toil. On this account I feel always, on a Saturday night, as though I also were released from some yoke of labour, had some wages to receive, and some luxury of repose to enjoy. For the sake, therefore, of witnessing, upon as large a scale as possible, a spectacle with which my sympathy was so entire, I used often, on Saturday nights, after I had taken opium, to wander forth, without much regarding the direction or the distance, to all the markets, and other parts of London, to which the poor resort on a Saturday night, for laying out their wages. Many a family party, consisting of a man, his wife, and sometimes one or two of his children, have I listened to, as they stood consulting on their ways and means, or the strength of their exchequer, or the price of household articles. Gradually I became familiar with their wishes, their difficulties, and their opinions. Sometimes there might be heard murmurs of discontent: but far oftener expressions on the countenance, or uttered in words, of patience, hope, and tranquility. And, taken generally, I must say, that, in this point at least, the poor are far more philosophic than the rich—that they show a more ready and cheerful submission to what they consider as irremediable evils, or irreparable losses. Whenever I saw occasion, or could do it without appearing to be intrusive, I joined their parties; and gave my opinion upon the matter in discussion, which, if not always judicious, was always received indulgently. If wages were a little higher, or expected to be so, or the quartern loaf a little lower, or it was reported that onions and butter were expected to fall, I was glad: yet, if the contrary were true, I drew from opium some means of consoling myself. For opium (like the bee, that extracts its materials indiscriminately from roses and from the soot of chimneys) can overrule all feelings into a compliance with the master key. Some of these rambles led me to great distances: for an opium-eater is too happy to observe the motion of time. And

sometimes in my attempts to steer homewards, upon nautical principles, by fixing my eye on the pole-star, and seeking ambitiously for a
northwest passage, instead of circumnavigating all the capes and headlands I had doubled in my outward voyage, I came suddenly upon such
knotty problems of alleys, such enigmatical entries, and such sphinx's
riddles of streets without thoroughfares, as must, I conceive, baffle the
audacity of porters, and confound the intellects of hackney-coachmen.
I could almost have believed, at times, that I must be the first discoverer of some of these *terræ incognitæ*, and doubted, whether they had
yet been laid down in the modern charts of London. For all this,
however, I paid a heavy price in distant years, when the human face
tyrannized over my dreams, and the perplexities of my steps in London came back and haunted my sleep, with the feeling of perplexities
moral or intellectual, that brought confusion to the reason, or anguish
and remorse to the conscience.

Thus I have shown that opium does not, of necessity, produce inactivity or torpor; but that, on the contrary, it often led me into markets
and theatres. Yet, in candour, I will admit that markets and theatres are
not the appropriate haunts of the opium-eater, when in the divinest
state incident to his enjoyment. In that state, crowds become an oppression to him; music even, too sensual and gross. He naturally seeks
solitude and silence, as indispensable conditions of those trances, or
profoundest reveries, which are the crown and consummation of what
opium can do for human nature. I, whose disease it was to meditate too
much, and to observe too little, and who, upon my first entrance at college, was nearly falling into a deep melancholy, from brooding too
much on the sufferings which I had witnessed in London, was sufficiently aware of the tendencies of my own thoughts to do all I could to
counteract them.—I was, indeed, like a person who, according to the
old legend, had entered the cave of Trophonius; and the remedies I
sought were to force myself into society, and to keep my understanding in continual activity upon matters of science. But for these remedies, I should certainly have become hypochondriacally melancholy.
In after years, however, when my cheerfulness was more fully reestablished, I yielded to my natural inclination for a solitary life. And,
at that time, I often fell into these reveries upon taking opium; and
more than once it has happened to me, on a summer night, when I
have been at an open window, in a room from which I could overlook

the sea at a mile below me, and could command a view of the great town of L[iverpool], at about the same distance, that I have sat, from sun-set to sun-rise, motionless, and without wishing to move.

I shall be charged with mysticism, Behmenism, quietism, &c. but *that* shall not alarm me. Sir H. Vane, the younger, was one of our wisest men; and let my readers see if he, in his philosophical works, be half as unmystical as I am.—I say, then, that it has often struck me that the scene itself was somewhat typical of what took place in such a reverie. The town of L[iverpool] represented the earth, with its sorrows and its graves left behind, yet not out of sight, nor wholly forgotten. The ocean, in everlasting but gentle agitation, and brooded over by a dove-like calm, might not unfitly typify the mind and the mood which then swayed it. For it seemed to me as if then first I stood at a distance, and aloof from the uproar of life; as if the tumult, the fever, and the strife, were suspended; a respite granted from the secret burthens of the heart; a sabbath of repose; a resting from human labours. Here were the hopes which blossom in the paths of life, reconciled with the peace which is in the grave; motions of the intellect as unwearied as the heavens, yet for all anxieties a halcyon calm: a tranquility that seemed no product of inertia, but as if resulting from mighty and equal antagonisms; infinite activities, infinite repose.

Oh! just, subtle, and mighty opium! that to the hearts of poor and rich alike, for the wounds that will never heal, and for "the pangs that tempt the spirit to rebel," bringest an assuaging balm; eloquent opium! that with thy potent rhetoric stealest away the purposes of wrath; and to the guilty man, for one night givest back the hopes of his youth, and hands washed pure from blood; and to the proud man, a brief oblivion for

Wrongs unredress'd, and insults unavenged;

that summonest to the chancery of dreams, for the triumphs of suffering innocence, false witnesses; and confoundest perjury; and dost reverse the sentences of unrighteous judges:—thou buildest upon the bosom of darkness, out of the fantastic imagery of the brain, cities and temples, beyond the art of Phidias and Praxiteles—beyond the splendour of Babylon and Hekatómpylos: and "from the anarchy of dreaming sleep," callest into sunny light the faces of long-buried beauties, and the blessed household countenances, cleansed from the "dishonours of the grave." Thou only givest these gifts to man; and thou hast the keys of Paradise, oh, just, subtle, and mighty opium!

THE BLACK CAT

Edgar Allan Poe

1843

*An alcoholic and rumored opium eater, Edgar Allan Poe infused
many of his short stories with violent, sometimes hallucinatory
scenes. In his young adulthood he was forced to leave the University
of Virginia after drinking and gambling with the abandon of a true
addict. He later joined the army and eventually transferred to West
Point, where he studied French and mathematics. In time Poe was
court-martialed for disobeying orders and was expelled from the
military academy. Despite his eventual literary success, he was
plagued by financial troubles. He died at age forty, after drinking so
heavily that he slipped into a coma. In his classic short story "The
Black Cat," Poe's penchant for the perverse and surreal is amply
displayed as his narrator's intoxications spur unimaginable acts of
depravity.*

For the most wild yet most homely narrative which I am about to pen,
I neither expect nor solicit belief. Mad indeed would I be to expect it,
in a case where my very senses reject their own evidence. Yet, mad am
I not—and very surely do I not dream. But to-morrow I die, and today I would unburden my soul. My immediate purpose is to place
before the world, plainly, succinctly, and without comment, a series
of mere household events. In their consequences, these events have
terrified—have tortured—have destroyed me. Yet I will not attempt to
expound them. To me, they have presented little but horror—to many
they will seem less terrible than *baroques*. Hereafter, perhaps, some intellect may be found which will reduce my phantasm to the common-

place—some intellect more calm, more logical, and far less excitable than my own, which will perceive, in the circumstances I detail with awe, nothing more than an ordinary succession of very natural causes and effects.

From my infancy I was noted for the docility and humanity of my disposition. My tenderness of heart was even so conspicuous as to make me the jest of my companions. I was especially fond of animals, and was indulged by my parents with a great variety of pets. With these I spent most of my time, and never was so happy as when feeding and caressing them. This peculiarity of character grew with my growth, and, in my manhood, I derived from it one of my principal sources of pleasure. To those who have cherished an affection for a faithful and sagacious dog, I need hardly be at the trouble of explaining the nature or the intensity of the gratification thus derivable. There is something in the unselfish and self-sacrificing love of a brute, which goes directly to the heart of him who has had frequent occasion to test the paltry friendship and gossamer fidelity of mere *Man*.

I married early, and was happy to find in my wife a disposition not uncongenial with my own. Observing my partiality for domestic pets, she lost no opportunity of procuring those of the most agreeable kind. We had birds, gold-fish, a fine dog, rabbits, a small monkey, and a *cat*.

This latter was a remarkably large and beautiful animal, entirely black, and sagacious to an astonishing degree. In speaking of his intelligence, my wife, who at heart was not a little tinctured with superstition, made frequent allusion to the ancient popular notion, which regarded all black cats as witches in disguise. Not that she was ever *serious* upon this point—and I mention the matter at all for no better reason than that it happens, just now, to be remembered.

Pluto—this was the cat's name—was my favorite pet and playmate. I alone fed him, and he attended me wherever I went about the house. It was even with difficulty that I could prevent him from following me through the streets.

Our friendship lasted, in this manner, for several years, during which my general temperament and character—through the instrumentality of the Fiend Intemperance—had (I blush to confess it) experienced a radical alteration for the worse. I grew, day by day, more moody, more irritable, more regardless of the feelings of others. I suffered myself to use intemperate language to my wife. At length, I even offered her personal violence. My pets, of course, were made to feel the change in my disposition. I not only neglected, but ill-used them. For Pluto, however, I still retained sufficient regard to restrain me from maltreating him, as I made no scruple of maltreating the rabbits, the monkey, or even the dog, when, by accident, or through affection, they came in my way. But my disease grew upon me—for what disease is like Alcohol!—and at length even Pluto, who was now becoming old, and consequently somewhat peevish—even Pluto began to experience the effects of my ill temper.

One night, returning home, much intoxicated, from one of my haunts about town, I fancied that the cat avoided my presence. I seized him; when, in his fright at my violence, he inflicted a slight wound upon my hand with his teeth. The fury of a demon instantly possessed me. I knew myself no longer. My original soul seemed, at once, to take its flight from my body; and a more than fiendish malevolence, gin-nurtured, thrilled every fibre of my frame. I took from my waistcoat pocket a penknife, opened it, grasped the poor beast by the throat, and deliberately cut one of its eyes from the socket! I blush, I burn, I shudder, while I pen the damnable atrocity.

When reason returned with the morning—when I had slept off the fumes of the night's debauch—I experienced a sentiment half of horror, half of remorse, for the crime of which I had been guilty; but it was, at best, a feeble and equivocal feeling, and the soul remained untouched. I again plunged into excess, and soon drowned in wine all memory of the deed.

In the meantime the cat slowly recovered. The socket of the lost eye presented, it is true, a frightful appearance, but he no longer appeared to suffer any pain. He went about the house as usual, but, as might be expected, fled in extreme terror at my approach. I had so much of my old heart left, as to be at first grieved by this evident dislike on the part of a creature which had once so loved me. But this feeling soon gave place to irritation. And then came, as if to my final and irrevocable overthrow, the spirit of PERVERSENESS. Of this spirit philosophy takes no account. Yet I am not more sure that my soul lives, than I am that perverseness is one of the primitive impulses of the human heart—one of the indivisible primary faculties, or sentiments, which give direction to the character of Man. Who has not, a hundred times, found himself committing a vile or a stupid action, for no other reason than because he knows he should *not?* Have we not a perpetual inclination, in the teeth of our best judgment, to violate that which is *Law,* merely because we understand it to be such? This spirit of perverseness, I say, came to my final overthrow. It was this unfathomable longing of the soul *to vex itself*—to offer violence to its own nature—to do wrong for the wrong's sake only—that urged me to continue and finally to consummate the injury I had inflicted upon the unoffending brute. One morning, in cold blood, I slipped a noose about its neck and hung it to the limb of a tree;—hung it with the tears streaming from my eyes, and with the bitterest remorse at my heart;—hung it *because* I knew that it had loved me, and *because* I felt it had given me no reason of offence;—hung it *because* I knew that in so doing I was committing a sin—a deadly sin that would so jeopardize my immortal soul as to place it—if such a thing were possible—even beyond the reach of the infinite mercy of the Most Merciful and Most Terrible God.

On the night of the day on which this most cruel deed was done, I was aroused from sleep by the cry of fire. The curtains of my bed were in flames. The whole house was blazing. It was with great difficulty that my wife, a servant, and myself, made our escape from the conflagration. The destruction was complete. My entire worldly wealth was swallowed up, and I resigned myself thenceforward to despair.

I am above the weakness of seeking to establish a sequence of cause and effect, between the disaster and the atrocity. But I am detailing a chain of facts—and wish not to leave even a possible link imperfect. On the day succeeding the fire, I visited the ruins. The walls, with one exception, had fallen in. This exception was found in a compartment wall, not very thick, which stood about the middle of the house, and against which had rested the head of my bed. The plastering had here, in great measure, resisted the action of the fire—a fact which I attributed to its having been recently spread. About this wall a dense crowd were collected, and many persons seemed to be examining a particular portion of it with very minute and eager attention. The words "strange!" "singular!" and other similar expressions, excited my curiosity. I approached and saw, as if graven in *bas-relief* upon the white surface, the figure of a gigantic *cat.* The impression was given with an accuracy truly marvellous. There was a rope about the animal's neck.

When I first beheld this apparition—for I could scarcely regard it as less—my wonder and my terror were extreme. But at length reflection came to my aid. The cat, I remembered, had been hung in a garden adjacent to the house. Upon the alarm of fire, this garden had been immediately filled by the crowd—by some one of whom the animal must have been cut from the tree and thrown, through an open window, into my chamber. This had probably been done with the view of arousing me from sleep. The falling of other walls had compressed the victim of my cruelty into the substance of the freshly-spread plaster; the lime of which, with the flames, and the *ammonia* from the carcass, had then accomplished the portraiture as I saw it.

Although I thus readily accounted to my reason, if not altogether to my conscience, for the startling fact just detailed, it did not the less fail to make a deep impression upon my fancy. For months I could not rid myself of the phantasm of the cat; and, during this period, there came back into my spirit a half-sentiment that seemed, but was not, remorse. I went so far as to regret the loss of the animal, and to look about me, among the vile haunts which I now habitually frequented, for another pet of the same species, and of somewhat similar appearance, with which to supply its place.

One night as I sat, half stupefied, in a den of more than infamy, my attention was suddenly drawn to some black object, reposing upon the head of one of the immense hogsheads of gin, or of rum, which constituted the chief furniture of the apartment. I had been looking steadily at the top of this hogshead for some minutes, and what now caused me surprise was the fact that I had not sooner perceived the object thereupon. I approached it, and touched it with my hand. It was a black cat—a very large one—fully as large as Pluto, and closely resembling him in every respect but one. Pluto had not a white hair upon any portion of his body; but this cat had a large, although indefinite splotch of white, covering nearly the whole region of the breast.

Upon my touching him, he immediately arose, purred loudly, rubbed against my hand, and appeared delighted with my notice. This, then, was the very creature of which I was in search. I at once offered to purchase it of the landlord; but this person made no claim to it—knew nothing of it—had never seen it before.

I continued my caresses, and when I prepared to go home, the animal evinced a disposition to accompany me. I permitted it to do so;

occasionally stooping and patting it as I proceeded. When it reached the house it domesticated itself at once, and became immediately a great favorite with my wife.

For my own part, I soon found a dislike to it arising within me. This was just the reverse of what I had anticipated; but—I know not how or why it was—its evident fondness for myself rather disgusted and annoyed me. By slow degrees these feelings of disgust and annoyance rose into the bitterness of hatred. I avoided the creature; a certain sense of shame, and the remembrance of my former deed of cruelty, preventing me from physically abusing it. I did not, for some weeks, strike, or otherwise violently ill use it; but gradually—very gradually— I came to look upon it with unutterable loathing, and to flee silently from its odious presence, as from the breath of a pestilence.

What added, no doubt, to my hatred of the beast, was the discovery, on the morning after I brought it home, that, like Pluto, it also had been deprived of one of its eyes. This circumstance, however, only endeared it to my wife, who, as I have already said, possessed, in a high degree, that humanity of feeling which had once been my distinguishing trait, and the source of many of my simplest and purest pleasures.

With my aversion to this cat, however, its partiality for myself seemed to increase. It followed my footsteps with a pertinacity which it would be difficult to make the reader comprehend. Whenever I sat, it would crouch beneath my chair, or spring upon my knees, covering me with its loathsome caresses. If I arose to walk it would get between my feet and thus nearly throw me down, or, fastening its long and sharp claws in my dress, clamber, in this manner, to my breast. At such times, although I longed to destroy it with a blow, I was yet withheld from so doing, partly by a memory of my former crime, but chiefly—let me confess it at once—by absolute *dread* of the beast.

This dread was not exactly a dread of physical evil—and yet I should be at a loss how otherwise to define it. I am almost ashamed to own—yes, even in this felon's cell, I am almost ashamed to own that the terror and horror with which the animal inspired me, had been heightened by one of the merest chimeras it would be possible to conceive. My wife had called my attention, more than once, to the character of the mark of white hair, of which I have spoken, and which constituted the sole visible difference between the strange beast and the one I had destroyed. The reader will remember that this mark, although large, had been originally very indefinite; but, by slow degrees—degrees nearly imperceptible, and which for a long time my reason struggled to reject as fanciful—it had, at length, assumed a rigorous distinctness of outline. It was now the representation of an object that I shudder to name—and for this, above all, I loathed, and dreaded, and would have rid myself of the monster *had I dared*—it was now, I say, the image of a hideous—of a ghastly thing—of the GALLOWS!—oh, mournful and terrible engine of Horror and of Crime—of Agony and of Death!

And now was I indeed wretched beyond the wretchedness of mere Humanity. And *a brute beast*—whose fellow I had contemptuously destroyed—*a brute beast* to work out for *me*—for me, a man fashioned in the image of the High God—so much of insufferable woe! Alas! neither by day nor by night knew I the blessing of rest any more! During the former the creature left me no moment alone, and in the latter I started hourly from dreams of unutterable fear to find the hot breath of *the thing* upon my face, and its vast weight—an incarnate nightmare that I had no power to shake off—incumbent eternally upon my *heart*!

Beneath the pressure of torments such as these the feeble remnant of the good within me succumbed. Evil thoughts became my sole intimates—the darkest and most evil of thoughts. The moodiness of my usual temper increased to hatred of all things and of all mankind; while from the sudden, frequent, and ungovernable outbursts of a fury to which I now blindly abandoned myself, my uncomplaining wife, alas, was the most usual and the most patient of sufferers.

One day she accompanied me, upon some household errand, into the cellar of the old building which our poverty compelled us to inhabit. The cat followed me down the steep stairs, and, nearly throwing me headlong, exasperated me to madness. Uplifting an axe, and forgetting in my wrath the childish dread which had hitherto stayed my hand, I aimed a blow at the animal, which, of course, would have proved instantly fatal had it descended as I wished. But this blow was arrested by the hand of my wife. Goaded by the interference into a rage more than demoniacal, I withdrew my arm from her grasp and buried the axe in her brain. She fell dead upon the spot without a groan.

This hideous murder accomplished, I set myself forthwith, and with entire deliberation, to the task of concealing the body. I knew that I could not remove it from the house, either by day or by night, without the risk of being observed by the neighbors. Many projects entered my mind. At one period I thought of cutting the corpse into minute fragments, and destroying them by fire. At another, I resolved to dig a grave for it in the floor of the cellar. Again, I deliberated about casting it in the well in the yard—about packing it in a box, as if merchandise, with the usual arrangements, and so getting a porter to take it from the house. Finally I hit upon what I considered a far better expedient than either of these. I determined to wall it up in the cellar, as the monks of the Middle Ages are recorded to have walled up their victims.

For a purpose such as this the cellar was well adapted. Its walls were loosely constructed, and had lately been plastered throughout with a rough plaster, which the dampness of the atmosphere had prevented from hardening. Moreover, in one of the walls was a projection, caused by a false chimney, or fireplace, that had been filled up and made to resemble the rest of the cellar. I made no doubt that I could readily displace the bricks at this point, insert the corpse, and wall the whole up as before, so that no eye could detect any thing suspicious.

And in this calculation I was not deceived. By means of a crowbar I easily dislodged the bricks, and, having carefully deposited the body against the inner wall, I propped it in that position, while with little trouble I relaid the whole structure as it originally stood. Having procured mortar, sand, and hair, with every possible precaution, I prepared a plaster which could not be distinguished from the old, and with this I very carefully went over the new brick-work. When I had finished, I felt satisfied that all was right. The wall did not present the slightest appearance of having been disturbed. The rubbish on the floor was picked up with the minutest care. I looked around triumphantly, and said to myself: "Here at least, then, my labor has not been in vain."

My next step was to look for the beast which had been the cause of so much wretchedness; for I had, at length, firmly resolved to put it to death. Had I been able to meet with it at the moment, there could have been no doubt of its fate; but it appeared that the crafty animal had been alarmed at the violence of my previous anger, and forbore to present itself in my present mood. It is impossible to describe or to imagine the deep, the blissful sense of relief which the absence of the detested creature occasioned in my bosom. It did not make its appearance during the night; and thus for one night, at least, since its introduction into the house, I soundly and tranquilly slept; aye, *slept* even with the burden of murder upon my soul.

The second and the third day passed, and still my tormentor came not. Once again I breathed as a freeman. The monster, in terror, had fled the premises for ever! I should behold it no more! My happiness was supreme! The guilt of my dark deed disturbed me but little. Some few inquiries had been made, but these had been readily answered. Even a search had been instituted—but of course nothing was to be discovered. I looked upon my future felicity as secured.

Upon the fourth day of the assassination, a party of the police came, very unexpectedly, into the house, and proceeded again to make rigorous investigation of the premises. Secure, however, in the inscrutability of my place of concealment, I felt no embarrassment whatever. The officers bade me accompany them in their search. They left no nook or corner unexplored. At length, for the third or fourth time, they descended into the cellar. I quivered not in a muscle. My heart beat calmly as that of one who slumbers in innocence. I walked the cellar from end to end. I folded my arms upon my bosom, and roamed easily to and fro. The police were thoroughly satisfied and prepared to depart. The glee at my heart was too strong to be restrained. I burned to say if but one word, by way of triumph, and to render doubly sure their assurance of my guiltlessness.

"Gentlemen," I said at last, as the party ascended the steps, "I delight to have allayed your suspicions. I wish you all health and a little more courtesy. By the bye, gentlemen, this—this is a very well-constructed house," (in the rabid desire to say something easily, I scarcely knew what I uttered at all),—"I may say an *excellently* well-constructed house. These walls—are you going, gentlemen?—these walls are solidly put together"; and here, through the mere frenzy of bravado, I rapped heavily with a cane which I held in my hand, upon that very portion of the brick-work behind which stood the corpse of the wife of my bosom.

But may God shield and deliver me from the fangs of the Arch-Fiend! No sooner had the reverberation of my blows sunk into silence, than I was answered by a voice from within the tomb!—by a cry, at first muffled and broken, like the sobbing of a child, and then quickly swelling into one long, loud, and continuous scream, utterly anomalous and inhuman—a howl—a wailing shriek, half of horror and half of triumph, such as might have arisen only out of hell, conjointly from the throats of the damned in their agony and of the demons that exult in the damnation.

Of my own thoughts it is folly to speak. Swooning, I staggered to the opposite wall. For one instant the party on the stairs remained motionless, through extremity of terror and awe. In the next a dozen stout arms were toiling at the wall. It fell bodily. The corpse, already greatly decayed and clotted with gore, stood erect before the eyes of the spectators. Upon its head, with red extended mouth and solitary eye of fire, sat the hideous beast whose craft had seduced me into murder, and whose informing voice had consigned me to the hangman. I had walled the monster up within the tomb.

FROM

THE COCAINE PAPERS

Sigmund Freud

1884

In addition to founding psychoanalysis, Sigmund Freud devoted a significant portion of his professional life to experimentation with drugs. As a medical investigator, he proclaimed cocaine to be an effective treatment for morphine and alcohol addiction as well as other ailments ranging from stomach disorders to syphilis. Though many of Freud's beliefs about cocaine use have since been discredited, his writings document the medical establishment's early efforts to understand the drug's effect. In The Cocaine Papers *he chronicles his groundbreaking experiments.*

I have carried out experiments and studied, in myself and others, the effect of coca on the healthy human body. . . .

The first time I took 0.05g of *cocaïnum muriaticum* in a 1% water solution was when I was feeling slightly out of sorts from fatigue. This solution is rather viscous, somewhat opalescent, and has a strange aromatic smell. At first it has a bitter taste, which yields afterwards to a series of very pleasant aromatic flavors. Dry cocaine salt has the same smell and taste, but to a more concentrated degree.

A few minutes after taking cocaine, one experiences a sudden exhilaration and feeling of lightness. One feels a certain furriness on the lips and palate, followed by a feeling of warmth in the same areas; if one now drinks cold water, it feels warm on the lips and cold in the throat. On other occasions the predominant feeling is a rather pleasant coolness in the mouth and throat.

During this first trial I experienced a short period of toxic effects, which did not recur in subsequent experiments. Breathing became slower and deeper and I felt tired and sleepy; I yawned frequently and felt somewhat dull. After a few minutes the actual cocaine euphoria began, introduced by repeated cooling eructation. Immediately after taking the cocaine I noticed a slight slackening of the pulse and later a moderate increase.

I have observed the same physical signs of the effect of cocaine in others, mostly people of my own age. The most constant symptom proved to be the repeated cooling eructation. This is often accompanied by a rumbling which must originate from high up in the intestine; two of the people I observed, who said they were able to recognize movements of their stomachs, declared emphatically that they had repeatedly detected such movements. Often, at the outset of the cocaine effect, the subjects alleged that they experienced an intense feeling of heat in the head. I noticed this in myself as well in the course of some later experiments, but on other occasions it was absent. In only two cases did coca give rise to dizziness. On the whole the toxic effects of coca are of short duration, and much less intense than those produced by effective doses of quinine or salicylate of soda; they seem to become even weaker after repeated use of cocaine....

The psychic effect of *cocaïnum muriaticum* in doses of 0.05–0.10g consists of exhilaration and lasting euphoria, which does not differ in any way from the normal euphoria of a healthy person. The feeling of excitement which accompanies stimulus by alcohol is completely lacking; the characteristic urge for immediate activity which alcohol produces is also absent. One senses an increase of self-control and feels more vigorous and more capable of work; on the other hand, if one works, one misses that heightening of the mental powers which alcohol, tea, or coffee induce. One is simply normal, and soon finds it difficult to believe that one is under the influence of any drug at all.

This gives the impression that the mood induced by coca in such doses is due not so much to direct stimulation as to the disappearance of elements in one's general state of well-being which cause depression. One may perhaps assume that the euphoria resulting from good health is also nothing more than the normal condition of a well-nourished cerebral cortex which "is not conscious" of the organs of the body to which it belongs.

During this stage of the cocaine condition, which is not otherwise distinguished, appear those symptoms which have been described as the wonderful stimulating effect of coca. Long-lasting, intensive mental or physical work can be performed without fatigue; it is as though the need for food and sleep, which otherwise makes itself felt peremptorily at certain times of the day, were completely banished. While the effects of cocaine last one can, if urged to do so, eat copiously and without revulsion; but one has the clear feeling that the meal was superfluous. Similarly, as the effect of coca declines it is possible to sleep on going to bed, but sleep can just as easily be omitted with no unpleasant consequences. During the first hours of the coca effect one cannot sleep, but this sleeplessness is in no way distressing.

I have tested this effect of coca, which wards off hunger, sleep, and fatigue and steels one to intellectual effort, some dozen times on myself; I had no opportunity to engage in physical work.

A very busy colleague gave me an opportunity to observe a striking example of the manner in which cocaine dispels extreme fatigue and a well justified feeling of hunger; at 6:00 P.M. this colleague, who had not eaten since the early morning and who had worked exceedingly hard during the day, took 0.05g of *cocaïnum muriaticum*. A few minutes later he declared that he felt as though he had just eaten an ample meal, that he had no desire for an evening meal, and that he felt strong enough to undertake a long walk. . . .

The effect of a moderate dose of coca fades away so gradually that, in normal circumstances, it is difficult to define its duration. If one works intensively while under the influence of coca, after from three to five hours there is a decline in the feeling of well-being, and a further dose of coca is necessary in order to ward off fatigue. The effect of coca seems to last longer if no heavy muscular work is undertaken. Opinion is unanimous that the euphoria induced by coca is not followed by any feeling of lassitude or other state of depression. I should be inclined to think that after moderate doses (0.05–0.10g) a part at least of the coca effect lasts for over twenty-four hours. In my own case, at any rate, I have noticed that even on the day after taking coca my condition compares favorably with the norm. I should be inclined to explain the possibility of a lasting gain in strength, such as has often been claimed for coca by the totality of such effects. . . .

THE THERAPEUTIC USES OF COCA

It was inevitable that a plant which had achieved such a reputation for marvelous effects in its country of origin should have been used to treat the most varied disorders and illnesses of the human body. The first Europeans who became aware of this treasure of the native population were similarly unreserved in their recommendation of coca. On the basis of wide medical experience, Mantegazza* later drew up a list of the therapeutic properties of coca, which one by one received the acknowledgment of other doctors. In the following section I have tried to collate the recommendations concerning coca, and, in doing so, to distinguish between recommendations based on successful treatment of illnesses and those which relate to the psychological effects of the stimulant. In general the latter outweigh the former. At present there seems to be some promise of widespread recognition and use of coca preparations in North America, while in Europe doctors scarcely know them by name. The failure of coca to take hold in Europe, which in my opinion is unmerited, can perhaps be attributed to reports of unfavorable consequences attendant upon its use, which appeared shortly after its introduction into Europe; or to the doubtful quality of the preparations, their relative scarcity and consequent high price. Some of the evidence which can be found in favor of the use of coca has been proved valid beyond any doubt, whereas some warrants at least an unprejudiced investigation....

a) *Coca as a stimulant.* The main use of coca will undoubtedly remain that which the Indians have made of it for centuries: it is of value in all cases where the primary aim is to increase the physical capacity of the body for a given short period of time and to hold strength in reserve to meet further demands—especially when outward circumstances exclude the possibility of obtaining the rest and nourishment normally necessary for great exertion. Such situations arise in wartime, on journeys, during mountain climbing and other expeditions, etc.—indeed, they are situations in which the alcoholic stimulants are also generally recognized as being of value. Coca is a far more potent and far less harmful stimulant than alcohol, and its widespread utilization is

---

* *Paola Mantegazza (1831–1910) was an Italian physician.*—RS

hindered at present only by its high cost. . . . If cocaine is given as a stimulant, it is better that it should be given in small effective doses (0.05–0.10g) and repeated so often that the effects of the doses overlap. Apparently cocaine is not stored in the body; I have already stressed the fact that there is no state of depression when the effects of coca have worn off.

At present it is impossible to assess with any certainty to what extent coca can be expected to increase human mental powers. I have the impression that protracted use of coca can lead to a lasting improvement if the inhibitions manifested before it is taken are due only to physical causes or to exhaustion. To be sure, the instantaneous effect of a dose of coca cannot be compared with that of a morphine injection; but, on the good side of the ledger, there is no danger of general damage to the body as is the case with the chronic use of morphine.

Many doctors felt that coca would play an important role by filling a gap in the medicine chest of the psychiatrists. It is a well-known fact that psychiatrists have an ample supply of drugs at their disposal for reducing the excitation of nerve centers, but none which could serve to increase the reduced functioning of the nerve centers. Coca has consequently been prescribed for the most diverse kinds of psychic debility—hysteria, hypochondria, melancholic inhibition, stupor, and similar maladies. . . .

On the whole, the efficacy of coca in cases of nervous and psychic debility needs further investigation, which will probably lead to partially favorable conclusions. According to Mantegazza coca is of no use, and is sometimes even dangerous, in cases of organic change and inflammation of the nervous system.

b) *The use of coca for digestive disorders of the stomach.* This is the oldest and most firmly founded use of coca, and at the same time it is the most comprehensible to us. . . .

. . . I have experienced personally how the painful symptoms attendant upon large meals—viz, a feeling of pressure and fullness in the stomach, discomfort and a disinclination to work—disappear with eructation following small doses of cocaine (0.025–0.05). Time and again I have brought such relief to my colleagues; and twice I observed how the nausea resulting from gastronomic excesses responded in a short time to the effects of cocaine, and gave way to a normal desire to eat and a feeling of bodily well-being. I have also learned to spare myself stomach troubles by adding a small amount of cocaine to salicylate of soda.

My colleague, Dr. Josef Pollak, has given me the following account of an astonishing effect of cocaine, which shows that it can be used to treat not merely local discomfort in the stomach but also serious reflex reactions; one must therefore assume that cocaine has a powerful effect on the mucous membrane and the muscular system of this organ.

"A forty-two-year-old, robust man, whom the doctor knew very well, was forced to adhere most strictly to a certain diet and to prescribed mealtimes; otherwise he could not avoid the attacks about to be described. When traveling or under the influence of any emotional strain he was particularly susceptible. The attacks followed a regular pattern: They began in the evening with a feeling of discomfort in the epigastrium, followed by flushing of the face, tears in the eyes, throbbing in the temples and violent pain in the forehead, accompanied by a feeling of great depression and apathy. He could not sleep during the night; toward morning there were long painful spasms of vomiting which lasted for hours. Round about midday he experienced some relief, and on drinking a few spoonfuls of soup had a feeling 'as though the stomach would at last eject a bullet which had lain in it for a long time.' This was followed by rancid eructation, until, toward evening, his condition returned to normal. The patient was incapable of work throughout the day and had to keep to his bed.

"At 8:00 P.M. on the tenth of June the usual symptoms of an attack began. At ten o'clock, after the violent headache had developed, the patient was given 0.075g *cocaïnum muriaticum*. Shortly thereafter he experienced a feeling of warmth and eructation, which seemed to him to be 'still too little.' At 10:30 a second dose of 0.075g of cocaine was given; the eructations increased; the patient felt some relief and was able to write a long letter. He alleged that he felt intensive movement in the stomach; at twelve o'clock, apart from a slight headache, he was normal, even cheerful, and walked for an hour. He could not sleep until 3:00 A.M., but that did not distress him. He awoke the next morning healthy, ready for work, and with a good appetite."

The effect of cocaine on the stomach—Mantegazza assumes this as well—is two-fold: stimulation of movement and reduction of the organ's sensitivity. The latter would seem probable not only because of the local sensations in the stomach after cocaine has been taken but because of the analogous effect of cocaine on other mucous membranes. Mantegazza claims to have achieved the most brilliant successes in treatments of gastralgia and enteralgia, and all painful and cramping afflictions of the stomach and intestines, which he attributes to the anesthetizing properties of coca. On this point I cannot confirm Mantegazza's experiences; only once, in connection with a case of gastric catarrh, did I see the sensitivity of the stomach to pressure disappear after the administration of coca. On other occasions I have observed myself, and also heard from other doctors, that patients suspected of having ulcers or scars in the stomach complained of increased pain after using coca; this can be explained by the increased movement of the stomach.

Accordingly, I should say that the use of coca is definitely indicated in cases of atonic digestive weakness and the so-called nervous stomach disorders; in such cases it is possible to achieve not merely a relief of the symptoms but a lasting improvement.

c) *Coca in cachexia.* Long-term use of coca is further strongly recommended—and allegedly has been tried with success—in all diseases which involve degeneration of the tissues, such as severe anemia, phthisis, long-lasting febrile diseases, etc.; and also during recovery from such diseases. . . .

One might wish to attribute such successes partly to the undoubted favorable effect of coca on the digestion, but one must bear in mind that a good many of the authors who have written on coca regard it as a "source of savings"; i.e., they are of the opinion that a system which has absorbed even an extremely small amount of cocaine is capable, as a result of the reaction of the body to coca, of amassing a greater store of vital energy which can be converted into work than would have been possible without coca. If we take the amount of work as being constant, the body which has absorbed cocaine should be able to manage with a lower metabolism, which in turn means a smaller intake of food. . . . I should add here that coca has been warmly praised in connection with the treatment of syphilis. . . .

d) *Coca in the treatment of morphine and alcohol addiction.* In America the important discovery has recently been made that coca preparations possess the power to suppress the craving for morphine in habitual addicts, and also to reduce to negligible proportions the serious symptoms of collapse which appear while the patient is being weaned away from the morphine habit. ...

There are some sixteen reports of cases in which the patient has been successfully cured of addiction; in only one instance is there a report of failure of coca to alleviate morphine addiction, and in this case the doctor wondered why there had been so many warm recommendations for the use of coca in cases of morphine addiction. The successful cases vary in their conclusiveness. Some of them involve large doses of opium or morphine and addictions of long standing. There is not much information on the subject of relapses, as most cases were reported within a very short time of the cure having been effected. Symptoms which appear during abstention are not always reported in detail. There is especial value in those reports which contain the observation that the patients were able to dispense with coca after a few weeks without experiencing any further desire for morphine. Special attention is repeatedly called to the fact that morphine cachexia gave way to excellent health, so that the patients were scarcely recognizable after their cure. Concerning the method of withdrawal, it should be made clear that in the majority of cases a gradual reduction of the habitual dose of the drug, accompanied by a gradual increase of the coca dose, was the method chosen; however, sudden discontinuation of the drug was also tried. ...

I once had occasion to observe the case of a man who was subjected to the type of cure involving the sudden withdrawal of morphine, assisted by the use of coca; the same patient had suffered severe symptoms as a result of abstinence in the course of a previous cure. This time his condition was tolerable; in particular, there was no sign of depression or nausea as long as the effects of coca lasted; chills and diarrhea were now the only permanent symptoms of his abstinence. The patient was not bedridden, and could function normally. During the first days of the cure he consumed 3dg of *cocaïnum muriaticum* daily, and after ten days he was able to dispense with the coca treatment altogether.

The treatment of morphine addiction with coca does not, therefore, result merely in the exchange of one kind of addiction for another—it does not turn the morphine addict into a *coquero;* the use of coca is only temporary. Moreover, I do not think that it is the general toughening effect of coca which enables the system weakened by morphine to withstand, at the cost of only insignificant symptoms, the withdrawal of morphine. I am rather inclined to assume that coca has a directly antagonistic effect on morphine, and in support of my view I quote the following observations of Dr. Josef Pollak on a case in point:

"A thirty-three-year-old woman has been suffering for years from severe menstrual migraine which can be alleviated only by morphia injections. Although the lady in question never takes morphia or experiences any desire to do so when she is free of migraine, during the attacks she behaves like a morphine addict. A few hours after the injection she suffers intense depression, biliousness, attacks of vomiting, which are stopped by a second morphine injection; thereupon, the symptoms of intolerance recur, with the result that an attack of migraine, along with all its consequences, keeps the patient in bed for three days in a most wretched condition. Cocaine was then tried to combat the migraine, but the treatment proved unsuccessful. It was necessary to resort to morphine injections. But as soon as the symptoms of morphine intolerance appeared, they were quickly relieved by 1dg of cocaine, with the result that the patient recovered from her attack in a far shorter time and consumed much less morphine in the process."

Coca was tried in America for the treatment of chronic alcoholism at about the same time as it was introduced in connection with morphine addiction, and most reports dealt with the two uses conjointly. In the treatment of alcoholism, too, there were cases of undoubted success, in which the irresistible compulsion to drink was either banished or alleviated, and the dyspeptic complaints of the drinkers were relieved. In general, however, the suppression of the alcohol craving through the use of coca proved to be more difficult than the suppression of morphomania; in one case ... the drinker became a *coquero.* One need only suggest the immense economic significance which coca would acquire as a "source of savings" in another sense, if its effectiveness in combating alcoholism were confirmed. ...

f) *Coca as an aphrodisiac.* The natives of South America, who represented their goddess of love with coca leaves in her hand, did not doubt the stimulative effect of coca on the genitalia. Mantegazza confirms that the *coqueros* sustain a high degree of potency right into old age; he even reports cases of the restoration of potency and the disappearance of functional weaknesses following the use of coca, although he does not believe that coca would produce such an effect in all individuals. . . .

Among the persons to whom I have given coca, three reported violent sexual excitement which they unhesitatingly attributed to the coca. A young writer, who was enabled by treatment with coca to resume his work after a longish illness, gave up using the drug because of the undesirable secondary effects which it had on him.

HOW THE OPIUM HABIT IS ACQUIRED

Virgil G. Eaton

1888

Concerned about the growing number of opium users who populated the Boston area in the late nineteenth century, the newspaperman Virgil G. Eaton offers a concise yet forceful prescription for reform in "How the Opium Habit Is Acquired," published in The Popular Science Monthly. *"Opium-slaves," as he calls them, "will resort to every trick and art which human ingenuity can invent." To prove his point, Eaton recounts the story of a prisoner who feeds his habit with opium that has been smuggled to him inside walnut shells. After analyzing the problem, Eaton points the finger at physicians for their willingness to prescribe opium for trivial ailments. To reverse the community's growing drug dependence, he recommends legislation and a renewed commitment to healthful living.*

I am not one of the persons who raise a great cry about the evils of the "opium-habit." I have no doubt that the continued use of narcotics, whether they be tobacco or opium, is injurious to the nervous system; but I also firmly believe that the recuperative powers of the body are such that they can largely overcome any harmful results coming from the regular use of these substances. For instance, I know a stonecutter who resides at Cape Elizabeth, Me., who for the past twenty years has used twenty cents' worth of black "navy plug" tobacco every day. He is a large, vigorous man, weighing over two hundred pounds. His appetite is good; he sleeps well, and, save for a little heart disturbance caused by overstimulation, he is perfectly healthy, and is likely to live until he is fourscore. He is now fifty-one years of age, and he assures me he has used tobacco since he was fourteen, and never had a fit of "swearing off" in his life. A peculiar and, I should say, a rather troublesome habit of his, is to go to bed every night with a big "quid" of hard "plug" tobacco between his molars. As this is always gone in the morning, and the pillow shows no traces of the weed, he thinks he chews it and swallows it in his sleep, though he never knows anything about the process.

There is a widow who keeps a lodging-house in Oak Street, Boston, Mass., who takes three drachms of morphia sulphate every day, in three one-drachm doses, morning, noon, and night. When it is remembered that an eighth of a grain is the usual dose for an adult, while two grains are sufficient to kill a man, the amount she takes seems startling. I asked her why she did not try and substitute tobacco, or bromide, or chloral hydrate for morphine, and she said they made her sick, so she could not use them. This woman is sixty years old, very pale and emaciated. Her appetite is poor. She attends to her duties faithfully, however, and is able, with the help of a girl, to carry on a large lodging-house.

I might give scores of instances similar to the above, but these will do for my purpose. I believe that the person who takes liquor or tobacco or opium, in regular quantities at stated intervals, is able to withstand their effect after getting fixed in the habit, and that it is the irregular, spasmodic use of these articles which brings delirium and death. It is the man who goes on a "spree," and then quits for a time, who has the weak stomach and aching head. His neighbor, who takes his regular toddy and his usual smoke, feels no inconvenience.

For the past year or more I have studied the growth of the opium-habit in Boston. It is increasing rapidly. Not only are there more Chinese "joints" and respectable resorts kept by Americans than there were a year ago, but the number of individuals who "hit the pipe" at home and in their offices is growing very fast. A whole opium "layout," including pipe, fork, lamp, and spoon, can now be had for less than five dollars. This affords a chance for those who have acquired the habit to follow their desires in private, without having to reveal their secret to anyone. How largely this is practiced I do not know, but, judging from the telltale pallor of the faces I see, I feel sure the habit is claiming more slaves every day.

In order to approximate the amount of opium in its various forms which is used in Boston, I have made a thorough scrutiny of the physicians' recipes left at the drugstores to be filled. As is well known, all recipes given by physicians are numbered, dated, and kept on file at the drugstores, so that they may be referred to at any time. To these I went in search of information.

I was surprised to learn how extensively opium and its alkaloids— particularly sulphate of morphia—are used by physicians. I found them prescribed for every ailment which flesh is heir to. They are used for headache, sore eyes, toothache, sore throat, laryngitis, diphtheria, bronchitis, congestion, pneumonia, consumption, gastritis, liver-complaint, stone in the gall-duct, carditis, aneurism, hypertrophy, peritonitis, calculus, kidney trouble, rheumatism, neuralgia, and all general or special maladies of the body. It is the great panacea and cure-all.

During my leisure time I have looked up more than 10,000 recipes. It has been my practice to go to the files, open the book, or take up a spindle at random, and take 300 recipes just as they come. The first store I visited found 42 recipes which contained morphine out of the 300 examined. Close by, a smaller store, patronized by poorer people, had 36. Up in the aristocratic quarters, where the customers call in carriages, I found 49 morphine recipes in looking over 300. At the North End, among the poor Italian laborers, the lowest proportion of 32 in 300 was discovered. Without detailing all the places visited, I will summarize by saying that, in 10,200 recipes taken in 34 drugstores, I found 1,481 recipes which prescribed some preparation of opium, or an average of fourteen and one half percent of the whole.

This was surprising enough; but my investigations did not end here. Of the prescriptions furnished by physicians I found that forty-two percent were filled the second time, and of those refilled twenty-three percent contained opium in some form. Again, twenty-eight percent of all prescriptions are filled a third time; and of these, sixty-one percent were for opiates; while of the twenty percent taken for the fourth filling, seventy-eight percent were for the narcotic drug, proving, beyond a doubt, that it was the opiate qualities of the medicine that afforded relief and caused the renewal.

From conversations with the druggists, I learned that the proprietary or "patent" medicines which have the largest sales were those containing opiates. One apothecary told me of an old lady who formerly came to him as often as four times a week and purchased a fifty-cent bottle of "cough-balsam." She informed him that it "quieted her nerves" and afforded rest when everything else had failed. After she had made her regular visits for over a year, he told her one day that he had sold out of the medicine required, and suggested a substitute, which was a preparation containing about the same amount of morphine. On trial, the woman found the new mixture answered every purpose of the old. The druggist then told her she had acquired the morphine-habit, and from that time on she was a constant morphine-user.

It was hard to learn just what proportion of those who began by taking medicines containing opiates became addicted to the habit. I should say, from what I learned, that the number was fully twenty-five percent—perhaps more. The proportion of those who, having taken up the habit in earnest, left it off later on, was very small—not over ten percent. When a person once becomes an opium-slave, the habit usually holds through life.

I was told many stories about the injurious effects of morphine and opium upon the morals of those who use it. One peculiarity of a majority is that, whenever a confirmed user of the narcotic obtains credit at the drugstore, he at once stops trading at that place and goes elsewhere. All the druggists know this habit very well, and take pains to guard against it. Whenever a customer asks for credit for a bottle of morphine, the druggist informs him that the store never trusts anyone; but if he has no money with him the druggist will gladly give him enough to last a day or two. In this way the druggist keeps his customer, whereas he would have lost his trade if the present had not been made at the time credit was refused.

Of course, I heard much about the irresistible desire which confirmed slaves to the habit have for their delight. There is nothing too degrading for them to do in order to obtain the narcotic. Many druggists firmly believe that a majority of the seemingly motiveless crimes which are perpetrated by reputable people are due to this habit. In pursuit of opium the slaves will resort to every trick and art which human ingenuity can invent. There is a prisoner now confined in the Concord (Mass.) Reformatory who has his opium smuggled in to him in the shape of English walnuts donated by a friend. The friend buys the opium and, opening the walnut-shells, extracts the meat, and fills up the spaces with the gum. Then he sticks the shells together with glue and sends them to the prison.

At present our clergymen, physicians, and reformers are asking for more stringent laws against the sale of these narcotics. The law compelling every person who purchases opium or other poisons to "register," giving his name and place of residence to the druggist, has been in force in Massachusetts for several years, and all this time the sales have increased. No registration law can control the traffic.

The parties who are responsible for the increase of the habit are the physicians who give the prescriptions. In these days of great mental strain, when men take their business home with them and think of it from waking to sleeping, the nerves are the first to feel the effects of overwork. Opium effects immediate relief, and the doctors, knowing this, and wishing to stand well with their patients, prescribe it more and more. Their design is to effect a cure. The result is to convert their patients into opium-slaves. The doctors are to blame for so large a consumption of opium, and they are the men who need reforming.

Two means of preventing the spread of the habit suggest themselves to every thoughtful person:

1. Pass a law that no prescriptions containing opium or its preparations can be filled more than once at the druggist's without having the physician renew it. The extra cost of calling on a doctor when the medicine ran out would deter many poor people from acquiring the habit. Such a law would also make the doctors more guarded in prescribing opiates for trivial ailments. With the law in force, and the druggists guarded by strict registration laws, we could soon trace the responsibility to its proper source, and then, if these safeguards were not enough, physicians could be fined for administering opiates save in exceptional cases.

2. The great preventive to the habit is to keep the body in such a state that it will not require sedatives or stimulants. The young men and women in our cities have too big heads, too small necks, and too flabby muscles. They should forsake medicine, and patronize the gymnasium. Let them develop their muscles and rest their nerves, and the family doctor, who means well, but who cannot resist the tendency of the age, can take a protracted vacation. Unless something of the kind is done soon, the residents of our American cities will be all opium-slaves.

THE ETHICS OF WINE-DRINKING AND TOBACCO-SMOKING

Leo Tolstoy

1891

While writing Anna Karenina, *the famed Russian novelist Leo Tolstoy embarked on a period of profound self-examination. Although he had spent time during his earlier years drinking and gambling, he began to ponder what he considered to be the important moral issues of life. This spiritual crisis ultimately led to Tolstoy's rigorous autobiographical essay* A Confession (1882). *Nine years later he focused his keen moral sensibilities on the prevalence of drinking and smoking in the late nineteenth century. In "The Ethics of Wine-Drinking and Tobacco-Smoking" he suggests an underlying motivation for these practices: "People drink and smoke . . . simply and solely in order to drown the warning voice of conscience."*

What is the true explanation of the use which people make of stupefying stimulants and narcotics, of brandy, wine, beer, hashish, opium, and of others less extensively indulged in, such as morphia, ether, fly-agaric? How did it first originate, and what caused it to spread so rapidly and to hold its own so tenaciously among all sorts and conditions of men, savage and civilised? To what are we to attribute the incontrovertible fact that wherever brandy, wine, beer, are unknown, there opium, hashish, fly-agaric, &c., are sure to be common, while the consumption of tobacco is universal?

What is it that impels people to stupefy themselves? Ask any man you meet what it was that first induced him to drink alcoholic liquors and why he drinks them now. He will reply: "It is pleasant to do so; every one drinks"; and he may possibly add, "to keep up my spirits." There is another category of persons—those who never take the trouble to ask themselves the question whether it is right or wrong to drink alcoholic liquors—who will urge as an all-sufficient reason, that wine is wholesome and imparts strength to him who drinks it—viz., they plead as a satisfactory ground a statement which has been long ago proved to be utterly false.

Put the same question to a smoker: ask him what first led him to smoke and what compels or induces him to keep up the habit now, and the answer will be the same: "To drive away melancholy; besides, the habit is universal; everybody smokes." The same or some analogous pleas would most probably be advanced by those who indulge in opium, hashish, morphia, and fly-agaric.

"To drive off the blues; to keep up my spirits; because every one does the same." Reasons of this kind might, without glaring absurdity, be advanced as grounds for the habit of twirling one's fingers, of whistling, of humming tunes, of playing a tin whistle, in a word, of occupying oneself in any one of a thousand ways that do not entail the destruction of natural riches, nor necessitate an enormous expenditure of human labour, of doing something in fine, which is not fraught with mischief to oneself and others. But none of the habits in question are of this harmless character. In order that tobacco, wine, hashish, opium, may be produced in sufficient quantities to keep pace with the present enormous rate of consumption, millions and millions of acres of the best soil, among populations sorely in need of land, are set apart for the cultivation of rye, potatoes, hemp, poppy, vines, and tobacco, and millions of human beings—in England, one-eighth of the entire population—devote all their lives to the manufacture of these stupefying stimulants. Nor is this all. The consumption of these products is, beyond all doubt, highly pernicious, is fraught with terrible evils, the reality of which are admitted by all—evils that work the ruin of more men and women than are laid low by all the bloody wars and infectious diseases that decimate the human race. And people are aware of this; so perfectly well aware of it, indeed, that the statement cannot for a moment be credited that they set in motion the baneful cause of it all; *merely to drive away melancholy to keep up their spirits,* or solely because *every one does it.*

It is obvious, therefore, that there must be some other explanation of this strange phenomenon. On all the highways and byways of life we are continually meeting with affectionate parents who though perfectly ready to make any—the heaviest—sacrifice for the welfare of their offspring, do not hesitate one moment to squander upon brandy, wine, beer, opium, hashish, and tobacco, a sum of money amply sufficient to feed their miserable, hunger-stricken children; or at least to insure them against the worst kinds of privation. It is perfectly evident, therefore, that the man who, placed by circumstances or his own acts in a position that imposes upon him the necessity of choosing between the infliction of hardship and misery upon the family that is dear to him, on the one hand, and abstinence from stupefying stimulants and narcotics, on the other, chooses the former alternative, is impelled to this choice by something far more potent than the desire to keep up his spirits, or the speculative consideration that every one else does the same. And so far as I am competent to hazard an opinion—and my qualifications consist solely in a theoretical knowledge of the judgments of others, gleaned from book-reading and in close personal observation of men, of my own self in particular at a time when I still drank wine and smoked tobacco—I would formulate that potent cause as follows:

Man, during the course of his conscious existence, has frequent opportunities for discerning in himself two distinct beings: the one blind and sensuous; the other endowed with sight, spiritual. The former eats, drinks, rests, sleeps, perpetuates itself, and moves about just like a machine duly wound up for a definite period; the seeing, spiritual being, which is linked to the sensuous, does nothing itself, but merely weighs and appreciates the conduct of the sensuous being, actively co-operating when it approves, and holding aloof when it disapproves the actions of the latter.

We may liken the being endowed with sight to the needle of a compass, one extremity of which points to the north and the other to the south, and the entire length and breadth of which is covered by a layer of some opaque substance. The needle thus remains invisible so long as the ship or vehicle that carries the compass is moving in the direction towards which the needle is pointing; nor does it move or become visible until the vessel or vehicle deviates from that direction.

In like manner, the seeing, spiritual being, whose manifestations we are wont in the language of every-day life to term conscience, always points with one extremity to good, and with the opposite one to evil, nor do we perceive it until such time as we swerve from the direction it indicates—viz., from good to evil. But no sooner have we performed an action contrary to the direction of our conscience than the consciousness of the spiritual being manifests itself, indicating the degree of the deviation from the direction pointed out by conscience. And as the mariner who has discovered that he is not moving towards the port for which he is bound cannot continue to work with his oars, his engines, or his sails until he either rights the vessel and steers her in accordance with the indications of the compass, or else succeeds in shutting his eyes to the fact that there is a deviation, so also the man who discerns the discord between his conscience and his sensual activity cannot continue to exercise that activity until he either brings it once more into harmony with the dictates of his conscience, or else hides from himself the testimony borne by his conscience to the irregularity of his animal life.

All human life may be truly said to be made up of one of two kinds of activity: (1) the bringing of one's conduct into harmony with the dictates of conscience; or (2) the concealing from oneself the manifestations of conscience, in order to make it possible to continue to live as one is living.

Some people are engaged in the former occupation, others in the latter. There is but one way to accomplish the former: moral enlightenment, increase of light within ourselves, and of attention to what the light reveals. There are two methods of attaining the second object— that of concealing from ourselves the manifestations of conscience: an external and an internal method. The former leads us to engage in occupations calculated to withdraw our attention from the teachings of conscience, while the latter consists in darkening the conscience itself.

Just as a man has it in his power to blind himself to an object that is immediately under his eyes in one of two ways: either by fixing them upon other and more striking objects, or by obstructing the organs of vision—thrusting some foreign body upon them—so, in like manner, a man can hide from himself the manifestations of his conscience, either by having all his attention engrossed by occupations of various kinds, cares, amusements, pastimes, or else by obstructing the organ of attention itself. When it is a question of persons of a blunted or limited moral sense, outward distractions are frequently quite sufficient to hinder them from noting the testimony borne by their consciences to the irregularity of their lives. With people of sensitive moral organisation such mechanical devices are seldom enough.

External means do not entirely draw off the attention, or wholly prevent it from recognising the discord between actual life and the requisitions of conscience. And the knowledge of this antagonism hinders people from living; in order, therefore, to remove this obstacle, and continue to live irregularly, they have recourse to the unfailing internal method of darkening conscience itself. And this is effectually accomplished by poisoning the brain by means of stupefying stimulants and narcotics.

Let us suppose, for instance, that a man's life is not what, according to the prompting of conscience, it should be, and he does not possess the force necessary to remould and reform it in accordance with these exigencies. On the other hand, the distractions which should have diverted his attention from the consciousness of this antagonism are either insufficient in themselves, or else repetition has worn off their point, and they no longer produce the looked for result. It is then that a man, desirous of continuing to live in spite of the testimony of his conscience to the irregularity of his life, determines to poison, to paralyse completely for a time, that organ through which the warnings of conscience are made manifest, just as a person might throw a handful of flour or snuff in his eyes in order to deliver himself from the sight of a disagreeable object.

II

It is not inclination, therefore, nor pleasure, nor distraction, nor amusement that gives us the clue to the universal habit of consuming hashish, opium, wine, and tobacco, but the necessity of concealing from oneself the records of one's conscience.

One day, while walking along a street, I passed by a number of *droschky*-drivers, who were gathered together in groups conversing, when I was struck by the remark which one of them addressed to another: "Who doubts it? Of course he would have been ashamed to do it if he'd been sober."

A sober man scruples to do that which a drunken man will execute without hesitation. These words embody the essential motive that induces people to have recourse to stupefying drugs and drinks. People employ them either for the purpose of stifling remorse, after having performed an action disapproved by their conscience, or else in order to induce a state of mind in which they shall be capable of doing something contrary to the dictates of their conscience, and to which the animal nature of man is impelling him.

A sober man has conscientious scruples to visit lewd women, to steal, to commit murder. A drunken man, on the contrary, is troubled with no such scruples. Hence it is that if a person wishes to do something which his conscience forbids him to do, he first stupefies his faculties.

I recollect being struck by the statement made by a man-cook on his trial for the murder of the old lady—a relative of mine—in whose service he had been living. From the account he gave of the crime, and the manner in which it was perpetrated, it appears that when he had sent his paramour, the maid-servant, out of the house, and the time had come for him to do the deed, he seized a knife and repaired to the bedroom where his intended victim was; but as he drew near he felt that in his sober senses he could not possibly perpetrate such a crime. "A sober man has conscientious scruples." He turned back, gulped down two tumblers of brandy that he had provided beforehand, and then, and not before, felt that he was ready to do the deed, and did it.

Nine-tenths of the total number of crimes that stain humanity are committed in the same way: "First take a drink to give you courage."

Of all the women who fall, fully one-half yield to the temptation under the influence of alcohol. Nearly all the visits made by young men to disorderly houses take place when the faculties have been blunted and dulled by intoxicating liquor. People are well acquainted with this property of alcohol to deaden the voice of conscience, and they deliberately make use of it for this very purpose.

Nor is this all. Not only do people cloud their own faculties, in order to stifle the voice of conscience, but, knowing what the effect of alcohol is, whenever they wish to make other people perform an act that is contrary to the dictates of their conscience, they purposely stupefy them, in order to render them temporarily deaf to its remonstrances. In war, soldiers are always made drunk, when they are about to be sent into close hand-to-hand combat. During the storming of

Sebastopol, all the French soldiers were completely intoxicated. After the storming of a fortress in the Central Asian War, when the Russian soldiers showed no inclination to plunder and kill the defenceless old men and children of the place, Skobeleff ordered them to be duly plied with brandy till they were drunk. Then they rushed out to accomplish the ghastly work.

Every one is acquainted with individuals who have drunk themselves out of their social sphere in consequence of crimes that tortured their conscience. It requires no extraordinary powers of observation to remark that people who in their lives set at naught the moral laws are much more addicted than others to stupefying stimulants and narcotics. Brigands, gangs of robbers, prostitutes, cannot dispense with alcohol.

Every one knows and acknowledges that indulgence in these things is a consequence of the remorse of conscience; that in certain immoral avocations stimulants are employed for the purpose of stifling the conscience. In like manner, every one knows and avows that the use of these stimulants does effectually deaden the voice of conscience, that a drunken man is capable of accomplishing acts, from the very contemplation of which in his sober moments he would have shrunk back in horror. About this there is no conflict of opinion. It is admitted on all hands without demur or reserve. And yet, strange to say, whenever the consumption of stupefying stimulants does not result in such acts as robbery, murder, violence, &c.; whenever they are indulged in, not as a consequence of remorse for terrible crimes, but by persons who follow professions which we do not regard as immoral, and are taken not all at once in large quantities, but continually, in moderate doses, it is taken for granted—no man can say why—that these stupefying stimulants have no effect upon the conscience, and certainly do not stifle or even deaden its voice.

Thus it is taken for granted that the daily consumption by a Russian in easy circumstances of a small glass of brandy before each meal, and of a tumbler of wine during the repast; by a Frenchman of his daily allowance of absinthe; by an Englishman of his port wine and porter; by a German of his lager-beer, and the smoking by a well-to-do Chinaman of a moderate dose of opium, besides a certain quantity of tobacco, are indulged in solely for pleasure, and have the desired effect on the animal spirits, but none at all on the conscience.

It is furthermore taken for granted that if after this customary stupefaction no robbery, murder, or other heinous crime is perpetrated, but only foolish and evil acts are performed, these acts are spontaneous, and are in no way the result of the stupefaction. It is taken for granted that if these persons committed no criminal act, they had therefore no need to gag their consciences, and that the life led by people addicted to the continual use of stimulants and narcotics is in every way excellent, and would have been in no respect different if these people had abstained from thus clouding their faculties. It is taken for granted, in fine, that the continuous consumption of stupefying stimulants does not in the least obscure the conscience of those who thus indulge in them.

On the one hand, then, every one knows by experience that his frame of mind, his mental mood, undergoes a change after he has indulged in alcohol and tobacco, and that what he was, or would have been, ashamed of before this artificial excitation, he has absolutely no scruples about afterwards; that after every sting of conscience, after the least painful of its pricks, one is possessed by a violent longing for some stimulant or narcotic; that under the influence of such stimulants it is very difficult to survey one's life and position; and that the continual consumption of an invariable moderate quantity of stimulants produces precisely the same kind of physiological effect as the instantaneous consumption of an excessive quantity. And on the other hand, people who indulge moderately in drinking alcohol and smoking tobacco flatter themselves that they take these things, not at all to silence their conscience, but solely to please their taste and obtain pleasure.

But one has only to give the matter a little serious, unprejudiced consideration—without attempting to cover and excuse one's own action—in order to acquire the conviction, in the first place, that if a man's conscience be deadened by his taking a large dose of alcoholic or narcotic preparations, the result is identical when he indulges in them continuously, though in smaller doses; for stimulants and narcotics always produce the same physiological action, which begins by abnormally intensifying, and ends by proportionately dulling and blunting the activity of the brain; and this, independently of the circumstance whether they are taken in greater or smaller quantities. In the second place, if these stimulants and narcotics possess at any time the property of benumbing the conscience, they are equally endowed with this property at all times, to the same extent if murder, robbery, and violence be perpetrated under their influence, as when only a word is spoken, a thought harboured, a feeling cherished, which would not have been spoken, harboured, or cherished without their influence. In the third place, if these brain-poisoning stimulants or narcotics are indispensable to robbers, brigands, and professional courtesans in order to drown the voice of their consciences, they are not less necessary to persons who follow certain other professions which are condemned by their own consciences, although regarded as legal and honourable by the vast majority of their fellow men.

In a word, it is impossible not to see that the habit of indulging in intoxicating stimulants in large or small doses, periodically or continuously, in the higher or the lower social circles, is always induced by the same cause, namely, the need of muffling the voice of conscience, in order not to be compelled to take notice of the jarring discord between actual life and the requisitions of conscience.

III

Therein lies the true cause of the universality of the habit of indulging in brain-poisoning stimulants, among others in tobacco, which is probably the most wide-spread and baneful of all.

It is claimed for tobacco that it gladdens the heart of the smoker, clears up his thoughts, attracts and gratifies him in precisely the same manner as any other habit he may have acquired, but that under no circumstances has it the effect possessed by alcohol of paralysing the activity of conscience. But it is only necessary to analyse more carefully than is the wont, the conditions under which a peculiarly strong craving for tobacco manifests itself, to acquire the conviction that brain-clouding by means of tobacco fumes, like brain-clouding by means of alcohol, exerts a direct action on the conscience, and that the need for this kind of stimulant is peculiarly intense precisely when the desire to stifle the voice of conscience is at its height. If it were true that tobacco only gladdens the heart and clears up the thoughts, no such passionate craving for it would be felt under such clearly defined circumstances, and people would not be heard averring that they are ready to dispense with food rather than deny themselves a smoke, a statement which, in many cases, we know to be literally true.

The male cook already alluded to, who murdered his mistress, told the court, on his trial, that when he had entered the bedroom and cut her throat with the knife, and seen her fall back uttering a hoarse, guttural sound, while the blood spurted out in a torrent, he was struck aghast at what he had done. "I had not the courage to finish her," he exclaimed, "so I went out of the bedroom, into the parlour, sat down, and smoked a cigarette." It was only after he had clouded his brain with tobacco fumes that he summoned up the force necessary to return to the bedroom and ply the knife until his victim was dead, when he began to ransack her movable property.

Now, it is obvious that the craving he felt to have a smoke under these peculiar circumstances was not due to a desire on his part to clear his thoughts or gladden his heart, but to the necessity of stifling a voice that was hindering him from consummating the deed he had planned and partially executed.

Every smoker can, if he will, discern the same clearly defined need of stupefying his thinking faculties with tobacco fumes at certain critical moments of his life. Speaking for myself, I can distinctly call to mind the times when I, while yet a smoker, felt this peculiarly pressing need of tobacco. It was always on occasions when I was desirous not to remember things that were thrusting themselves upon my memory, when I was anxious to forget, to suspend all thought. At one time I would be sitting alone, doing nothing, conscious that I ought to be engaged at my work, but averse to all occupations. I would then light a cigarette, smoke it, and continue to sit in idleness. Another time I would remember that I had an engagement for five o'clock, but that I had lingered too long in another place and it was now too late. The thought that it was too late being disagreeable to me, I would take out a cigarette and drive it away in tobacco fumes. If I felt cross and peevish, and was offending another man by the tone or contents of my speech, and recognising my duty to cease, yet resolved to give way to my peevishness, I would smoke and continue to show my ill-temper. When sitting at the card-table I had lost more than the sum to which I had determined to limit my losses, I would light a cigarette and play on. Whenever I had placed myself in an awkward position, had done anything reprehensible, had made a blunder, and feeling myself bound to acknowledge the true state of affairs in order to extricate myself from it, was yet unwilling to do so, I shifted the blame on to others, took out a cigarette and smoked. If, when working at a book or story I felt dissatisfied with what I was writing, and saw it to be my duty to cease, but felt an inclination to finish what I had thought out, I took out a cigarette and smoked. Was I discussing some question, and did I see that my opponent and myself, viewing the matter from different angles of vision, did not and could not understand each other, if I felt a strong desire to make him hear me out notwithstanding, I began to smoke and continued to talk.

The characteristic that distinguishes tobacco from other kinds of brain-clouding stimulants, besides the rapidity with which it stupefies the faculties, and its apparent harmlessness, consists in what may be termed its portativeness, in the ease with which it can be employed upon every trivial occasion. Thus the consumption of opium, alcohol, hashish involves certain arrangements which one cannot make at all times and in all places, whereas the tobacco and paper necessary for making cigarettes you can always carry about with you without the slightest personal inconvenience. Then, again, the opium-smoker and the drunkard excite loathing and horror, whereas there is nothing repulsive about the tobacco-smoker as such; but, over and above these advantages, tobacco possesses another property that materially contributes to render it popular; while the stupefaction induced by opium, hashish, alcohol, extends to all impressions received, and to all actions performed over a relatively long period of time, the deadening effect on the brain of tobacco can be regulated in accordance with the exigencies of each particular case. Do you wish, for instance, to do something which you know you ought not to do? Smoke a cigarette, muddle your faculties just to the extent that is absolutely indispensable to enable you to do what you should have left undone, and you are at once as fresh as ever, and can think and speak with your wonted clearness. Are you too painfully conscious that you have done something which you should have refrained from doing? Smoke a cigarette, and the gnawing worm of conscience will be quickly smothered in the fumes of your tobacco, and you can turn forthwith to another occupation, and forget what occasioned your annoyance.

But making an abstract from all those particular cases in which every smoker has recourse to tobacco, not for the purpose of satisfying a habitual craving, or of whiling away the time, but as a means of silencing the voice of his conscience, which protests against certain acts that he has already performed or intends to perform, do we not clearly discern the strictly defined relation and interdependence between people's way of living and their passionate love of smoking?

When do boys begin to smoke? Almost invariably when they have lost the innocence of childhood. Why is it that people addicted to smoking can leave it off the moment they raise themselves up to a higher moral level, and others recommence as soon as they drift into a dissolute social circle? Why is it that almost all gamblers are smokers? Why is it that among the female sex the women who lead blameless, regular lives are the least frequently addicted to smoking? Why do courtesans and the insane all smoke without exception? Habit, no doubt, is a factor in these cases which cannot be ignored, but after having given it our fullest consideration, we must still admit that there is a certain well-defined, undeniable interdependence between smoking and the need for silencing one's conscience, and that smoking does undoubtedly produce that effect.

To what extent can smoking stifle the voice of conscience? We have no need to seek for the materials for a solution of this question in exceptional cases of crime and remorse; it is simply sufficient to observe the behaviour of the ordinary—one might almost say of any—smoker. Every smoker abandoning himself to his passion, loses sight of, or rides roughshod over, certain of the most elementary rules of social life, the observance of which he demands from others; and which he himself respects in all other cases, whenever his conscience is not completely silenced by tobacco. Every person of moderately good breeding in our social sphere holds it to be unseemly, ill-mannered, churlish, merely for his own pleasure to interfere with the peace and comfort of others, and *á fortiori* to injure their health. No one would take the liberty to flood with water a room in which people were sitting; to scream and yell in it; to turn on hot, cold, or foetid air, or to perform any other acts tending to disturb or injure others; and yet out of a thousand smokers scarcely one will hesitate to fill with noxious fumes a room the atmosphere of which is being breathed by women and children who do not smoke. If before lighting their cigarette or cigar, they ask the company present, "Have you any objection?" every one knows that he or she is expected to answer, "Not the least!" (although it is inconceivable that it should be anything but disagreeable to a non-smoker to have the air he respires poisoned, and to find stinking cigarette ends in glasses, tumblers, cups, plates, candlesticks, or even were it only in ashtrays). And even if we suppose that non-smoking adults can support the discomforts in question, surely no one will maintain that it is agreeable or wholesome for children, whose permission nobody ever thinks of asking. And yet people who are perfectly honourable and humane in all other respects smoke in the company of children, at table, in small rooms, poisoning the air with fumes of tobacco, and never feel the faintest prick of conscience.

It is commonly urged in favour of the practice—and I used to advance the plea myself—that smoking conduces to efficient mental work; and there is no doubt that if we confine our consideration to the quantity of intellectual work done, we shall find this plea well grounded. To a man who is smoking, and who has consequently ceased to gauge and weigh his thoughts, it naturally seems that his mind has suddenly become thronged with ideas. As a mere matter of fact, however, his ideas have not become more numerous, but he has simply lost all control over them.

A man who works is always conscious of two beings within himself—the one who is engaged in work, and the one who sits in judgment upon the work done. The severer the judgment he passes, the slower and the more perfect is the work done, and *vice versa*. If the judge be under the influence of a stimulant or a narcotic, there will be more work done, but of an inferior quality.

"If I do not smoke, I cannot work; I cannot get my thoughts upon paper; and even when I have begun, I cannot go on." So people commonly say, and so I said myself in times gone by. Now, what is the meaning of this statement? It means that you have nothing to say, or that the ideas to which you are endeavouring to give expression have not matured in your consciousness—are only dimly dawning upon you—and the living critic within you, unclouded by tobacco fumes, tells you so. Now, if you were not a smoker, you would, under these circumstances, either wait patiently until you had acquired a clear conception of the subject about which you wished to write, or else you would strive, by throwing yourself manfully into it, to master it thoroughly, weighing and discussing the objections that suggest themselves to your mind, and generally elucidating your thoughts to yourself. Instead of this, however, you take out a cigarette, and smoke; the living critic within you becomes clouded, stupefied, and the hitch in your work is removed; that which seemed petty, unworthy, while your brain was still fresh and clear, now appears great, excellent; that which struck you as obscure is no longer so; you make light of the objections that occur to you, and you continue to write, and find to your joy that you can write quickly and much.

IV

"But can it be possible that such a slight, almost imperceptible, change as is produced by the mild flush of excitement that ensues upon our moderately indulging in wine or tobacco should work such grave results? No doubt, to a person who smokes opium, takes hashish, drinks alcohol so immoderately that he falls down helpless and bereft of his reason, the consequences may be very grave indeed; but it is very different when a person only takes as much as suffices to cause a pleasurable excitement. This state can surely be productive of no such wide-reaching results." This is the objection that people usually make. It seems to them that mere incipient inebriation—the partial eclipsing, or rather the mellowing, of the light of consciousness cannot entail serious results of any kind. Now, it is as reasonable to think thus as to imagine that, although a watch may be seriously injured by striking it against a stone, it is not liable to any damage whatever from the introduction of a splinter of wood, or some other foreign body, into its internal mechanism.

It should not be lost sight of that the labour which is mainly instrumental in moving and moulding human life does not consist in the movement of human hands, feet, or backs, but in modifications of consciousness. Before a man can perform anything with his hands and feet a certain change must necessarily have taken place in his conscience. And this change determines all the ensuing actions of the man. Now, these modifications of human consciousness are always slight, well-nigh imperceptible.

The Russian painter Bruloff was once engaged in correcting a drawing of one of his pupils. He touched it very slightly with his pencil here and there, with the result that his pupil cried out: "Why you have only given the drawing one or two scarcely appreciable touches, and it has undergone a complete transformation!" Bruloff sententiously replied: "Art begins only there where scarcely perceptible touches effect great changes."

This saying is strikingly true; and not merely when restricted to art, but when applied to all human existence. We are justified in affirming that true life begins only where scarcely perceptible touches begin to tell, where such changes as are produced are infinitesimally small; and seem to us of no account. It is not where vast outward changes take place, where people move backwards and forwards, crossing each other, clashing with each other, fighting and slaying each other, that true life is to be found; it is where infinitesimal differential changes occur.

Take Rasskolnikoff,* for instance. His true life did not coincide with the moment when he killed the old woman or her sister. When he set about murdering the old woman, and especially when he was killing her sister, he was not instinct with genuine life; he was acting as a wound-up machine acts, doing what he could not possibly refrain from doing; firing off the charge that he had accumulated within himself long before. One old woman lay killed before him, the other stood there in his presence, and the axe was ready in his hand.

Rasskolnikoff's true life coincided not with the moment when he met the old woman's sister, but the time when he had not yet killed either of the two, when he had not yet entered a stranger's lodging bent upon murder; when he had no axe in his hands, no loop in his greatcoat on which to hang it, when he had no thoughts of the old woman whatever; it coincided with the time when, lying on the sofa in his own room, not thinking of the old woman, nor of the question whether it was lawful or not in obedience to the will of one human being to wipe out the earthly existence of another unworthy human being, but was debating with himself whether he should or should not live in St. Petersburg, whether he should or should not take his mother's money, and meditating upon other matters that had no reference whatever to the old woman. It is at such conjunctures that the greatest attainable clearness of mental vision is of the very utmost importance for the right solution of such questions as may then arise; it is at such moments that one glass of beer drunk, one little cigarette smoked, can

* The hero of Dostoyevsky's novel *Crime and Punishment.*

hinder that solution, can cause it to be put off, can silence the voice of conscience, and can bring about a solution of the question in a sense favourable to our baser nature, as was the case with Rasskolnikoff.

Upon what takes place after a man has already formed his decision and has begun to embody it in action, many important issues of a material order may, no doubt, depend; edifices may be pulled down in consequence, riches may be scattered to the winds of heaven, human bodies may be deprived of life; but absolutely nothing can be done but what was already included in the consciousness of the man himself. The limits of what can take place are fixed by this consciousness.

Let me not be misunderstood. What I am saying now has nothing in common with the question of free will and determinism. The discussion of such matters is superfluous here, seeing that it has no connection with the question at issue, and I believe I may say it is quite superfluous for any intelligible purpose whatever. Putting aside, then, the question whether a man is or is not free to act as he pleases (a problem which, it seems to me, is not properly stated), all that I am here concerned to maintain is, that as human activity is determined by scarcely appreciable changes in consciousness, it follows (whether we admit so-called free will or not) that too much attention cannot possibly be given to the state of mind in which these changes occur, just as the most scrupulous care should be taken of the condition of the scales in which we are about to weigh precious objects. It is incumbent upon us, as far as in us lies, to surround ourselves and others with the conditions most favourable to that precision and clearness of thought which are so indispensable to the proper working of our consciousness; and we should certainly refrain most scrupulously from hindering and clogging this action of consciousness by the consumption of brain-clouding stimulants and narcotics.

For man is at once a spiritual and an animal being. His activity can be set in motion by influencing his spiritual nature, and it can likewise receive an impulse by influencing his animal nature. In this he resembles a watch which can be moved by moving either the hands or the main wheel. And as it is much more expedient to regulate the movement of a watch by its internal mechanism than by moving its hands, so it is far more judicious to determine a man's activity by means of his consciousness than by means of his animal nature. And as in a watch we should be most concerned to maintain those conditions which ensure the smooth working of the inner mechanism, so in man we should lay most stress on the attainment and maintenance of unclouded purity and sharpness of consciousness, through which man's activity is most easily and most conveniently determined. Of this there can be no doubt; every one feels and knows that it is true. But very often people also feel the necessity of deceiving themselves. They are not so much concerned that their consciousness should work smoothly and well, as that they should persuade themselves that what they are bent on doing is right and good; and in order to acquire that persuasion they deliberately have recourse to means which they know will interfere with the right working of their consciousness.

V

People drink and smoke, therefore, not merely for want of something better to do to while away the time, or to raise their spirits; not because of the pleasure they receive, but simply and solely in order to drown the warning voice of conscience. And if that be so, how terrible are the consequences that must ensue! In effect, just fancy what a curious building the people would construct who, in order to adjust the walls to a perpendicular, should refuse to employ a straight plumb-line, and for the purpose of measuring the angles should object to use an ordinary carpenter's square, preferring to the former a soft plastic plumb-rule, that bends and adjusts itself to all the irregularities of the walls, and to the latter a carpenter's square that folds and yields to the touch and adjusts itself equally well to an acute and an obtuse angle!

And yet this is exactly what is done in every-day life by those who stupefy themselves. Life is not regulated by conscience, it is conscience that plies and adjusts itself to life.

This is what we see taking place in the life of private individuals. This it is which also takes place in the life of all humanity—which is but the sum total of the lives of private individuals.

In order thoroughly to realise all that is involved in this clouding of one's consciousness, the reader has only to call distinctly to mind his frame of mind at each of the chief periods of his life. He will remember that at each of these periods he found himself face to face with certain moral problems which he was bound to solve in one sense or the other, and upon the right solution of which the well-being of his whole life depended. To arrive at this solution after an exhaustive survey of all the factors and phases of the problem is an utter impossibility without putting a very severe strain upon the attention. Now, this effort of attention constitutes work. Whatever work we put our hands to, there is always a period in its progress—generally the commencement—when its disagreeable features very strongly impress us, when it seems peculiarly arduous and irksome, and human nature in its weakness suggests the wish to abandon it altogether. Physical work seems irksome in the beginning, intellectual labour appears still more irksome. As Lessing remarks, people have the habit of ceasing to think as soon as the process of thinking becomes difficult, and in my opinion precisely when it becomes fruitful. A man feels instinctively that the problems that come up before him clamouring for a solution, the Sphinx's riddles that must be answered on pain of death, cannot be properly thought out without strenuous and, in many cases, painful labour, and this he would gladly shirk. Now, if he were bereft of the means of clouding his mental faculties, it would be impossible for him to expunge from the tablets of his conscience the questions on the order of the day, and, *nolens volens,* he would find himself in conditions that necessitated an answer, and admitted neither of excuse nor delay. But, behold, he discovers an effective means of putting off these questions whenever they present themselves for a solution; and he does not fail to make use of it. The moment life demands an answer to these questions, and they begin to worry and harass him, he has recourse to those artificial means, and delivers himself from the vexation of spirit engendered by the disquieting questions. His consciousness no longer presses for a speedy solution, and the problems remain unsolved until the next interval of lucidity. But when the following period of lucidity comes round the same thing is repeated, and the individual continues to stand for months, for years, sometimes during his whole life, face to face with the same moral problems without moving one step forward in the direction of a solution. And yet all the movement and progress of human life consists exclusively in the right solution of moral problems. This curious mode of procedure presents considerable analogy with the conduct of a man employed to recover a lost pearl lying at the bottom of a shallow river, who, to escape entering the cold water, prevents himself from seeing the pearl by deliberately stirring up the mud, and repeating the process whenever the water shows signs of becoming clear again. A man addicted to the habit of stupefying his fac-

ulties by artificial means will often continue stagnant during the whole
course of his existence, standing in the same place, looking out upon the
world through the mist of the vague self-contradictory life-philosophy
that he once accepted; at the beginning of every new period of lucidity
pressing hard against the same wall, against which he pressed in the
same way ten, fifteen, twenty years before, and in which he lacks the
means to make a breach, because he persists in deliberately blunting
the edge of the thought which alone was capable of effecting it.

Every one has it in his power to verify the truth of this assertion
upon himself and upon others. Let him conjure up before his mind's
eye the principal events of his own life for the period during which
he has been indulging in smoking and drinking, and let him pass in
review the same period in the life of others. He will then clearly
perceive the line of demarcation, the characteristic trait that separates
smokers and tipplers from people who are free from those habits.
For the more a man stupefies himself with these stimulants and narcotics the more stolid, quiescent, and stagnant he becomes intellectu-
ally and morally.

VI

Terrible indeed are the evils that have been more than once described
to us, which opium and hashish bring upon those who consume them;
terrible, likewise, are the effects—which we can every day observe—
of alcoholism upon the inveterate drunkard; but more terrible beyond
comparison for the entire community at large are the effects of moderate drinking and smoking, habits largely indulged in as harmless by
the majority of the people, more especially by the so-called educated
classes of our social world.

These consequences cannot be otherwise than terrible if we
admit what it is impossible to deny, that the guiding force of the
community—political, administrative, scientific, literary, artistic—is
wielded for the most part by men who are not in a normal condition of
mind, by men who, to call things by their names, are in a state of intoxication. It is usually taken for granted that a man who, like most of
the members of our well-to-do classes, indulges in a little spirits every
day before each meal, is during the hours of work next day in a perfectly normal state of mind. This is a grievous error. The man who

yesterday drank a bottle of wine, a tumbler of *vodka,* or two large measures of beer, is to-day in a state of subsiding intoxication or incipient sobriety, a state of dejection which follows upon yesterday's excitement; consequently, he is mentally oppressed as well as depressed, and this feeling is but intensified by smoking. A man who drinks and smokes moderately but regularly every day, requires—in order to restore his brain to its normal condition—at least one week, probably more than a week, of total abstinence from spirits and tobacco. Now, no smoker or bibbler ever voluntarily abstains for such a long time.

It follows, therefore, that by far the greatest part of all that is done in this world of ours, both by those whose profession it is to guide and teach others and by those who are thus guided and taught, is done in a state of ebriety.

And I trust this will not be taken either as a joke or an exaggeration: the extravagant disorder, and especially the senselessness and folly of our life springs mainly from the state of continuous inebriation in which the majority of people deliberately place themselves. Is it conceivable that people not drunk should calmly set about doing all the extraordinary things that are being accomplished in our world, from the Eiffel Tower to obligatory military service? It is utterly inconceivable. Without the slightest need, or even semblance of need, a company is formed, a large capital subscribed; people go to work to make estimates and draw plans; millions of working days and millions of *poods* of iron are spent in the construction of a tower; and, when finished, millions of persons consider it their duty to repair to the summit of this tower, stay a short time, and then crawl down again, and the only effect produced on the minds of men by this tower, and the frequency with which ascents are made in it, is the desire and the resolve to go and erect still loftier towers in other places. Now, is it conceivable that these things should be done by sober people? Or, take another case; all European States are, and have for scores of years been, busily engaged in inventing and perfecting effectual weapons to kill people; and they carefully teach the science of organised murder to all young men who have reached manhood's estate. All are well aware that incursions of barbarians are no longer possible, and that these preparations for murder are intended by Christian, civilised nations to be employed against each other; all feel that this is unseemly, painful, nefarious, ruinous, immoral, impious, and senseless; and yet all persist in carrying out their preparations for mutual destruction: some by arranging political combinations, making alliances, and settling who is to slaughter whom; others by directing the work of those who are engaged in getting things ready for the slaughter; and others, again, by submitting against their own will, against their conscience, against their reason, to these preparations for murder. Now, could sober men act in this way? None but drunken men, men who never have a lucid interval of sobriety, could do these things, could live on in spite of this perpetual, irreconcilable, terrible conflict between life and conscience, in which not only in this matter, but in all other respects, the people of our world live and have their being.

At no other period of the world's history, I feel convinced, did mankind lead an existence in which the dictates of conscience and their deliberate actions were in such evident conflict as at present.

It seems as if the human race in our days had got fastened to something that is holding it back, impeding its progress. There would seem to be some external cause which hinders it from attaining the position that belongs to it of right, in virtue of consciousness. The cause in question—or, if there be several, the main cause—is the physical state of stupefaction to which the overwhelming majority of human beings reduce themselves by means of alcohol and tobacco.

The deliverance of humanity from this terrible evil will arrive in epoch in the life of the race, and, apparently, this epoch will arrive in the near future. The evil is already recognised. A change in the consciousness of men in reference to the use of brain-poisoning stimulants and narcotics has already taken place: people are beginning to realise the terrible mischief they produce, and they are manifesting this feeling in acts; and this imperceptible change in their consciousness must inevitably bring in its train the emancipation of humanity from the influence of all such brain poisons. This emancipation of mankind from the thraldom of brain poisons will open their eyes to the demands of their consciousness, and they will forthwith begin to put their life in harmony with its dictates.

This process seems to have already begun. And, as is usual in such cases, it is beginning in the higher social classes, after all the lower orders have become infected with the evil.

How Children Are Made Drunkards

William Lee Howard

1907

In response to the untimely death of a thirty-eight-year-old patient, Dr. William Lee Howard wrote a sentimental account of the young man's path to alcohol addiction for Ladies' Home Journal. *After investigating the man's family history, Dr. Howard concludes that he had been "poisoned" as an infant by "soothing syrups" containing opium and baby's milk laced with gin. In this article he implores mothers of young children never to resort to the popular sleep cures of the day.*

The other day I attended the funeral of a dear friend and patient. When twenty years of age he promised to be one of the literary lights of this country.

The pace he set for himself was not rapid for an individual physiologically balanced, yet he could not maintain it without artificial assistance. So he was compelled—mark you, I say compelled—to keep propped by stimulants. It is a long story to a short end. The sad termination came at thirty-eight.

His mother, sister and closest friends could not account for this fine boy's merging into the drunken man. I worked hard over that boy! But I had nothing to build upon. His nervous structure was sand—quicksand.

"But," said his mother to me, "how could Robert become such a slave to drink? What was the cause?"

Of course, there was a cause; there must be a cause for every effect. I did not know it, but I determined to find it.

The essential thing to know when treating instability is the family history of the patient. In this case the family history was excellent. He came of sturdy Scotch stock. No nervous affliction on either side as far back as could be traced. Grandparents, father and mother were all temperate people. The sister, three years older than the brother, was a normal woman, the mother of three healthy boys, athletes and strictly temperate in all things.

Yet here we had an extraordinarily brilliant young man whose career was ruined because he had to have stimulants. He abhorred the stuff, made mighty efforts to get along without it, but it was a physiological impossibility.

After long and minute investigations I discovered the truth—the awful, warning truth, which, when it reached the heart of his mother, brought her to the grave. She had allowed his delicate, baby nerve-cells to be poisoned, distorted, by opium and alcohol—innocently, ignorantly, of course.

This mother of Robert was very ill immediately after his birth. He was given to a supposedly-responsible nurse. The best-intentioned nurse cannot feel the future responsibility to the child. If the child disturbs her rest and annoys her by its cries what is more natural than that she should give the baby a dose of one of the much-advertised "harmless soothing syrups"? Of course, baby sleeps quietly: he is in an opium sleep. Of course, he looks fat and well-nourished: he is drug-bloated.

In this case I found that a little gin was frequently put into the baby's milk. "It is good for the kidneys," the old nurse said. Then she said that it was the custom to give a little "soothing syrup" to all babies. "It helps to soften up the gums." It did. And it also helped to soften up the delicate tissues of the brain.

When the mother recovered the babe was given to her. But he missed his opium; he yelled and went into spasms; every tiny nerve-cell was crying out for its poison. But there was a "cure" for his agony. A "soothing syrup" was given to him, and he "sweetly" slept, only to be poisoned again when the effect had worn off and he cried for more.

So we buried this young man—a man poisoned by drugs when a

babe and ostracised as a drunkard when a man because his nerve-cells never grew to manhood's necessities.

How many mothers, and good mothers, too, are innocently and ignorantly allowing their sons and daughters to start on a drunkard's career, commencing at the cradle in the same way! These mothers forget one thing: that every healthy baby should cry and kick. That is its way of filling the lungs and developing the muscles. To "soothe" it with anything but pure food, fresh air and loving arms is to send it out into the world an undeveloped, helpless being.

To give a baby any of the so-called "soothing syrups" is worse than murder—a living death. For, mark you this well: the principal ingredient in the average "soothing syrup" is some form, some derivative, of opium, laudanum or morphine. There may be one or two exceptions, but don't even allow these in the house. If it is called "tincture" remember that the average tincture contains alcohol.

No drug known is so poisonous, none so quickly works irreparable damage to the infant, as opium and its derivatives. It devours the nerve-cell substance; it weakens the tissues of the brain; it eats out a man's capacity to think or act except when he is under its influence; it is the drug that throws on to the world the poor, helpless beings who fill our reform schools, insane asylums and drunkards' graves.

The sad part of this drugging of infants is that it occurs for the greatest part among those who need all the advantages of pure food, fresh air and hygienic attention. The ignorant mothers believe the delusive advertisements, have implicit faith in the unscrupulous druggist, and the baby is opiumed from the day of its birth.

It is useless to look for moral and mental defects in the public-school children when the real cause, drugging in the cradle, is overlooked.

Nor is this cruel murder of children confined to one class. Who is most to blame—the woman of wealth who simply gives her child over to a hired nurse and does not take the trouble to give her baby the soothing caresses that soon lull it to sleep, or the worn-out mother of the tenement, who, seeing her fretting child, ignorantly gives it opium—or, in other words, a "soothing syrup"?

I know a man whose mother believed in "soothing syrups." She would not believe that they were "doped." So, whenever the child cried, it was given a spoonful of the "syrup." Of course, it made him sleep. When his "soothing-syrup" days had passed by she discovered that he was nervous and fretful. He was given a "tonic" to "tone him up"—the tonic contained opium again, and alcohol. Of course, it "toned him up." But soon the system refused to respond to the "tonic." It was not strong enough, and yet the moment he stopped the "tonic" he became listless and incapable of work. Finally, he had to resort to the next more powerful drug—morphine. He became a morphine fiend. He had reached a desirable professorship—one of the most successful professors in the college. But soon it was noticed that the brilliancy of his eye was unnatural, and, to make a long story short, the truth came out. He lost his professorship, he got morose, his mother died from a broken heart, and the man is today in an insane asylum. There you have a direct line from the "soothing syrups" of the cradle to the "morphine" of the man, and to the asylum.

I have said that babies get alcohol through nurses' milk. I have directly traced cases of habitual drunkenness to this cause.

Quite frequently you will find a nurse who is feeding a child, who takes a glass of beer or ale with her meals and at night. She tells you that her doctor told her she needed some such tonic to keep up her strength. Now, it is not probable that a glass of beer at mealtimes will have any appreciable effect on the milk. Nevertheless, it is tampering with a dangerous possibility.

The human system can, physiologically, burn up a certain amount of alcohol during twenty-four hours. But just what that quantity is for different individuals is uncertain. One nurse may be able to consume several bottles of beer during the twenty-four hours and use up in her system every drop of the alcohol so that none is left in the secretions. But—and here is the important point—she may at any time exceed this amount. She may take in more alcohol than the tissues can burn and the residue will be found in the secretions. In the nursing woman the milk secretions are the most active; hence, here the excess alcohol will be found, and your little baby gets its first poisonous drink. And if your baby is getting any of the by-products of beer or whisky it will soon become fretful and irritable. It is then only a short step to the bottle of "soothing syrup."

Thousands of babies are started on drunkards' careers in this way. And there is but one way to avoid it. Never "soothe" a child except by

Nature's own ways. The moment a "syrup," a "liniment," a "cure" of any sort is advertised as putting a baby to sleep, or soothing it, look out for it. That is the article, of all others, you do not want in your home to give your child. From such concoctions, with their morphine, opium or laudanum, do we make drunkards of our children!

THE ENEMY

Margarita Spalding Gerry

1909

Harper's Monthly Magazine *published Margarita Spalding Gerry's harrowing account of a lonely woman's struggle to overcome morphine addiction. The wife of a navy officer who is at sea, Mrs. Campbell steadfastly denies her problem before finally admitting to the unhappiness and destruction of her life. With the help of a private nurse, she makes desperate attempts to free herself from the drug and the physical suffering it inflicts upon her. Slowly, Mrs. Campbell reduces her daily intake of morphine in anticipation of her husband's homecoming. Sadly, she ultimately fails to overcome her lethal habit.*

I followed the doctor into the reception-room and closed the door behind me.

"Doctor Dietrich, who is to take the responsibility in this case?"

"You and I."

I gasped.

"I'm afraid it's rather a high-handed performance on my part"—I was surprised to see what a boyish smile he had—"but there was no time to be lost. I found when I got a square look at her last night—I forgot to tell you that she came to my office at eleven—alone—begging for a morphine hypodermic—with one of the usual stories, of course—that I had seen her before. I know her husband. Lieutenant Campbell, a fine fellow—"

"You didn't give it to her!"

"Oh yes. I gave her a hypodermic—of water—coward, of course—didn't want a scene. But she was too habituated to be put off that way, so I had my scene, after all." He shrugged his shoulders so as to make himself look brutal. But I was beginning to know Doctor Dietrich too well to be deceived by his brusque mannerisms.

"And then?" I prompted him.

"Oh—I talked with her while I was getting her home—got hold of her a little. It won't last, you know; maybe it didn't ten minutes after I left her. But I just put the thing to her—played she was a reasoning human being for a few minutes. You know, just what any one would have done." He almost stammered in his haste to get himself out of the conversation.

"You needn't be afraid of me, Doctor Dietrich," I laughed. "Honestly, I am not going to praise you. You have convinced me. I know it is less than nothing to get hold of a morphine victim when she is frantic for the drug, send her away without it, and get her to consent to undergo treatment. Having settled this point, I must say that I don't like to nurse Mrs. Campbell without consulting some of her relatives."

"But she hasn't any people that can be counted on," he said, irritably. "Campbell cruising around the Pacific somewhere—doesn't know anything about the morphine, she says. Nothing but a stepmother on Campbell's side and a brother on hers. And he's out on the Pacific coast somewhere. She's in Washington only because Campbell's last station was Annapolis; they know only a few of the navy people here, and those only slightly. Some one had to take hold."

I felt as if a two-hundred-pound weight had settled down on my shoulders. But it would never occur to you to refuse a case if Doctor Dietrich wanted you to take it.

"But," I said, in depression, "I'm afraid she wasn't sincere in her desire to reform—"

"'Reform'!" he interrupted me, laughing. "Dear me, how moral you are! You surely wouldn't expect her to stay in the same mind all this time. That's one of the features of the disease."

I felt as if he were taking me too much for granted. And that made me want to say something unpleasant.

"I think it very probable," I remarked, stiffly, "that she put herself under your charge in order to get the morphine you would allow her in addition to what she had managed to hide. Sometime between the hour when you left her and ten this morning when I arrived she must have bought a quantity of the powder—"

"Oh yes, there are always druggists that pander to anything with a profit—'my poverty and not my will consents'—that sort of thing. Did you discover where she put it?"

"Yes: in the brass knobs of one of the bedsteads."

"Clever hiding-place," nodded the doctor, approvingly. "She probably has another; they usually count on discovery. You'll watch her closely, of course. If she has another store, she won't stay long from her base of supplies"—he was looking absent-mindedly for his gloves.

"But, doctor! What am I to do if she won't try to do better? It's dreadful to think any one is trying to deceive you all the time."

Doctor Dietrich looked me over in his dispassionate way.

"You're a good deal of a little girl, after all, aren't you?" he demanded. Then his face grew stern. "Now, see here, I will not have Mrs. Campbell treated as if she were a criminal. This cunning, this apparent destruction of the moral nature, is as much a feature of the disease as the contraction of the pupil of the eye. As for the beginnings of these things—that's all beyond you or me. I think it very probable that, under the same circumstances, I'd be five times worse than she is. Enough physicians are," he threw in grimly. "I asked you to take the case because I thought that, even though you are a nurse, you might manage to be a little human—and then, there was the question of class. If you nurse Mrs. Campbell—are you going to do it?"

"Yes," I replied, meekly.

"Well, then, you can't sleep or breathe without the load of this woman's sick body on your conscience. You've got to realize that it's your *conscience* and her *body*—you mustn't dare to judge her. You've got to be nurse and keeper and entertainer and sister. And you've even got to take it on trust that she is worth saving. For you didn't see her as she was when she married Campbell. Poor little bride!" he turned to say under his breath.

I felt ashamed of myself.

"I'm sorry," I said, in the silliest way. "And I won't judge her. Honestly, I won't."

His face cleared.

"That's better," he said briskly. "Now, just now, the only thing you can do is to try to find out how much she has been in the habit of taking during the twenty-four hours; of course you can't trust what she says—probably she doesn't know. Get her down to five grains at two fixed hours as soon as you can. Wish I knew who prescribed morphine for her in the first place—it was for some slight neuralgic trouble, I believe. But I suppose I have no business to know. There are enough of us who never think beyond 'relieving' the immediate pain," he added, sadly.

He took up his hat.

"If you could contrive to feel some real fondness for her," he said, his hand on the knob of the hall door, "that would be the best thing yet—"

"Oh, Doctor Dietrich!" said a sweet, husky voice from the head of the stairs. "Vulnerable, after all?"

We both turned and looked where Mrs. Campbell stood, one nervous delicate hand on the balustrade. Her brown eyes gazed deliberately from the doctor to me. Their brilliant gaze would have been arch had they not been suffused with a restful languor. When I had seen her the moment before, she had been tense and restlessly irritable.

"Vulnerable—oh, yes," assented the doctor, absently. Then, as he telegraphed, "She has had it!" to me, he straightened himself and said gallantly, "But where weapons are irresistible, what man is not?" with a magnificent sweep of his hat, which served the double purpose of announcing his departure and conveying another warning to me.

Mrs. Campbell laughed, a low, infinitely contented laugh.

"Funny, square man, Doctor Dietrich is, isn't he?" she said, lightly. "And so clever, so terrifyingly clever!" She darted a side glance at me, full of the playful cunning of a child, and the first thing I knew I was laughing with her. That seemed to clear the atmosphere—she had bit her lip when I first appeared in my nurse's uniform. But now she gave me a soft, caressing pat on the hand.

"What shall we do with ourselves this April day?" she asked. "I think I want something different."

"The country?" I suggested.

"Yes, that's it. I want to see the spring beauties and anemones. I'd like to be where they are when—when I usually take—it. I know it will be better for me!" She was on fire with enthusiasm. "Come!" She turned her head as she preceded me up the stairs to say, "I wasn't very nice to you when you came, but I think it is very good of you to stay with me and help me get well." There was something appealing in the confident little smile she threw me.

"How would it do to take a house in the country for these weeks?" I began, knowing that it was a good plan to break up associations connected with the drug.

Her face fell.

"Oh no, I couldn't—it wouldn't do—Lex wouldn't like it not to find me here when he returns. I—like this house!" She was trembling with fear and excitement, and it took some moments to reassure her.

I delayed only long enough in my room to pick up my hat before I followed her into her own exquisitely fresh and simple bedroom. It's a humiliating thing to have to act as keeper; but Mrs. Campbell gave no sign of resentment. She was changing her house gown for a tailored white linen walking-dress—in which there was less difference to be observed from my uniform. And both were suitable enough for the warm day. She looked so slender and girlish as she stood, with arms upraised pinning on her hat, that compassion filled me. Whether or not she saw something of it as my eyes met hers in the mirror I don't know. But she lifted her chin proudly and said to my reflection:

"Of course you understand I require assistance only for the baths and massage and things like that while I reduce the amount of morphine I have been forced to take." She turned around and faced me. "I have quite enough willpower to drop it any moment I choose," she said, haughtily.

My heart sank. It would be so much more difficult to deal with her in that mood. She so needed to realize her danger. And I thought the doctor had convinced her the night before.

For the first half-hour of our walk Mrs. Campbell's enthusiasm hurried her forward at a pace I found it difficult to equal. As soon as her interest slackened and she began to drag, I hailed a car, which took us within a short distance of Piney Branch and spring flowers. There for a time she was happy. She darted here and there, by the side of the road, half-way across a field, greeting with joyous and caressing cries each new patch of purple pansy-violets or delicate bloodroot. But in the midst of pursuit interest left her as freakishly as it had been evoked. She dropped the already faded flowers and stood locking and unlocking her emptied hands, eyes turned broodingly toward the city we had left.

"Mrs. Campbell," I said, thinking that this might be the time to find out the quantity of the drug she had been accustomed to use, "do you feel that you must have a hypodermic? What have you been accustomed to take? And at what intervals? I have brought the medicine with me."

Her lips parted eagerly and she turned feverish eyes to me. The next moment the instinct of secrecy prevailed.

"No, no. I shall get along very nicely until this evening. Then—just a grain or so—to make me sleep. But only if the neuralgia troubles me. You mustn't think I am addicted to it." She spoke with a fine air of candor and a gracious smile.

But, with the words, the spirit of restlessness seized her, and she was as eager to get back home as she had been to leave it. In spite of hurry and the help of a passing taxicab she was exhausted before we reached shelter. When I had made her comfortable in bed she still protested that she did not want the morphine. So I went for a glass of milk to bridge over the hour before dinnertime, but found that she had fallen asleep. I listened to her quiet breathing for a few minutes, covered her up, and left her, delighted that she was having natural slumber. It all looked encouraging.

I utilized the unexpected freedom by making a systematic search for possible hiding-places for morphine. Mrs. Campbell's was one of the usual small houses on the outskirts of a fashionable quarter that represent the eternal compromise between the purses and the position of the navy. Both the maids denied having ever bought the drug for Mrs. Campbell, and, when I had explained the circumstances, promised that they never would. The elder woman followed me into the ₋utler's pantry.

"Indade, I wndn't do annything to hurt Mrs. Campbell for the wur-ruld," she said, with a sudden softness in her hard face. "And I'm glad some one has come to take care of her, poor little lady. She's been that kind to me, nobody knows, takin' me and my boy in whin nobody else wud!"

The house was full of photographs of a naval officer in all sorts of settings, some of them Eastern enough. Mr. Campbell must have been a vain personage—or else he must have been responding to constant demands from home. I concluded, after a glance or so at the straight-forward face, that the second was the explanation.

This had all taken but a short time; and yet, when I heard a slight noise from Mrs. Campbell's room and ran to her, she must have been up for many minutes, for the room was in the most amazing confusion. Sitting in the midst of a heap of scattered things, she explained casually that she had been hunting for "one of Lex's old letters."

I think I have never seen a being more pitifully changed by the ravages of a sorry half-hour than Mrs. Campbell had become during the time she had been left alone. The pupils of her eyes, contracted to mere points, were uncanny in the faded brown of the iris; "witch-eyed"—the old phrase occurred to me. The skin, whose pallor was a compound of blue-white and yellow-white and gray—all blanched and unwholesome tones—the haunted pallor that is the visible blight of morphine—stretched taut over an expressionless face, stranger still because of the disorder of hanging locks of dark hair, of stained and creased negligee and linen. She had evidently started to write, for letters were heaped upon the desk and ink smeared fingers and hanging sleeves. One disfiguring blotch was brushed across her cheek. How the dainty room could have harbored as much grime as made unrecognizable her graceful beauty and its once fresh and exquisite setting, and what quest had matched the disorder of tumbled possessions with the disorder of a wandering will; I could only guess. But it was all so tragically pitiful that for the moment I could only ache with sympathy.

Where she had obtained the morphine, whether it had been brought to her or concealed, I could only surmise—until I caught a glimpse of a skirt with hem half ripped tossed carelessly upon the floor of a closet. A small heap of tablets and a needle were lying quite openly on the desk by the side of the letters. I remembered that I had heard of a hospital patient having carried the drug with her in the hem of a dressing-gown. But a more important question pressed. Was there any means by which I might make an impression that should last longer than the instant upon the diseased will?

I glanced around the room, saddened afresh by its testimony to the chaos in the soul of her who sat and smiled at me out of the depths of some drugged and mysterious peace. I raised the window-shade, and the austere sunlight pierced to every corner of the desecrated shrine. Its rays reached her—and she shrank and pressed her hands before her eyes. It reached one of the numberless photographs of her husband in its cathedral-like frame. In the white summer uniform of the navy he stood, miraculously trim and cleanly, suggesting in his grooming the taut readiness of a strung bow.

I took the wife's hand and led her before the dresser, determined that the narcotic that bound her mind should yield enough to let her see. I held her with my eyes, that something of the normal might penetrate. Then, when the immobility of her fixed and silly smile had given way to a childish dismay, I pointed to the dirt and disorder that she had wrought—the room, her clothes, her hair, the needle-punctures, dull wounds in the firm young flesh of her arms where the sleeves of her negligee had fallen away. And then I held before her the whiteness of the stern young figure.

For a space she followed my eyes to the room, herself in the glass, her husband, back and forth in a wondering round. Then at last her face quivered, and she burst into a storm of immoderate and hysterical weeping, hiding her face in her hair, throwing herself into my arms, clinging there, shaking, holding out the poor dishonored hands.

"Oh, Miss Alyson," she wailed, "make them clean, make them clean!" And, striking her hands fiercely against each other: "Help me! Make me clean! Make me clean!"

I held her for a long time, silently, warmly—for there are moments when nothing can heal but the insistence of human nearness; and she clung to me, the storm ebbing away in broken words, sobs, long indrawn breaths. "I will do anything—I will tell you where it is—I have been so vain of my strength, but I am afraid—afraid. Let us go away—where nothing will remind me of it—the crazy hunger—the wicked peace of it. Let us go away. You will help me—never leave me alone—I am too weak to be alone—it finds me out when I think I am so strong. And Lex—my husband—Lex— You will *never* let him see me—like this!" And again the storm of weeping came, and she tried to pull herself from my arms to the floor.

But I held her strongly, no room for mere pity, nothing but the will that she should be helped in my heart. And by degrees this tempest ebbed as the first had done, and her poor head lay quietly on my breast. There came a moment when she raised calmed eyes to mine, saying, simply:

"You will help me? You will? I want to be cured. I will be good."

—

"Let me see, how many days have we before Campbell turns up? To-day is Monday; he comes Thursday. Oh, I ought to have had the case a year ago!" It was four weeks later. Doctor Dietrich bent over to crank up his runabout with an impatient jerk.

"But she has gone through the month without a setback."

"I never saw any one put up such a fight." The doctor turned toward me. "That's what I'm afraid of. A woman like that, all emotion and nerves, and possessed with a determination to be free— The question is whether her heart will hold out. I'll tell you now that's what I'm worried about. I tested it again to-day—and it doesn't suit me!" He threw his little leather bag on the seat and jumped in.

"I'm sure her husband's coming will help her." I was thinking of her face when his telegram had come.

"Don't know whether it will help or hinder," said Doctor Dietrich, shortly. "She can't stand any additional emotional strain. But we'll all work together." His hand was on the steering-wheel and his voice had taken on its usual inspiriting heartiness. "Programme is, to drop the evening half-grain to-day. The effects are going to be worse than at any stage we have gone through. Watch her heart. Have all the stimulants ready. You never can tell which one of them won't work. I shall keep within telephone communication after seven—that's the time you have been giving the dose, isn't it? And I shall be here at eleven." The runabout was already raising a cloud of dust along the driveway.

I found Mrs. Campbell so transported with joy that she laughed recklessly at the idea of any difficulty "now Lex is coming." She darted in and out of the house inspecting the floors—we had made the change into Maryland, and fitting up the little country place had been a great resource. She came in to tell me excitedly that she was sure three of the roses would be in bloom by Thursday; she telephoned to the city for "some of the things that Lex likes." She pulled muslin curtains down to have them done up; the blank that was usually filled by writing to her husband was spent over an utterly unintelligible pile of time-tables. Finally, fearing the reaction that was certain to come, I put her to bed, and lay down on a couch just outside her door to see if my example would make her feel drowsy. She was quiet for a short time, then began turning restlessly from side to side. I bent over her.

"I am so sorry, Miss Alyson," she said, penitently. "But I can't feel sleepy. I'm too happy. Do let me get up and dress for dinner. I feel all the time as if Lex might get here a few days earlier by mistake!" She laughed; but she was shutting and opening her slender hands feverishly.

"Take a long time, then, and make yourself look your prettiest—and let me brush your hair and do it low. Then we can see whether we like it before Lieutenant Campbell comes."

When all was done there was still an hour and a half before seven. And into her voice had begun to come the edge that tells of strained nerves and a craving body.

We spent a forced half-hour in the garden, trying to revive the earlier enthusiasm about the roses. Then we used up a few plates taking photographs of each other and Jimmie, the cook's little boy. I had brought my camera with me, thinking that a fad might be useful. At that point Mrs. Campbell was sure she was very hungry, but when we went in to a really tempting dinner she played with it and piteously said she couldn't eat. She began to look strained and gray under all her gayety, and I, trying to imagine in my own person the nervous unrest that was consuming her, braced myself for the conflict that was coming.

Seven o'clock was on us! Neither spoke of it, but the thought was between us. There was first a walk to be taken. This evening a steady pace was impossible to Mrs. Campbell; she either darted forward or lagged. And soon she lagged so persistently that I knew further fatigue in the close damp air would be dangerous, and got her home. Then I read to her for a time, but the warm country evening had brought forward its visitation of flying and creeping things which the ill-fitting screens were powerless to exclude. And the attention of the drooping figure opposite to me fluttered and lapsed with the dance of the moths and beetles around the light. There came a point where she jumped up with an impatient cry and began pacing up and down the room. I closed the book, put my arm through hers, and walked up and down and round the room with her. For a few rounds she said nothing. Then:

"You won't leave me alone?"—without turning her head.

"Not a minute," I said, holding her hand firmly.

"Because"—she spoke in a muffled voice and still without meeting my eyes—"I am afraid the time is coming when I won't be able to help—won't be able to think of anything—not even Lex—but— That!"

"I understand—I know—" I tried to make my voice commonplace and confident. "I will think for you—the doctor too. He will be here after a while—whenever you need him."

"Oh—." This was a long breath, half of relief, half of dismay.

"Eight o'clock!" I announced, cheerfully, as the tender chimes of a little clock down-stairs began the hour.

"Eight!" she cried, in dismay, and her voice was sharp and anguished. "Only one hour gone! And all the rest of the night! And all the rest of all time!"

"But it is only for a tiny fraction of time that it will be so hard," I soothed her. "And after a few days you will have your husband to make you forget everything else."

"Yes, yes," she assented, happily, and was quiet.

"Show me how to knit, won't you?" I asked, with spontaneous enthusiasm. "I have some white wool here, and some needles. I'd like to have the pattern of that sweater." That caught her attention. She had knit half of the neckband, when she began to lose stitches. Suddenly she threw the work down.

"I can't do anything," she half sobbed. "My hands are too unsteady." As I caught the needles from her I saw her hands twitch violently. While I was putting the things away she screamed out:

"I can't keep still— Oh, come here and keep me still!" Her feet were clattering on the floor in a jerking spasm. The rigors of the crisis were upon us.

I went to the frightened woman and put my arms around her.

"Mrs. Campbell, I know that you would rather know that we have a fight before us. We will have to expect all sorts of painful symptoms. But we will find something to ease each feature. You must trust to us."

"Have other people borne it?" she asked, frightened eyes on mine.

I nodded my head.

She made an effort to steady her quivering lips.

"Then I will do all I can. But it seems as if I would die or go mad with the hunger—and weakness—and I don't want to die—before Lex comes—"

"We will not let you suffer beyond your strength—the doctor will come whenever we call him—and each minute lived through is a gain. Now, first, you must promise me to eat something." She shook her head. "Then you must drink some hot milk."

I read out loud until Norah brought the milk. Mrs. Campbell did not listen, and I hardly knew what the book was, but the sound of my voice was a faint distraction. Mrs. Campbell tried valiantly to drink the milk, but her throat contracted spasmodically, and it was a long and painful process. And the end of it was a violent nausea which left her weak and trembling. I half carried her to her bed, gave her a warm sponge and an alcohol rub and then tried to control the nervous spasms by an energetic massage—sedatives seemed to have no effect. She became somewhat more quiet under this. Although her face was set and gray and her eyes painfully open, she faced the night with more courage, knowing that she had met the enemy face to face.

It was in this mood that she met the recurring attacks that made of the heavy night a battle-ground. It was in a moment of comparative ease that the doctor came. She was lying with her cheek on her hand, in her face a gentle happiness that was born of the respite.

"Miss Alyson, I really believe I can sleep," she was saying.

There was delight on the doctor's face as he came forward and read the situation with his keen eyes. Under cover of a congratulatory hand-clasp he read her pulse and nodded thoughtfully to me. It was while Mrs. Campbell was laughing over his account of some medical meeting he had left in town that her hand went to her head.

"Oh—!" she shrieked— "I can't bear it!" And she clasped her head and rocked herself in the effort to endure.

Doctor Dietrich waited for her to be able to speak.

"Is it the old neuralgic trouble?" he asked, gently.

"Yes," she gasped. "only worse—worse than it has ever been— Oh, help me—if I must bear it. Give me something—or I am afraid—I am afraid—" She writhed with agony.

The doctor beckoned to me. "Keep your hand on her pulse," he muttered. "Let me know the instant it grows worse. She can bear very little more." Then he sought in his medicine-case for the thing that might soothe.

In the half-hour that followed we tried one expedient after another: hot applications, cold compresses, sedative after sedative. Nothing served. I had left her for an instant to hurry Norah with hot water, and the doctor was looking for another vial, when we both heard a sound. Mrs. Campbell was at the door of the old-fashioned wardrobe in her room. Before I could reach her she had pulled down a skirt, had run her fingers desperately along the hem, and had put it in her mouth, sucking it as a famished baby sups his milk.

"Mrs. Campbell!" I cried, snatching it away. I recognized the old skirt in which she had hidden the morphine when I came to her. She burst into tears.

"You won't give me anything—and I am dying—I must have it—Look! See how strong I am!" She picked up a pencil that lay on the desk and snapped it between her slender fingers. "I don't know what I'll do to you or to myself if you don't give it to me. You are cruel—cruel!" And she fell back on the bed, sobbing helplessly.

We brought her out of that state of half-delirium, but it left her in a state of alarming collapse. Sweat drenched her, and while the doctor waited in suspense the pulse under my hand gave a throb and began to leap forward with feeble but tumultuous speed. I looked at the doctor, and he understood. She was too weak to swallow either the coffee or the brandy that we plied her with. We gave her a grain of morphine, defeat in our souls. But when she lay back and slept, peace in her face at last, we loved the drug that we had fought. There lies the strength of the Enemy.

Mrs. Campbell's fresh morning face made me wonder if I had dreamed the scenes of the night before. An unexpected letter from Lieutenant Campbell, mailed in San Francisco after he had sent his telegram, added tonic to the calm of a long and refreshing sleep. She was confident, jubilant.

"Nothing can be as bad as last night," she said. "And, even then, I held out for four hours. To-night I will stand it just so much longer. And then—last night I hadn't had the letter. When the craving comes—even if the pain comes too—I shall look at this. And I won't want anything in the world but Lex. Then I will read it again and know he is coming!"

And the day and the evening did go better. When at last I got her to bed and she had dropped into what seemed to be a peaceful doze, my heart beat high with hope.

I was sitting by her, knitting, when a choking gasp brought me to my feet. When I bent over her she grasped my hand frantically.

"I was in a sort of a sleep," she said, "and in it seemed to know that I was asleep and was happy. But all at once something screamed at me in the din, 'Now it's time to wake and dance—and dance—and dance.' And a phantasmagoria of everything awful that could be imagined went before my eyes swiftly, blindingly. In every scene Lex and I were hunting each other, always longing, always missing; horrors and death came in between—sometimes Lex stumbled and fell—sometimes I. And everywhere people being wrecked and torn— Oh— it was horrible— Don't let me sleep again. Don't!" And she clung to me with hysterical sobbing.

I soothed her as best I could, with dismay in my heart. For with what could we fight this horror of sleep itself, when sleep was the one thing that could save her? And for this tumult of the mysterious physical there was nothing that could cure save the slow, discouraging, wonted physical methods that so mock the hunted soul! Over it all we went: walking up and down the room, bed when that had exhausted, sponging and rubbing and sponging again, then a cupful of hot broth, a glass of milk— And the constant appeal of the shattered human: "Can I bear it? Have others borne it and lived? No—not sleep—don't let me sleep. When I'm defenceless the dreadful things will crowd on me again. There's nothing that helps but the touch of your warm, pulsing hand. Don't let go of me—Nancy. Just be sorry for me—that helps—"

So we clung together, hands lax and slippery with sweat when exhaustion brought a pallid substitute for peace, hands wringing and grinding when the convulsions were upon her, but always together. When eleven brought Doctor Dietrich she lay upon her bed, hair streaming damp and tangled over the pillow, her pallor distinct from the mere whiteness of the pillow, her eyes desperately, hopelessly open. Even the doctor's cheerfulness, native and acquired, wavered for an instant and he bit his lip. He raised his eyebrows. My hand was on her pulse at that moment and I nodded my head warningly—it was rapidly becoming alarming. He tested it himself.

"Brandy," he ordered, chafing her hands—I had hot water at her feet. We got a little of the brandy between the gray lips, but the little that she could swallow brought no response from the feeble and intermittent pulse. The doctor drew in his breath with a slight noise.

"Fill the needle," he ordered. "One grain."

She moved her head, a glimmer of inquiry in her eyes.

"Yes, it's necessary, Mrs. Campbell," he said, tenderly. He bent over her to say with cheerfulness, "Better luck next time."

Tears stood in her eyes and brimmed over. One hand outstretched for the needle, the doctor dried them on his big man's handkerchief, accurately using his surgeon's fingers, but with a gentleness greater than that of a woman.

———

It was at a later hour the next night, nearly midnight, that the hope that had again flared up because of a good day and a most heroic fight during the early hours of the night flickered out. When all had looked promising, and Mrs. Campbell, inspired by the habit of resisting, was beginning to be hopeful, the neuralgia began to encroach on the region about her heart. We three fought it grimly, desperately, until the too familiar danger signals warned us that we must fall back—warned two of us. For Mrs. Campbell, when she heard the doctor's low order to me, roused herself to say, "No!" The word fluttered out, breathed rather than spoken, but it was the most inflexible sound I have ever heard.

Doctor Dietrich bent over her. His voice trembled.

"We must, Mrs. Campbell," he said, a depth of reverence in his tone. She was too far spent to speak again; her body swayed itself toward the thing it craved; but one weak hand tried to grasp the mattress to hold herself away. And, even while they begged, her eyes denied.

The doctor hung over her tensely until he saw her eyes close, and rest descend upon her like the benediction of a false prophet. He threw the needle across the room and it shivered, delicately.

"*Damn* the man who gave it to her!" said the doctor, between his closed teeth. And I felt *honored* that he didn't feel it necessary to beg my pardon when he looked up and realized that I was there!

———

"Nancy," said Mrs. Campbell, while she was still in bed the next morning, "why did the doctor give it to me last night?"

I could not look in her face as I answered. "It was necessary."

"What could make it necessary? I thought you two were pledged to help me." She did not raise her voice, but I felt on the defensive.

"We are in honor bound to take every measure to save life."

"*Life!*" she said, under her breath. Her tone made me lift my head. It was so worse than contemptuous, impersonal, and remote. But as I looked she turned away from me with her cheek on her palm. "It would have been so much kinder not to." And her lip quivered.

"Now, now, you mustn't talk that way," I said, taking up the burden of impersonal cheerfulness. "The next time—"

She faced me.

"Did Doctor Dietrich say to you last night that there was still hope?" she demanded. Then, when I could not answer, "Do you think there is still hope?"

No one could have said the falsely reassuring thing to those expectant eyes.

"We think that—now—until your heart is stronger at least—you will have to take a very small amount."

"Will my heart ever be stronger?"

"We can't—"

"Has any one been known to recover from morphine whose heart was affected?"

"I—don't know."

"Does Doctor Dietrich think I can recover from the morphine?"

"He—thinks the best we can do is to keep it down."

"Oh—" this was a long-drawn breath. "Well, one can believe—him."

She turned her face away again; and I tried to lighten the weight on my heart by laying out the prettiest clothes I could find. At last, without looking at me, she said:

"Sit here by me, please. I am thinking—and I do not want to feel alone."

I took one hand between mine and smoothed it.

"I suppose," she said, meditatively, "there must have been some one moment when I was weak and could have resisted it—"

"It wasn't your—" I began, indignantly, but she silenced me by a pressure of her fingers.

"Let us think," she said. "I want to think."

Again there was silence before she went on, her face still turned away.

"Of course, when the doctor gave it to me first I didn't know what it was. I was crazy with the pain and he said he could help me. There was a prick—and then—Heaven!" Her voice had become joyous with the memory. "The next time, of course, I asked for the same medicine. It was a long time before I knew what it was. And then I saw the name, by chance, on a box. And I said, 'Isn't morphine a dangerous thing to use, doctor?' And he laughed and said: 'Not when it is used by a physician's order and for pain. I think *you* needn't worry, Mrs. Campbell.' "

She turned her wedding-ring around and around her finger.

"When Lex went away, four months after we were married, I was so miserable and so lonely. Night after night I lay and strained my arms out in the blank darkness and cried and begged Lex—or God; they meant just about the same thing to me—to let me know his poor body was not beating up against some shore—" She shuddered.

"My dear, you mustn't." I lay down on the bed beside her and took her in my arms. She brushed a grateful kiss against my cheek.

"Well, I won't. But I was at some seashore place and the glare of the sun on the sea nearly blinded me—I suppose crying had something to do with it. The pain came again. And I remembered the name of the medicine that had cured me the year before. So I got some. That must have been the time I was at fault!" Her tone was triumphant at the discovery.

"After that"—she hurried over this part—"somehow every time I took it I seemed to have to have it. I suppose I really didn't—but it seemed so." The thing in Mrs. Campbell that made your heart go out to her—all hers—was the child that lay hidden somewhere back of the beautiful woman. "But then—there's—pain!" she said, in a startled tone. "I suppose God knows why He made pain so great and then made us weak—and let us know the thing that soothes and—kills!"

I had been glad that she could not see my face on the pillow beside hers, but now something in her tone made me seek her face. Her great eyes were wide open, and there was a calm strength in her face that I had never seen there before.

"I think you'd better get up," I said, in a business-like tone. "We have ever so much to do to-day."

"All right—in a minute. How much morphine am I to have this morning—"

"Oh, we have got it down to almost nothing—half a grain—and at night."

"Better give me a little more—now. I want just enough to make me normal—myself—as nearly myself as I can ever be—" Again the tone was too detached to be either contemptuous or despairing—and yet it made me feel desolate. "Can you imagine what it would be to have that always between his face and mine—his heart and mine—and daily growing worse—Nancy! I want you to tell him about it!"

I was startled.

"But surely you would want to—" I began to stammer.

"No, I want you to tell him. You can make him understand better—better even than the doctor."

"If you wish, dear, after you have had your meeting."

"Oh—that!" Her face contracted.

"Neuralgia?" I asked, anxiously.

She shook her head indifferently.

"You know Lex will never be able to understand—really," she went on. "He is too strong—too master of himself to ever be a mere victim—" again the cutting, impersonal tone. "No, he will love me, but he will pity me—*pity*!" This time she lost control of herself and sobbed.

"It may be pity if you make your eyes red," I said, briskly.

For an hour we were busy with our morning programme. I never worked harder over any one than I did over Mrs. Campbell. I was as anxious as she could have been to have her her beautiful self. Hopeless as it all was, I couldn't help wanting her to have her one perfect moment. When I had finished her I gave her a hypodermic and anxiously watched the effect. She was in the still, cold mood, and white.

"I think it will take another grain to bring me up to normal," she said, coolly. "And I must be that to-day." So I gave it to her and saw the life come back into her face. After breakfast she said:

"I want to try on the gown that I will wear to-night." I brought it, glad that she could think of it; it made her seem more human. It was one of white crêpe that Lieutenant Campbell had had embroidered for her in China, and the frock was very well made. When she was dressed I looked at her. She scrutinized me.

"You think I am looking—myself?" she asked, simply.

"If yourself is a very beautiful woman," I replied, as baldly.

"You are sure that I am not excited or hysterical or anything that is not controlled?" Her eyes narrowed as she questioned me.

"I have never seen you calmer."

"I look like a normal, sane woman, not flawed—fit to be the mother of his children?"

Her eyes were still on me. But I couldn't bear it and turned away my head.

She waited until I had nodded.

"Then, I think I want you to take my photograph—as I am—right now—without waiting a moment!" For the first time it was evident that intense feeling was behind the whim.

We went out on the lawn and I posed her carefully with a good background of shrubbery. And it certainly was in a moment of inspiration that I snapped Mrs. Campbell just as you could fairly see the pride and the beauty and the love in her leap to her eyes to greet her husband. When she saw it she nodded, satisfied. We made a few prints. And after that she seemed to sag into a settled indifference.

So when she said she wanted to lie down after lunch I was only glad she felt drowsy. I stayed with her until she had fallen asleep; her breathing was regular, and when I spoke to her she did not answer, but stirred and sighed softly. I ran down-stairs to give the maids some orders about things. I must have been away half an hour telephoning and arranging things down-stairs.

When I ran up-stairs, anxious because there was scant time to get Mrs. Campbell ready for six o'clock, the shades were still drawn. I raised them and saw—her— I have never been able to speak of it. It is only God who can feel calm in the face of such things. But—the drained bottle of poison had fallen on the floor. And on the table, the paper seal unbroken, was a box, with enough morphine to have set her free—untouched.

Before I had time to more than catch at the bed on which she partly lay to keep myself from falling, Norah's voice, glad with Irish heartiness, rang from below, welcoming Lieutenant Campbell.

Something came back to me: There was the husband. To be told.

There were footsteps, coming up, two at a time— I was out in the hall, the door of her room locked and the key in my pocket, when he reached the landing.

He looked at me with a flicker of disappointment—evidently he thought I was some guest who would be a third in his home-coming. But in an instant he held out his hand, smiling. He was a big Viking sort of a fellow, with light hair, so ash-colored that it looked gray, and strong straight brows that were slaty over the brilliant blue of his eyes.

And his smile was as dazzling as the sun on snow-crust. I couldn't take his hand.

"Don't go in, Lieutenant Campbell— You mustn't go in!" I can see now the arrested smile.

"What's the matter? Is she ill?"

I told him—something—I have never known what I said. But after the first few words he whirled me away from the door and tried to force it. And—somehow—I held him aside and made him be still while I said:

"You mustn't see her. You must never see her—" all the while thinking. Then I remembered that in the pocket of the nurse's apron I had on was her picture—I had had it on to develop the plates—and I took it out.

"This is what she wants you to see. It is herself. That—in there— isn't. She made me take this to show it to you. I know she did." And— with his dazed eyes on it, not on me—I told him—the rest.

———

I had done some of the things that had to be gone through when I gave out. I managed to get to the telephone and ask Doctor Dietrich to come, without telling him anything. When I heard his good reassuring, "All *right*!" I hung the receiver up somehow and put my head on the table and cried and cried and cried.

LET ME FEEL YOUR PULSE

O. Henry

1910

A former Texas bank teller and newspaper columnist, William Sydney Porter (pseudonym O. Henry) was known for his humorous depictions of everyday life. Early in his career he was accused of embezzling funds from the Austin bank where he worked—a charge for which he served three years in prison. It was during his imprisonment that he honed his craft and emerged as an accomplished writer. Upon his release, O. Henry traveled to New York, where he established himself as a prolific writer of ironically plotted stories. In "Let Me Feel Your Pulse," O. Henry examines the life of a man whose emotional frailties fuel his addiction to alcohol.

So I went to a doctor.

"How long has it been since you took any alcohol into your system?" he asked.

Turning my head sidewise, I answered, "Oh, quite awhile."

He was a young doctor, somewhere between twenty and forty. He wore heliotrope socks, but he looked like Napoleon. I liked him immensely.

"Now," said he, "I am going to show you the effect of alcohol upon your circulation." I think it was "circulation" he said; though it may have been "advertising."

He bared my left arm to the elbow, brought out a bottle of whiskey, and gave me a drink. He began to look more like Napoleon. I began to like him better.

Then he put a tight compress on my upper arm, stopped my pulse with his fingers, and squeezed a rubber bulb connected with an apparatus on a stand that looked like a thermometer. The mercury jumped up and down without seeming to stop anywhere; but the doctor said it registered two hundred and thirty-seven or one hundred and sixty-five or some such number.

"Now," said he, "you see what alcohol does to the blood-pressure."

"It's marvelous," said I, "but do you think it a sufficient test? Have one on me, and let's try the other arm." But, no!

Then he grasped my hand. I thought I was doomed and he was saying good-bye. But all he wanted to do was to jab a needle into the end of a finger and compare the red drop with a lot of fifty-cent poker chips that he had fastened to a card.

"It's the hæmoglobin test," he explained. "The color of your blood is wrong."

"Well," said I, "I know it should be blue; but this is a country of mix-ups. Some of my ancestors were cavaliers; but they got thick with some people on Nantucket Island, so—"

"I mean," said the doctor, "that the shade of red is too light."

"Oh," I said, "it's a case of matching instead of matches."

The doctor then pounded me severely in the region of the chest. When he did that I don't know whether he reminded me most of Napoleon or Battling or Lord Nelson. Then he looked grave and mentioned a string of grievances that the flesh is heir to—mostly ending in "itis." I immediately paid him fifteen dollars on account.

"Is or are it or some or any of them necessarily fatal?" I asked. I thought my connection with the matter justified my manifesting a certain amount of interest.

"All of them," he answered, cheerfully. "But their progress may be arrested. With care and proper continuous treatment you may live to be eighty-five or ninety."

I began to think of the doctor's bill. "Eighty-five would be sufficient, I am sure," was my comment. I paid him ten dollars more on account.

"The first thing to do," he said, with renewed animation, "is to find a sanitarium where you will get a complete rest for a while, and allow your nerves to get into a better condition. I myself will go with you and select a suitable one."

So he took me to a mad-house in the Catskills. It was on a bare mountain frequented only by infrequent frequenters. You could see nothing but stones and boulders, some patches of snow, and scattered pine trees. The young physician in charge was most agreeable. He gave me a stimulant without applying a compress to the arm. It was luncheon time, and we were invited to partake. There were about twenty inmates at little tables in the dining room. The young physician in charge came to our table and said: "It is a custom with our guests not to regard themselves as patients, but merely as tired ladies and gentlemen taking a rest. Whatever slight maladies they may have are never alluded to in conversation."

My doctor called loudly to a waitress to bring some phosphoglycerate of lime hash, dog-bread, bromo-seltzer pancakes, and nux vomica tea for my repast. Then a sound arose like a sudden wind storm among pine trees. It was produced by every guest in the room whispering loudly, "Neurasthenia!"—except one man with a nose, whom I distinctly heard say, "Chronic alcoholism." I hope to meet him again. The physician in charge turned and walked away.

An hour or so after luncheon he conducted us to the workshop— say fifty yards from the house. Thither the guests had been conducted by the physician in charge's understudy and sponge-holder—a man with feet and a blue sweater. He was so tall that I was not sure he had a face; but the Armour Packing Company would have been delighted with his hands.

"Here," said the physician in charge, "our guests find relaxation from past mental worries by devoting themselves to physical labor— recreation, in reality."

There were turning-lathes, carpenters' outfits, clay-modelling tools, spinning-wheels, weaving-frames, treadmills, bass drums, enlarged-crayon-portrait apparatuses, blacksmith forges, and everything, seemingly, that could interest the paying lunatic guests of a first-rate sanitarium.

"The lady making mud pies in the corner," whispered the physician in charge, "is no other than—Lulu Lulington, the authoress of the novel entitled 'Why Love Loves.' What she is doing now is simply to rest her mind after performing that piece of work."

I had seen the book. "Why doesn't she do it by writing another one instead?" I asked.

As you see, I wasn't as far gone as they thought I was.

"The gentleman pouring water through the funnel," continued the physician in charge, "is a Wall Street broker broken down from over-work."

I buttoned my coat.

Others he pointed out were architects playing with Noah's arks, ministers reading Darwin's "Theory of Evolution," lawyers sawing wood, tired-out society ladies talking Ibsen to the blue-sweatered sponge-holder, a neurotic millionaire lying asleep on the floor, and a prominent artist drawing a little red wagon around the room.

"You look pretty strong," said the physician in charge of me. "I think the best mental relaxation for you would be throwing small boulders over the mountainside and then bringing them up again."

I was a hundred yards away before my doctor overtook me.

"What's the matter?" he asked.

"The matter is," said I, "that there are no aeroplanes handy. So I am going to merrily and hastily jog the foot-pathway to yon station and catch the first unlimited-soft-coal express back to town."

"Well," said the doctor, "perhaps you are right. This seems hardly the suitable place for you. But what you need is rest—absolute rest and exercise."

That night I went to a hotel in the city, and said to the clerk: "What I need is absolute rest and exercise. Can you give me a room with one of those tall folding beds in it, and a relay of bellboys to work it up and down while I rest?"

The clerk rubbed a speck off one of his finger nails and glanced sidewise at a tall man in a white hat sitting in the lobby. That man came over and asked me politely if I had seen the shrubbery at the west entrance. I had not, so he showed it to me and then looked me over.

"I thought you had 'em," he said, not unkindly, "but I guess you're all right. You'd better go see a doctor, old man."

A week afterward my doctor tested my blood pressure again with-out the preliminary stimulant. He looked to me a little less like Napo-leon. And his socks were of a shade of tan that did not appeal to me.

"What you need," he decided, "is sea air and companionship."

"Would a mermaid—" I began; but he slipped on his professional manner.

"I myself," he said, "will take you to the Hotel Bonair off the coast of Long Island and see that you get in good shape. It is a quiet, comfortable resort where you will soon recuperate."

The Hotel Bonair proved to be a nine-hundred-room fashionable hostelry on an island off the main shore. Everybody who did not dress for dinner was shoved into a side dining room and given only a terrapin and champagne table d'hôte. The bay was a great stamping ground for wealthy yachtsmen. The *Corsair* anchored there the day we arrived. I saw Mr. Morgan standing on deck eating a cheese sandwich and gazing longingly at the hotel. Still, it was a very inexpensive place. Nobody could afford to pay their prices. When you went away you simply left your baggage, stole a skiff, and beat it for the mainland in the night.

When I had been there one day I got a pad of monogrammed telegraph blanks at the clerk's desk and began to wire to all my friends for get-away money. My doctor and I played one game of croquet on the golf links and went to sleep on the lawn.

When we got back to town a thought seemed to occur to him suddenly. "By the way," he asked, "how do you feel?"

"Relieved of very much," I replied.

Now a consulting physician is different. He isn't exactly sure whether he is to be paid or not, and this uncertainty insures you either the most careful or the most careless attention. My doctor took me to see a consulting physician. He made a poor guess and gave me careful attention. I liked him immensely. He put me through some coördination exercises.

"Have you a pain in the back of your head?" he asked. I told him I had not.

"Shut your eyes," he ordered, "put your feet close together, and jump backward as far as you can."

I always was a good backward jumper with my eyes shut, so I obeyed. My head struck the edge of the bathroom door, which had been left open and was only three feet away. The doctor was very sorry. He had overlooked the fact that the door was open. He closed it.

"Now touch your nose with your right forefinger," he said.

"Where is it?" I asked.

"On your face," said he.

"I mean my right forefinger," I explained.

"Oh, excuse me," said he. He reopened the bathroom door, and I took my finger out of the crack of it. After I had performed the marvelous digito-nasal feat I said:

"I do not wish to deceive you as to symptoms, Doctor; I really have something like a pain in the back of my head." He ignored the symptom and examined my heart carefully with a latest-popular-air-penny-in-the-slot ear-trumpet. I felt like a ballad. "Now," he said, "gallop like a horse for about five minutes around the room."

I gave the best imitation I could of a disqualified Percheron being led out of Madison Square Garden. Then, without dropping in a penny, he listened to my chest again.

"No glanders in our family, Doc," I said.

The consulting physician held up his forefinger within three inches of my nose. "Look at my finger," he commanded.

"Did you ever try Pears'—" I began; but he went on with his test rapidly.

"Now look across the bay. At my finger. Across the bay. At my finger. At my finger. Across the bay. Across the bay. At my finger. Across the bay." This for about three minutes.

He explained that this was a test of the action of the brain. It seemed easy to me. I never once mistook his finger for the bay. I'll bet that if he had used the phrases: "Gaze, as it were, unpreoccupied, outward—or rather laterally—in the direction of the horizon, underlaid, so to speak, with the adjacent fluid inlet," and "Now, returning—or rather, in a manner, withdrawing your attention, bestow it upon my upraised digit"—I'll bet, I say, that Henry James himself could have passed the examination.

After asking me if I had ever had a grand uncle with curvature of the spine or a cousin with swelled ankles, the two doctors retired to the bathroom and sat on the edge of the bath tub for their consultation. I ate an apple, and gazed first at my finger and then across the bay.

The doctors came out looking grave. More: they looked tombstones and Tennessee-papers-please-copy. They wrote out a diet list to which I was to be restricted. It had everything that I had ever heard of to eat on it, except snails. And I never eat a snail unless it overtakes me and bites me first.

"You must follow this diet strictly," said the doctors.

"I'd follow it a mile if I could get one-tenth of what's on it," I answered.

"Of next importance," they went on, "is outdoor air and exercise. And here is a prescription that will be of great benefit to you."

Then all of us took something. They took their hats, and I took my departure.

I went to a druggist and showed him the prescription.

"It will be $2.87 for an ounce bottle," he said.

"Will you give me a piece of your wrapping cord?" said I.

I made a hole in the prescription, ran the cord through it, tied it around my neck, and tucked it inside. All of us have a little superstition, and mine runs to a confidence in amulets.

Of course there was nothing the matter with me, but I was very ill. I couldn't work, sleep, eat, or bowl. The only way I could get any sympathy was to go without shaving for four days. Even then somebody would say: "Old man, you look as hardy as a pine knot. Been up for a jaunt in the Maine Woods, eh?"

Then, suddenly, I remembered that I must have outdoor air and exercise. So I went down South to John's. John is an approximate relative by verdict of a preacher standing with a little book in his hands in a bower of chrysanthemums while a hundred thousand people looked on. John has a country house seven miles from Pineville. It is at an altitude and on the Blue Ridge Mountains in a state too dignified to be dragged into this controversy. John is mica, which is more valuable and clearer than gold.

He met me at Pineville, and we took the trolley car to his home. It is a big, neighborless cottage on a hill surrounded by a hundred mountains. We got off at his little private station, where John's family and Amaryllis met and greeted us. Amaryllis looked at me a trifle anxiously.

A rabbit came bounding across the hill between us and the house. I threw down my suit-case and pursued it hotfoot. After I had run twenty yards and seen it disappear, I sat down on the grass and wept disconsolately.

"I can't catch a rabbit any more," I sobbed. "I'm of no further use in the world. I may as well be dead."

"Oh, what is it—what is it, Brother John?" I heard Amaryllis say.

"Nerves a little unstrung," said John, in his calm way. "Don't worry. Get up, you rabbit-chaser, and come on to the house before the biscuits get cold." It was about twilight, and the mountains came up nobly to Miss Murfree's descriptions of them.

Soon after dinner I announced that I believed I could sleep for a year or two, including legal holidays. So I was shown to a room as big and cool as a flower garden, where there was a bed as broad as a lawn. Soon afterward the remainder of the household retired, and then there fell upon the land a silence.

I had not heard a silence before in years. It was absolute. I raised myself on my elbow and listened to it. Sleep! I thought that if I only could hear a star twinkle or a blade of grass sharpen itself I could compose myself to rest. I thought once that I heard a sound like the sail of a catboat flapping as it veered about in a breeze, but I decided that it was probably only a tack in the carpet. Still I listened.

Suddenly some belated little bird alighted upon the window-sill, and, in what he no doubt considered sleepy tones, enunciated the noise generally translated as "cheep!"

I leaped into the air.

"Hey! what's the matter down there?" called John from his room above mine.

"Oh, nothing," I answered, "except that I accidentally bumped my head against the ceiling."

The next morning I went out on the porch and looked at the mountains. There were forty-seven of them in sight. I shuddered, went into the big hall sitting room of the house, selected "Pancoast's Family Practice of Medicine" from a bookcase, and began to read. John came in, took the book away from me, and led me outside. He has a farm of three hundred acres furnished with the usual complement of barns, mules, peasantry, and harrows with three front teeth broken off. I had seen such things in my childhood, and my heart began to sink.

Then John spoke of alfalfa, and I brightened at once. "Oh, yes," said I, "wasn't she in the chorus of—let's see—"

"Green, you know," said John, "and tender, and you plow it under after the first season."

"I know," said I, "and the grass grows over her."

"Right," said John. "You know something about farming, after all."

"I know something of some farmers," said I, "and a sure scythe will mow them down some day."

On the way back to the house a beautiful and inexplicable creature walked across our path. I stopped irresistibly fascinated, gazing at it. John waited patiently, smoking his cigarette. He is a modern farmer. After ten minutes he said: "Are you going to stand there looking at that chicken all day? Breakfast is nearly ready."

"A chicken?" said I.

"A white Orpington hen, if you want to particularize."

"A white Orpington hen?" I repeated, with intense interest. The fowl walked slowly away with graceful dignity, and I followed like a child after the Pied Piper. Five minutes more were allowed me by John, and then he took me by the sleeve and conducted me to breakfast.

After I had been there a week I began to grow alarmed. I was sleeping and eating well and actually beginning to enjoy life. For a man in my desperate condition that would never do. So I sneaked down to the trolley-car station, took the car for Pineville, and went to see one of the best physicians in town. By this time I knew exactly what to do when I needed medical treatment. I hung my hat on the back of a chair, and said rapidly:

"Doctor, I have cirrhosis of the heart, indurated arteries, neurasthenia, neuritis, acute indigestion, and convalescence. I am going to live on a strict diet. I shall also take a tepid bath at night and a cold one in the morning. I shall endeavor to be cheerful, and fix my mind on pleasant subjects. In the way of drugs I intend to take a phosphorus pill three times a day, preferably after meals, and a tonic composed of the tinctures of gentian, cinchona, calisaya, and cardamon compound. Into each teaspoonful of this I shall mix tincture of nux vomica, beginning with one drop and increasing it a drop each day until the maximum dose is reached. I shall drop this with a medicine-dropper, which can be procured at a trifling cost at any pharmacy. Good-morning."

I took my hat and walked out. After I had closed the door I remembered something that I had forgotten to say. I opened it again. The doctor had not moved from where he had been sitting, but he gave a slightly nervous start when he saw me again.

"I forgot to mention," said I, "that I shall also take absolute rest and exercise."

After this consultation I felt much better. The reëstablishing in my mind of the fact that I was hopelessly ill gave me so much satisfaction that I almost became gloomy again. There is nothing more alarming to a neurasthenic than to feel himself growing well and cheerful.

John looked after me carefully. After I had evinced so much interest in his white Orpington chicken he tried his best to divert my mind, and was particular to lock his hen house of nights. Gradually the tonic mountain air, the wholesome food, and the daily walks among the hills so alleviated my malady that I became utterly wretched and despondent. I heard of a country doctor who lived in the mountains near-by. I went to see him and told him the whole story. He was a gray-bearded man with clear, blue, wrinkled eyes, in a home-made suit of gray jeans.

In order to save time I diagnosed my case, touched my nose with my right forefinger, struck myself below the knee to make my foot kick, sounded my chest, stuck out my tongue, and asked him the price of cemetery lots in Pineville.

He lit his pipe and looked at me for about three minutes. "Brother," he said, after a while, "you are in a mighty bad way. There's a chance for you to pull through, but it's a mighty slim one."

"What can it be?" I asked, eagerly. "I have taken arsenic and gold, phosphorus, exercise, nux vomica, hydrotherapeutic baths, rest, excitement, codein, and aromatic spirits of ammonia. Is there anything left in the pharmacopœia?"

"Somewhere in these mountains," said the doctor, "there's a plant growing—a flowering plant that'll cure you, and it's about the only thing that will. It's of a kind that's as old as the world; but of late it's powerful scarce and hard to find. You and I will have to hunt it up. I'm not engaged in active practice now: I'm getting along in years; but I'll take your case. You'll have to come every day in the afternoon and help me hunt for this plant till we find it. The city doctors may know a lot about new scientific things, but they don't know much about the cures that nature carries around in her saddle bags."

So every day the old doctor and I hunted the cure-all plant among the mountains and valleys of the Blue Ridge. Together we toiled up steep heights so slippery with fallen autumn leaves that we had to catch every sapling and branch within our reach to save us from falling. We waded through gorges and chasms, breast-deep with laurel and ferns; we followed the banks of mountain streams for miles, we wound our way like Indians through brakes of pine—road side, hill side, river side, mountain side we explored in our search for the miraculous plant.

As the old doctor said, it must have grown scarce and hard to find. But we followed our quest. Day by day we plumbed the valleys, scaled the heights, and tramped the plateaus in search of the miraculous plant. Mountain-bred, he never seemed to tire. I often reached home too fatigued to do anything except fall into bed and sleep until morning. This we kept up for a month.

One evening after I had returned from a six-mile tramp with the old doctor, Amaryllis and I took a little walk under the trees near the road. We looked at the mountains drawing their royal-purple robes around them for their night's repose.

"I'm glad you're well again," she said. "When you first came you frightened me. I thought you were really ill."

"Well again!" I almost shrieked. "Do you know that I have only one chance in a thousand to live?"

Amaryllis looked at me in surprise. "Why," said she, "you are as strong as one of the plow-mules, and sleep ten or twelve hours every night, and you are eating us out of house and home. What more do you want?"

"I tell you," said I, "that unless we find the magic—that is, the plant we are looking for—in time, nothing can save me. The doctor tells me so."

"What doctor?"

"Doctor Tatum—the old doctor who lives halfway up Black Oak Mountain. Do you know him?"

"I have known him since I was able to talk. And is that where you go every day—is it he who takes you on these long walks and climbs that have brought back your health and strength? God bless the old doctor."

Just then the old doctor himself drove slowly down the road in his rickety old buggy. I waved my hand at him and shouted that I would be on hand the next day at the usual time. He stopped his horse and called to Amaryllis to come out to him. They talked for five minutes while I waited. Then the old doctor drove on.

When we got to the house Amaryllis lugged out an encyclopædia and sought a word in it. "The doctor said," she told me, "that you needn't call any more as a patient, but he'd be glad to see you any time as a friend. And then he told me to look up my name in the ency-clopædia and tell you what it means. It seems to be the name of a genus of flowering plants, and also the name of a country girl in Theocritus and Virgil. What do you suppose the doctor meant by that?"

"I know what he meant," said I. "I know now."

A word to a brother who may have come under the spell of the unquiet Lady Neurasthenia.

The formula was true. Even though gropingly at times, the physi-cians of the walled cities had put their fingers upon the specific medica-ment.

And so for the exercise one is referred to good Doctor Tatum on Black Oak Mountain—take the road to your right at the Methodist meeting house in the pine-grove.

Absolute rest and exercise!

What rest more remedial than to sit with Amaryllis in the shade, and, with a sixth sense, read the wordless Theocritan idyl of the gold-bannered blue mountains marching orderly into the dormitories of the night?

JOHN BARLEYCORN

Jack London

1913

By the time Jack London published his autobiographical portrait,
John Barleycorn, *he was well known as the dashing young novelist of* The Call of the Wild *and* White Fang. *His popularity gave* Barleycorn *an immediate audience, and he surprised many readers with its confessional account of his history with alcohol. The publication of London's personal story challenged the scornful notions about drinking that prevailed during the early twentieth century. Although London resisted calling himself an alcoholic, he acquiesced to his publisher's demand that the work be subtitled "Alcoholic Memoirs." Three years after the book's release, London died at the age of forty. Family members contend that he was the victim of kidney failure, while others believe that he died from an overdose of morphine. The following excerpt comprises Chapters III–VI of* John Barleycorn.

I was five years old the first time I got drunk. It was on a hot day, and my father was plowing in the field. I was sent from the house, half a mile away, to carry to him a pail of beer. "And be sure you don't spill it," was the parting injunction.

It was, as I remember it, a lard pail, very wide across the top, and without a cover. As I toddled along, the beer slopped over the rim upon my legs. And as I toddled, I pondered. Beer was a very precious thing. Come to think of it, it must be wonderfully good. Else why was I never permitted to drink of it in the house? Other things kept from me by the grown-ups I had found good. Then this, too, was good. Trust the grown-ups. They knew. And anyway, the pail was too full. I was slopping it against my legs and spilling it on the ground. Why waste it? And no one would know whether I had drunk or spilled it.

I was so small that in order to negotiate the pail, I sat down and gathered it into my lap. First I sipped the foam. I was disappointed. The preciousness evaded me. Evidently it did not reside in the foam. Besides, the taste was not good. Then I remembered seeing the grown-ups blow the foam away before they drank. I buried my face in the foam and lapped the solid liquid beneath. It wasn't good at all. But still I drank. The grown-ups knew what they were about. Considering my diminutiveness, the size of the pail in my lap, and my drinking out of it with my breath held and my face buried to the ears in foam, it was rather difficult to estimate how much I drank. Also, I was gulping it down like medicine, in nauseous haste to get the ordeal over.

I shuddered when I started on, and decided that the good taste would come afterward. I tried several times more in the course of that long half-mile. Then, astounded by the quantity of beer that was lacking, and remembering having seen stale beer made to foam afresh, I took a stick and stirred what was left till it foamed to the brim.

And my father never noticed. He emptied the pail with the wide thirst of the sweating plowman, returned it to me, and started up the plow. I endeavored to walk beside the horses. I remember tottering and falling against their heels in front of the shining share, and that my father hauled back on the lines so violently that the horses nearly sat down on me. He told me afterward that it was by only a matter of inches that I escaped disembowelling. Vaguely, too, I remember, my father carried me in his arms to the trees on the edge of the field, while all the world reeled and swung about me and I was aware of deadly nausea mingled with an appalling conviction of sin.

I slept the afternoon away under the trees, and when my father roused me at sundown it was a very sick little boy that got up and dragged wearily homeward. I was exhausted, oppressed by the weight of my limbs, and in my stomach was a harp-like vibration that extended to my throat and brain. My condition was like that of one who had gone through a battle with poison. In truth, I had been poisoned.

In the weeks and months that followed I had no more interest in beer than in the kitchen stove after it had burned me. The grown-ups were right. Beer was not for children. The grown-ups didn't mind it;

but neither did they mind taking pills and castor oil. As for me, I could manage to get along quite well without beer. Yes, and to the day of my death I could have managed to get along quite well without it. But circumstance decreed otherwise. At every turn in the world in which I lived, John Barleycorn beckoned. There was no escaping him. All paths led to him. And it took twenty years of contact, of exchanging greetings and passing on with my tongue in my cheek, to develop in me a sneaking liking for the rascal.

———

My next bout with John Barleycorn occurred when I was seven. This time my imagination was at fault, and I was frightened into the encounter. Still farming, my family had moved to a ranch on the bleak sad coast of San Mateo County south of San Francisco. It was a wild, primitive countryside in those days; and often I heard my mother pride herself that we were old American stock and not immigrant Irish and Italians like our neighbors. In all our section there was only one other old American family.

One Sunday morning found me, how or why I cannot now remember, at the Morrisey ranch. A number of young people had gathered there from the nearer ranches. Besides, the oldsters had been there, drinking since early dawn, and, some of them, since the night before. The Morriseys were a huge breed, and there were many strapping great sons and uncles, heavy-booted, big-fisted, rough-voiced.

Suddenly there were screams from the girls and cries of "Fight!" There was a rush. Men hurled themselves out of the kitchen. Two giants, flush-faced, with graying hair, were locked in each other's arms. One was Black Matt, who, everybody said, had killed two men in his time. The women screamed softly, crossed themselves, or prayed brokenly, hiding their eyes and peeping through their fingers. But not I. It is a fair presumption that I was the most interested spectator. Maybe I would see that wonderful thing, a man killed. Anyway, I would see a man-fight. Great was my disappointment. Black Matt and Tom Morrisey merely held on to each other and lifted their clumsy-booted feet in what seemed a grotesque, elephantine dance. They were too drunk to fight. Then the peacemakers got hold of them and led them back to cement the new friendship in the kitchen.

Soon they were all talking at once, rumbling and roaring as big-chested open-air men will when whisky has whipped their taciturnity.

And I, a little shaver of seven, my heart in my mouth, my trembling body strung tense as a deer's on the verge of flight, peered wonderingly in at the open door and learned more of the strangeness of men. And I marveled at Black Matt and Tom Morrisey, sprawled over the table, arms about each other's necks, weeping lovingly.

The kitchen-drinking continued, and the girls outside grew timorous. They knew the drink game, and all were certain that something terrible was going to happen. They protested that they did not wish to be there when it happened, and some one suggested going to a big Italian rancho four miles away, where they could get up a dance. Immediately they paired off, lad and lassie, and started down the sandy road. And each lad walked with his sweetheart—trust a child of seven to listen and to know the love affairs of his countryside. And behold, I, too, was a lad with a lassie. A little Irish girl of my own age had been paired off with me. We were the only children in this spontaneous affair. Perhaps the oldest couple might have been twenty. There were chits of girls, quite grown up, of fourteen and sixteen, walking with their fellows. But we were uniquely young, this little Irish girl and I, and we walked hand in hand, and, sometimes, under the tutelage of our elders, with my arm around her waist. Only that wasn't comfortable. And I was very proud, on that bright Sunday morning, going down the long bleak road among the sandhills. I, too, had my girl, and was a little man.

The Italian rancho was a bachelor establishment. Our visit was hailed with delight. The red wine was poured in tumblers for all, and the long dining-room was partly cleared for dancing. And the young fellows drank and danced with the girls to the strains of an accordeon. To me that music was divine. I had never heard anything so glorious. The young Italian who furnished it would even get up and dance, his arms around his girl, playing the accordeon behind her back. All of which was very wonderful for me, who did not dance, but who sat at a table and gazed wide-eyed at the amazingness of life. I was only a little lad, and there was so much of life for me to learn. As the time passed, the Irish lads began helping themselves to the wine, and jollity and high spirits reigned. I noted that some of them staggered and fell down in the dances, and that one had gone to sleep in a corner. Also, some of the girls were complaining and wanting to leave, and others of the girls were titteringly complacent, willing for anything to happen.

When our Italian hosts had offered me wine in a general sort of way, I had declined. My beer experience had been enough for me, and I had no inclination to traffic further in the stuff nor in anything related to it. Unfortunately, one young Italian, Peter, an impish soul, seeing me sitting solitary, stirred by a whim of the moment, half-filled a tumbler with wine and passed it to me. He was sitting across the table from me. I declined. His face grew stern, and he insistently proffered the wine. And then terror descended upon me—a terror which I must explain.

My mother had theories. First, she steadfastly maintained that brunettes and all the tribe of dark-eyed humans were deceitful. Needless to say, my mother was a blond. Next, she was convinced that the dark-eyed Latin races were profoundly sensitive, profoundly treacherous, and profoundly murderous. Again and again, drinking in the strangeness and the fearsomeness of the world from her lips, I had heard her state that if one offended an Italian, no matter how slightly and unintentionally, he was certain to retaliate by stabbing one in the back. That was her particular phrase—"stab you in the back."

Now, although I had been eager to see Black Matt kill Tom Morrisey that morning, I did not care to furnish to the dancers the spectacle of a knife sticking in *my* back. I had not yet learned to distinguish between facts and theories. My faith was implicit in my mother's exposition of the Italian character. Besides, I had some glimmering inkling of the sacredness of hospitality. Here was a treacherous, sensitive, murderous Italian, offering me hospitality. I had been taught to believe that if I offended him he would strike at me with a knife precisely as a horse kicked out when one got too close to its heels and worried it. Then, too, this Italian, Peter, had those terrible black eyes I had heard my mother talk about. They were eyes different from the eyes I knew, from the blues and grays and hazels of my own family, from the pale and genial blues of the Irish. Perhaps Peter had had a few drinks. At any rate his eyes were brilliantly black and sparkling with deviltry. They were the mysterious, the unknown, and who was I, a seven-year-old, to analyze them and know their prankishness? In them I visioned sudden death, and I declined the wine half-heartedly. The expression in his eyes changed. They grew stern and imperious as he shoved the tumbler of wine closer.

What could I do? I have faced real death since in my life, but never have I known the fear of death as I knew it then. I put the glass to my lips, and Peter's eyes relented. I knew he would not kill me just then. That was a relief. But the wine was not. It was cheap, new wine, bitter and sour, made of the leavings and scrapings of the vineyards and the vats, and it tasted far worse than beer. There is only one way to take medicine, and that is to take it. And that is the way I took that wine. I threw my head back and gulped it down. I had to gulp again and hold the poison down, for poison it was to my child's tissues and membranes.

Looking back now, I can realize that Peter was astounded. He half-filled a second tumbler and shoved it across the table. Frozen with fear, in despair at the fate which had befallen me, I gulped the second glass down like the first. This was too much for Peter. He must share the infant prodigy he had discovered. He called Dominick, a young mustached Italian, to see the sight. This time it was a full tumbler that was given me. One will do anything to live. I gripped myself, mastered the qualms that rose in my throat, and downed the stuff.

Dominick had never seen an infant of such heroic caliber. Twice again he refilled the tumbler, each time to the brim, and watched it disappear down my throat. By this time my exploits were attracting attention. Middle-aged Italian laborers, old-country peasants who did not talk English and who could not dance with the Irish girls, surrounded me. They were swarthy and wild-looking; they wore belts and red shirts; and I knew they carried knives; and they ringed me around like a pirate chorus. And Peter and Dominick made me show off for them.

Had I lacked imagination, had I been stupid, had I been stubbornly mulish in having my own way, I should never have got in this pickle. And the lads and lassies were dancing, and there was no one to save me from my fate. How much I drank I do not know. My memory of it is of an age-long suffering of fear in the midst of a murderous crew, and of an infinite number of glasses of red wine passing across the bare boards of a wine-drenched table and going down my burning throat. Bad as the wine was, a knife in the back was worse, and I must survive at any cost.

Looking back with the drinker's knowledge, I know now why I did not collapse stupefied upon the table. As I have said, I was frozen, I was paralyzed, with fear. The only movement I made was to convey that never-ending procession of glasses to my lips. I was a poised and motionless receptacle for all that quantity of wine. It lay inert in my fear-inert stomach. I was too frightened, even, for my stomach to turn. So all that Italian crew looked on and marveled at the infant phenomenon that downed wine with the *sang-froid* of an automaton. It is not in the spirit of braggadocio that I dare to assert they had never seen anything like it.

The time came to go. The tipsy antics of the lads had led a majority of the soberer-minded lassies to compel a departure. I found myself at the door, beside my little maiden. She had not had my experience, so she was sober. She was fascinated by the titubations of the lads who strove to walk beside their girls, and began to mimic them. I thought this was a great game, and I, too, began to stagger tipsily. But she had no wine to stir up, while my movements quickly set the fumes rising to my head. Even at the start, I was more realistic than she. In several minutes I was astonishing myself. I saw one lad, after reeling half a dozen steps, pause at the side of the road, gravely peer into the ditch, and gravely, and after apparent deep thought, fall into it. To me this was excruciatingly funny. I staggered to the edge of the ditch, fully intending to stop on the edge. I came to myself, in the ditch, in process of being hauled out by several anxious-faced girls.

I didn't care to play at being drunk any more. There was no more fun in me. My eyes were beginning to swim, and with wide-open mouth I panted for air. A girl led me by the hand on either side, but my legs were leaden. The alcohol I had drunk was striking my heart and brain like a club. Had I been a weakling of a child, I am confident that it would have killed me. As it was, I know I was nearer death than any of the scared girls dreamed. I could hear them bickering among themselves as to whose fault it was; some were weeping—for themselves, for me, and for the disgraceful way their lads had behaved. But I was not interested. I was suffocating, and I wanted air. To move was agony. It made me pant harder. Yet those girls persisted in making me walk, and it was four miles home. Four miles! I remember my swimming eyes saw a small bridge across the road an infinite distance away. In fact, it was not a hundred feet distant. When I reached it, I sank down and lay on my back panting. The girls tried to lift me, but I was helpless and suffocating. Their cries of alarm brought Larry, a drunken youth of seventeen, who proceeded to resuscitate me by jumping on my chest. Dimly I remember this, and the squalling of the girls as they struggled with him and dragged him away. And then I knew nothing, though I learned afterward that Larry wound up under the bridge and spent the night there.

When I came to, it was dark. I had been carried unconscious for four miles and been put to bed. I was a sick child, and, despite the terrible strain on my heart and tissues, I continually relapsed into the madness of delirium. All the content of the terrible and horrible in my child's mind spilled out. The most frightful visions were realities to me. I saw murders committed, and I was pursued by murderers. I screamed and raved and fought. My sufferings were prodigious. Emerging from such delirium, I would hear my mother's voice: "But the child's brain. He will lose his reason." And sinking back into delirium, I would take the idea with me and be immured in madhouses, and be beaten by keepers, and surrounded by screeching lunatics.

One thing that had strongly impressed my young mind was the talk of my elders about the dens of iniquity in San Francisco's Chinatown. In my delirium I wandered deep beneath the ground through a thousand of these dens, and behind locked doors of iron I suffered and died a thousand deaths. And when I would come upon my father, seated at table in these subterranean crypts, gambling with Chinese for great stakes of gold, all my outrage gave vent in the vilest cursing. I would rise in bed, struggling against the detaining hands, and curse my father till the rafters rang. All the inconceivable filth a child running at large in a primitive countryside may hear men utter, was mine; and though I had never dared utter such oaths, they now poured from me, at the top of my lungs, as I cursed my father sitting there underground and gambling with long-haired, long-nailed Chinamen.

It is a wonder that I did not burst my heart or brain that night. A seven-year-old child's arteries and nerve-centers are scarcely fitted to endure the terrific paroxysms that convulsed me. No one slept in the thin, frame farmhouse that night when John Barleycorn had his will of me. And Larry, under the bridge, had no delirium like mine. I am confident that his sleep was stupefied and dreamless, and that he awoke next day merely to heaviness and moroseness, and that if he lives to-day he does not remember that night, so passing was it as an incident. But my brain was seared forever by that experience. Writing now, thirty years afterward, every vision is as distinct, as sharp-cut, every pain as vital and terrible, as on that night.

I was sick for days afterward, and I needed none of my mother's in-junctions to avoid John Barleycorn in the future. My mother had been dreadfully shocked. She held that I had done wrong, very wrong, and that I had gone contrary to all her teaching. And how was I, who was never allowed to talk back, who lacked the very words with which to express my psychology—how was I to tell my mother that it was her teaching that was directly responsible for my drunkenness? Had it not been for her theories about dark eyes and Italian character, I should never have wet my lips with the sour, bitter wine. And not until man-grown did I tell her the true inwardness of that disgraceful affair.

In those after-days of sickness, I was confused on some points, and very clear on others. I felt guilty of sin, yet smarted with a sense of in-justice. It had not been my fault; yet I had done wrong. But very clear was my resolution never to touch liquor again. No mad dog was ever more afraid of water than was I of alcohol.

Yet the point I am making is that this experience, terrible as it was, could not in the end deter me from forming John Barleycorn's cheek-by-jowl acquaintance. All about me, even then, were the forces moving me toward him. In the first place, barring my mother, ever extreme in her views, it seemed to me all the grown-ups looked upon the affair with tolerant eyes. It was a joke, something funny that had happened. There was no shame attached. Even the lads and lassies giggled and snickered over their part in the affair, narrating with gusto how Larry had jumped on my chest and slept under the bridge, how So-and-So had slept out in the sandhills that night, and what had happened to the other lad who fell in the ditch. As I say, so far as I could see, there was no shame anywhere. It had been something ticklishly, devilishly fine—a bright and gorgeous episode in the monotony of life and labor on that bleak, fog-girt coast.

The Irish ranchers twitted me good-naturedly on my exploit, and patted me on the back until I felt that I had done something heroic. Peter and Dominick and the other Italians were proud of my drinking prowess. The face of morality was not set against drinking. Besides, everybody drank. There was not a teetotaler in the community. Even the teacher of our little country school, a graying man of fifty, gave us vacations on the occasions when he wrestled with John Barleycorn and was thrown. Thus there was no spiritual deterrence. My loathing for alcohol was purely physiological. I didn't like the damned stuff.

This physical loathing for alcohol I have never got over. But I have conquered it. To this day I re-conquer it every time I take a drink. The palate never ceases to rebel, and the palate can be trusted to know what is good for the body. But men do not knowingly drink for the effect alcohol produces on the body. What they drink for is the brain-effect; and if it must come through the body, so much the worse for the body.

And yes, despite my physical loathing for alcohol, the brightest spots in my child life were the saloons. Sitting on the heavy potato wagons, wrapped in fog, feet stinging from inactivity, the horses plodding slowly along the deep road through the sandhills, one bright vision made the way never too long. The bright vision was the saloon at Colma, where my father, or whoever drove, always got out to get a drink. And I got out to warm by the great stove and get a soda cracker. Just one soda cracker, but a fabulous luxury. Saloons were good for something. Back behind the plodding horses, I would take an hour in consuming that one cracker. I took the smallest of nibbles, never losing a crumb, and chewed the nibble till it became the thinnest and most delectable of pastes. I never voluntarily swallowed this paste. I just tasted it, and went on tasting it, turning it over with my tongue, spreading it on the inside of one cheek, then on the inside of the other cheek, until, at the end, it eluded me and in tiny drops and oozelets slipped and dribbled down my throat. Horace Fletcher had nothing on me when it came to soda crackers.

I liked saloons. Especially I liked the San Francisco saloons. They had the most delicious dainties for the taking—strange breads and crackers, cheeses, sausages, sardines—wonderful foods that I never saw on our meager home-table. And once, I remember, a barkeeper mixed me a sweet temperance drink of syrup and soda water. My father did not pay for it. It was the barkeeper's treat, and he became my ideal of a good, kind man. I dreamed day dreams of him for years. Although I was seven years old at the time, I can see him now with undiminished clearness, though I never laid eyes on him but that one time. The saloon was south of Market Street in San Francisco. It stood on the west side of the street. As you entered, the bar was on the left. On the right, against the wall, was the free-lunch counter. It was a long, narrow room, and at the rear, beyond the beer kegs on tap, were small round tables and chairs. The barkeeper was blue-eyed, and had fair, silky hair peeping out from under a black silk skull-cap. I remember he wore a brown Cardigan jacket, and I know precisely the spot, in the midst of the array of bottles, from which he took the bottle of red-colored syrup. He and my father talked long, and I sipped my sweet drink and worshiped him. And for years afterward I worshiped the memory of him.

Despite my two disastrous experiences, here was John Barleycorn, prevalent and accessible everywhere in the community, luring and drawing me. Here were connotations of the saloon making deep indentations in a child's mind. Here was a child, forming its first judgments of the world, finding the saloon a delightful and desirable place. Stores, nor public buildings, nor all the dwellings of men ever opened their doors to me and let me warm by their fires or permitted me to eat the food of the gods from narrow shelves against the wall. Their doors were ever closed to me; the saloon's doors were ever open. And always and everywhere I found saloons, on highway and byway, up narrow alleys and on busy thoroughfares, bright-lighted and cheerful, warm in winter and in summer dark and cool. Yes, the saloon was a mighty fine place, and it was more than that.

By the time I was ten years old, my family had abandoned ranching and gone to live in the city. And here, at ten, I began on the streets as a newsboy. One of the reasons for this was that we needed the money. Another reason was that I needed the exercise. I had found my way to the free public library, and was reading myself into nervous prostration. On the poor-ranches on which I had lived there had been no books. In ways truly miraculous, I had been lent four books, marvelous books, and them I had devoured. One was the life of Garfield; the second, Paul du Chaillu's African travels; the third, a novel by Ouida with the last forty pages missing; and the fourth, Irving's "Alhambra." This last had been lent me by a school-teacher. I was not a forward child. Unlike Oliver Twist, I was incapable of asking for more. When I returned the "Alhambra" to the teacher I hoped she would lend me another book. And because she did not—most likely she deemed me unappreciative—I cried all the way home on the three-mile tramp from the school to the ranch. I waited and yearned for her to lend me another book. Scores of times I nerved myself almost to the point of asking her, but never quite reached the necessary pitch of effrontery.

And then came the city of Oakland, and on the shelves of that free-library I discovered all the great world beyond the skyline. Here were thousands of books as good as my four wonder-books, and some were even better. Libraries were not concerned with children in those days, and I had strange adventures. I remember, in the catalogue, being impressed by the title, "The Adventures of Peregrine Pickle." I filled an application blank and the librarian handed me the collected and entirely unexpurgated works of Smollett in one huge volume. I read everything, but principally history and adventure, and all the old travels and voyages. I read mornings, afternoons, and nights. I read in bed, I read at the table, I read as I walked to and from school, and I read at recess while the other boys were playing. I began to get the "jerks." To everybody I replied: "Go away. You make me nervous."

And so, at ten, I was out on the streets, a newsboy. I had no time to read. I was busy getting exercise and learning how to fight, busy learning forwardness, and brass and bluff. I had an imagination and a curiosity about all things that made me plastic. Not least among the things I was curious about was the saloon. And I was in and out of many a one. I remember, in those days, on the east side of Broadway between Sixth and Seventh, from corner to corner, there was a solid block of saloons.

In the saloons life was different. Men talked with great voices, laughed great laughs, and there was an atmosphere of greatness. Here was something more than common every-day where nothing happened. Here life was always very live, and, sometimes, even lurid, when blows were struck, and blood was shed, and big policemen came shouldering in. Great moments, these, for me, my head filled with all the wild and valiant fighting of the gallant adventures on sea and land. There were no big moments when I trudged along the street throwing my papers in at doors. But in the saloons, even the sots, stupefied, sprawling across the tables or in the sawdust, were objects of mystery and wonder.

And more, the saloons were right. The city fathers sanctioned them and licensed them. They were not the terrible places I heard boys deem them who lacked my opportunities to know. Terrible they might be, but then that only meant they were terribly wonderful, and it is the terribly wonderful that a boy desires to know. In the same way pirates, and shipwrecks, and battles were terrible; and what healthy boy wouldn't give his immortal soul to participate in such affairs?

Besides, in saloons I saw reporters, editors, lawyers, judges, whose names and faces I knew. They put the seal of social approval on the saloon. They verified my own feeling of fascination in the saloon. They, too, must have found there that something different, that something beyond, which I sensed and groped after. What it was, I did not know; yet there it must be, for there men focused like buzzing flies about a honey pot. I had no sorrows, and the world was very bright, so I could not guess that what these men sought was forgetfulness of jaded toil and stale grief.

Not that I drank at that time. From ten to fifteen I rarely tasted liquor, but I was intimately in contact with drinkers and drinking places. The only reason I did not drink was because I didn't like the stuff. As the time passed, I worked as boy-helper on an ice-wagon, set up pins in a bowling-alley with a saloon attached, and swept out saloons at Sunday picnic grounds.

Big jovial Josie Harper ran a road-house at Telegraph Avenue and Thirty-ninth Street. Here for a year I delivered an evening paper, until my route was changed to the water-front and tenderloin of Oakland. The first month, when I collected Josie Harper's bill, she poured me a glass of wine. I was ashamed to refuse, so I drank it. But after that I watched the chance when she wasn't around so as to collect from her barkeeper.

The first day I worked in the bowling-alley, the barkeeper, according to custom, called us boys up to have a drink after we had been setting up pins for several hours. The others asked for beer. I said I'd take ginger ale. The boys snickered, and I noticed the barkeeper favored me with a strange, searching scrutiny. Nevertheless he opened a bottle of ginger ale. Afterward, back in the alleys, in the pauses between games, the boys enlightened me. I had offended the barkeeper. A bottle of ginger ale cost the saloon ever so much more than a glass of steam beer; and it was up to me, if I wanted to hold my job, to drink beer. Besides, beer was food. I could work better on it. There was no food in ginger ale. After that, when I couldn't sneak out of it, I drank beer and wondered what men found in it that was so good. I was always aware that I was missing something.

What I really liked in those days was candy. For five cents I could buy five "cannon-balls"—big lumps of the most delicious lastingness. I could chew and worry a single one for an hour. Then there was a

Mexican who sold big slabs of brown chewing taffy for five cents each. It required a quarter of a day properly to absorb one of them. And many a day I made my entire lunch off of one of those slabs. In truth, I found food there, but not in beer.

———

But the time was rapidly drawing near when I was to begin my second series of bouts with John Barleycorn. When I was fourteen, my head filled with the tales of the old voyagers, my vision with tropic isles and far sea-rims, I was sailing a small centerboard skiff around San Francisco Bay and on the Oakland Estuary. I wanted to go to sea. I wanted to get away from monotony and the commonplace. I was in the flower of my adolescence, athrill with romance and adventure, dreaming of wild life in the wild man-world. Little I guessed how all the warp and woof of that man-world was entangled with alcohol.

So, one day, as I hoisted sail on my skiff, I met Scotty. He was a husky youngster of seventeen, a runaway apprentice, he told me, from an English ship in Australia. He had just worked his way on another ship to San Francisco; and now he wanted to see about getting a berth on a whaler. Across the estuary, near where the whalers lay, was lying the sloop-yacht *Idler*. The caretaker was a harpooner who intended sailing next voyage on the whale ship *Bonanza*. Would I take him, Scotty, over in my skiff to call upon the harpooner?

Would I? Hadn't I heard the stories and rumors about the *Idler*?— the big sloop that had come up from the Sandwich Islands where it had been engaged in smuggling opium. And the harpooner who was care-taker! How often had I seen him and envied him his freedom. He never had to leave the water. He slept aboard the *Idler* each night, while I had to go home upon the land to go to bed. The harpooner was only nine-teen years old (and I have never had anything but his own word that he was a harpooner); but he had been too shining and glorious a person-ality for me ever to address as I paddled around the yacht at a wistful distance. Would I take Scotty, the runaway sailor, to visit the har-pooner, on the opium-smuggler *Idler*? Would I!

The harpooner came on deck to answer our hail, and invited us aboard. I played the sailor and the man, fending off the skiff so that it would not mar the yacht's white paint, dropping the skiff astern on a long painter, and making the painter fast with two nonchalant half-hitches. We went below. It was the first sea-interior I had ever seen.

The clothing on the wall smelled musty. But what of that? Was it not the sea-gear of men?—leather jackets lined with corduroy, blue coats of pilot cloth, sou'westers, sea-boots, oilskins. And everywhere was in evidence the economy of space—the narrow bunks, the swinging tables, the incredible lockers. There were the tell-tale compass, the sea-lamps in their gimbals, the blue-backed charts carelessly rolled and tucked away, the signal-flags in alphabetical order, and a mariner's dividers jammed into the woodwork to hold a calendar. At last I was living. Here I sat, inside my first ship, a smuggler, accepted as a comrade by a harpooner and a runaway English sailor who said his name was Scotty.

The first thing that the harpooner, aged nineteen, and the sailor, aged seventeen, did to show that they were men, was to behave like men. The harpooner suggested the eminent desirableness of a drink, and Scotty searched his pockets for dimes and nickels. Then the harpooner carried away a pink flask to be filled in some blind pig, for there were no licensed saloons in that locality. We drank the cheap rotgut out of tumblers. Was I any the less strong, and the less valiant, than the harpooner and the sailor? They were men. They proved it by the way they drank. Drink was the badge of manhood. So I drank with them, drink by drink, raw and straight, though the damned stuff couldn't compare with a stick of chewing taffy or a delectable "cannon-ball." I shuddered and swallowed my gorge with every drink, though I manfully hid all such symptoms.

Divers times we filled the flask that afternoon. All I had was twenty cents, but I put it up like a man, though with secret regret at the enormous store of candy it could have bought. The liquor mounted in the heads of all of us, and the talk of Scotty and the harpooner was upon running the Easting down, gales off the Horn and pamperos off the Plate, lower topsail breezes, southerly busters, North Pacific gales, and of smashed whaleboats in the Arctic ice.

"You can't swim in that ice water," said the harpooner confidentially to me. "You double up in a minute and go down. When a whale smashes your boat, the thing to do is to get your belly across an oar, so that when the cold doubles you you'll float."

"Sure," I said, with a grateful nod and an air of certitude that I, too, would hunt whales and be in smashed boats in the Arctic Ocean. And, truly, I registered his advice as singularly valuable information, and filed it away in my brain, where it persists to this day.

But I couldn't talk—at first. Heavens! I was only fourteen, and had never been on the ocean in my life. I could only listen to the two sea-dogs, and show my manhood by drinking with them, fairly and squarely, drink and drink.

The liquor worked its will with me; the talk of Scotty and the harpooner poured through the pent space of the *Idler*'s cabin and through my brain like great gusts of wide, free wind; and in imagination I lived my years to come and rocked over the wild, mad, glorious world on multitudinous adventures.

We unbent. Our inhibitions and taciturnities vanished. We were as if we had known each other for years and years, and we pledged ourselves to years of future voyagings together. The harpooner told of misadventures and secret shames. Scotty wept over his poor old mother in Edinburg—a lady, he insisted, gently born—who was in reduced circumstances, who had pinched herself to pay the lump sum to the ship-owners for his apprenticeship, whose sacrificing dream had been to see him a merchantman officer and a gentleman, and who was heart-broken because he had deserted his ship in Australia and joined another as a common sailor before the mast. And Scotty proved it. He drew her last sad letter from his pocket and wept over it as he read it aloud. The harpooner and I wept with him, and swore that all three of us would ship on the whaleship *Bonanza*, win a big pay-day, and, still together, make a pilgrimage to Edinburg and lay our store of money in the dear lady's lap.

And, as John Barleycorn heated his way into my brain, thawing my reticence, melting my modesty, talking through me and with me and as me, my adopted twin brother and *alter ego*, I, too, raised my voice to show myself a man and an adventurer, and bragged in detail and at length of how I had crossed San Francisco Bay in my open skiff in a roaring southwester when even the schooner sailors doubted my exploit. Further, I—or John Barleycorn, for it was the same thing—told Scotty that he might be a deep sea sailor and know the last rope on the great deep sea ships, but that when it came to small-boat sailing I could beat him hands down and sail circles around him.

The best of it was that my assertion and brag were true. With reticence and modesty present, I could never have dared tell Scotty my small-boat estimate of him. But it is ever the way of John Barleycorn to loosen the tongue and babble the secret thought.

Scotty, or John Barleycorn, or the pair, was very naturally offended by my remarks. Nor was I loath. I could whip any runaway sailor seventeen years old. Scotty and I flared and raged like young cockerels, until the harpooner poured another round of drinks to enable us to forgive and make up. Which we did, arms around each other's necks, protesting vows of eternal friendship—just like Black Matt and Tom Morrisey, I remembered, in the ranch kitchen in San Mateo. And remembering, I knew that I was at last a man—despite my meager fourteen years—a man as big and manly as those two strapping giants who had quarreled and made up on that memorable Sunday morning of long ago.

By this time the singing stage was reached, and I joined Scotty and the harpooner in snatches of sea songs and chanties. It was here, in the cabin of the *Idler,* that I first heard "Blow the Man Down," "Flying Cloud," and "Whisky, Johnny, Whisky." Oh, it was brave. I was beginning to grasp the meaning of life. Here was no commonplace, no Oakland Estuary, no weary round of throwing newspapers at front doors, delivering ice, and setting up ninepins. All the world was mine, all its paths were under my feet, and John Barleycorn, tricking my fancy, enabled me to anticipate the life of adventure for which I yearned.

We were not ordinary. We were three tipsy young gods, incredibly wise, gloriously genial, and without limit to our powers. Ah!—and I say it now, after the years—could John Barleycorn keep one at such a height, I should never draw a sober breath again. But this is not a world of free freights. One pays according to an iron schedule—for every strength the balanced weakness; for every high a corresponding low; for every fictitious godlike moment an equivalent time in reptilian slime. For every feat of telescoping long days and weeks of life into mad, magnificent instants, one must pay with shortened life, and, ofttimes, with savage usury added.

Intenseness and duration are as ancient enemies as fire and water. They are mutually destructive. They cannot co-exist. And John Barleycorn, mighty necromancer though he be, is as much a slave to organic chemistry as we mortals are. We pay for every nerve Marathon we run, nor can John Barleycorn intercede and fend off the just payment. He can lead us to the heights, but he cannot keep us there, else would we all be devotees. And there is no devotee but pays for the mad dances John Barleycorn pipes.

Yet the foregoing is all in after-wisdom spoken. It was no part of the knowledge of the lad, fourteen years old, who sat in the *Idler's* cabin between the harpooner and the sailor, the air rich in his nostrils with the musty smell of men's sea-gear, roaring in chorus: "Yankee ship come down de ribber—Pull, my bully boys, pull!"

We grew maudlin, and all talked and shouted at once. I had a splendid constitution, a stomach that would digest scrap-iron, and I was still running my Marathon in full vigor when Scotty began to fail and fade. His talk grew incoherent. He groped for words and could not find them, while the ones he found his lips were unable to form. His poisoned consciousness was leaving him. The brightness went out of his eyes, and he looked as stupid as were his efforts to talk. His face and body sagged as his consciousness sagged. (A man cannot sit upright save by an act of will.) Scotty's reeling brain could not control his muscles. All his correlations were breaking down. He strove to take another drink, and feebly dropped the tumbler on the floor. Then, to my amazement, weeping bitterly, he rolled into a bunk on his back and immediately snored off to sleep.

The harpooner and I drank on, grinning in a superior way to each other over Scotty's plight. The last flask was opened, and we drank it between us, to the accompaniment of Scotty's stertorous breathing. Then the harpooner faded away into his bunk, and I was left alone, unthrown, on the field of battle.

I was very proud, and John Barleycorn was proud with me. I could carry my drink, into unconsciousness. And I was still on my two feet, upright, making my way on deck to get air into my scorching lungs. It was in this bout on the *Idler* that I discovered what a good stomach and a strong head I had for drink—a bit of knowledge that was to be a source of pride in succeeding years, and that ultimately I was to come to consider a great affliction. The fortunate man is the one who cannot take more than a couple of drinks without becoming intoxicated. The unfortunate wight is the one who can take many glasses without betraying a sign; who *must* take numerous glasses in order to get the "kick."

The sun was setting when I came on the *Idler's* deck. There were plenty of bunks below. I did not need to go home. But I wanted to demonstrate to myself how much I was a man. There lay my skiff astern. The last of a strong ebb was running out in channel in the teeth of an ocean breeze of forty miles an hour. I could see the stiff white-caps, and the suck and run of the current was plainly visible in the face and trough of each one.

I set sail, cast off, took my place at the tiller, the sheet in my hand, and headed across channel. The skiff heeled over and plunged into it madly. The spray began to fly. I was at the pinnacle of exaltation. I sang "Blow the Man Down" as I sailed. I was no boy of fourteen, living the mediocre ways of the sleepy town called Oakland. I was a man, a god, and the very elements rendered me allegiance as I bitted them to my will.

The tide was out. A full hundred yards of soft mud intervened be-tween the boat-wharf and the water. I pulled up my centerboard, ran full tilt into the mud, took in sail, and, standing in the stern as I had often done at low tide, I began to shove the skiff with an oar. It was then that my correlations began to break down. I lost my balance and pitched headforemost into the ooze. Then, and for the first time, as I floundered to my feet covered with slime, the blood running down my arms from a scrape against a barnacled stake, I knew that I was drunk. But what of it? Across the channel two strong sailormen lay uncon-scious in their bunks where I had drunk them. I *was* a man. I was still on my legs, if they *were* knee deep in mud. I disdained to get back into the skiff. I waded through the mud, shoving the skiff before me and yammering the chant of my manhood to the world.

I paid for it. I was sick for a couple of days, meanly sick, and my arms were painfully poisoned from the barnacle scratches. For a week I could not use them, and it was a torture to put on and take off my clothes.

I swore, "Never again!" The game wasn't worth it. The price was too stiff. I had no moral qualms. My revulsion was purely physical. No ex-alted moments were worth such hours of misery and wretchedness. When I got back to my skiff, I shunned the *Idler*. I would cross the op-posite side of the channel to go around her. Scotty had disappeared. The harpooner was still about, but him I avoided. Once, when he landed on the boat-wharf, I hid in a shed so as to escape seeing him. I was afraid he would propose some more drinking, maybe have a flask full of whisky in his pocket.

And yet—and here enters the necromancy of John Barleycorn—that afternoon's drunk on the *Idler* had been a purple passage flung into the monotony of my days. It was memorable. My mind dwelt on it continually. I went over the details, over and over again. Among other things, I had got into the cogs and springs of men's actions. I had seen Scotty weep about his own worthlessness and the sad case of his Edinburg mother who was a lady. The harpooner had told me terribly wonderful things of himself. I had caught a myriad enticing and inflammatory hints of a world beyond my world, and for which I was certainly as fitted as the two lads who had drunk with me. I had got behind men's souls. I had got behind my own soul and found unguessed potencies and greatnesses.

Yes, that day stood out above all my other days. To this day it so stands out. The memory of it is branded in my brain. But the price exacted was too high. I refused to play and pay, and returned to my cannon-balls and taffy-slabs. The point is that all the chemistry of my healthy, normal body drove me away from alcohol. The stuff didn't agree with me. It was abominable. But despite this, circumstance was to continue to drive me toward John Barleycorn, to drive me again and again, until, after long years, the time should come when I would look up John Barleycorn in every haunt of men—look him up and hail him gladly as benefactor and friend. And detest and hate him all the time. Yes, he is a strange friend, John Barleycorn.

A Bartender Tells What Man Did to Booze, and Booze to Man

Anonymous

1919

As a sober witness to the culture of alcohol and its consumption, the bartender is in a unique position to investigate the behaviors and motivations of men and women whose efforts to find solace also bring them to the brink of self-destruction. This essay, published in the Dearborn Independent *by an anonymous New York bartender, provides as much insight into the drinker's psyche as any psychologist's erudite analysis. "Men liked to drink together because of the way alcohol let down the bars," the bartender surmises. "I have seen timid men become bold; and men of few words, 'hard boiled' fellows, become voluble talkers."*

To me there was always a fascination in tending bar. I liked to study the various ingredients with which I made drinks, and their effect upon different kinds of men. I think that in twenty years I came to know "booze" intimately. It has secrets. These I shall tell you.

There has always been more or less mystery about drinking. The swinging doors to every café and saloon suggested secrecy. They hid the drinkers from the world. Behind the bar, on my side of it, the side where were the bottles with their varicolored contents, that was a mystery. What was really in those bottles? Why the colors? Why did men like cocktails, fizzes, rickeys, juleps, highballs, punches, toddys, cordials, wine, whisky, beer?

Frankly, I liked the bottles behind the bar—not all of them, for I shall tell you, too, how men were cheated. I liked to choose, from a large number of bottles, certain bottles which my experience told me to take. I enjoyed pouring from these bottles just the exact quantity of liquors to produce a drink satisfactory to my patrons. I consider the mixing of drinks an art. I know the taste a certain mixture will produce, also the effect. For twenty years I watched the effect of alcohol upon men.

I have heard a lot about what booze does to men. Get one thing straight. There is one reason, and only one, why men drank. I have seen them demand of me a certain brand of whisky and show pettishness when we were out of it. I have seen them call for a particular make of gin. I have seen wine drinkers—who, in America, are rare—hold up a glass to the light and go into delights about its color and odor. I have heard men speculate upon the shadings of color and "creaminess" of beer. I have heard the virtues of "juleps" argued against those of "rickeys." But don't fool yourself that a man drank whisky or gin because a certain brand offered some mysterious piquancy of flavor. Don't fool yourself that men drank wine because of the bouquet; that men drank beer for its color or creaminess; that men drank "juleps" for the mint, or "rickeys" for the lime-juice. Men drank for the alcohol in the drink and for no other reason. Believe me, I know. The sole reason for the existence of these various drinks was to induce the body to accept them.

Were a man to mix alcohol with water and drink it, the palate, the stomach, would rebel. So it became a profession for the makers of booze and for us bartenders to disguise alcohol with odors and flavors so that men could more readily accept it. Also, different drinks provided men with different quantities of alcohol, as they wanted. It was for the alcohol alone, what it did to them, that men drank.

About inducing the stomach to accept drink. Rare indeed is the man whose first drink was strong in alcohol. The average person taking whisky for the first time gagged. His body resented it. More easy was it to down, the first time, beer or wine or a cocktail, with the alcohol taste carefully camouflaged by fruit. I have seen these "first drinkers." Most of them began on beer and then came a day when they wanted more alcohol and they went to whisky, to distilled spirits, gin or rum, with their higher percentages of alcohol. But they began on beer. Their body would not stand for them beginning on whisky. Nature had to be "eased in." First, it accepted a drink with about five per cent alcohol; then it wanted thirty-five per cent.

Of course, you know what alcohol is. I made it my business to find out about everything in the booze game. Alcohol is a liquid without color, sharp and repellent of taste, and quite suave of odor. Before telling you what it did to men—as I have watched it from behind the bar—I shall tell you what we did to alcohol so it would please men. After we colored and perfumed alcohol, it reminded me sometimes of a woman of the night, adorned to attract.

I shall begin with a dynamite drink. You know brandy, cognac? They made it by distilling wine. When distilled, it was colorless and had about fifty per cent alcohol. Then it was put in a cask from the wood of which it took an amber or brown color. In the cask it lost some of the alcohol, and when it came to us at the bar in bottles it had about forty per cent alcohol. I have served brandy, however, that was as high as fifty-two per cent alcohol. Whisky was not quite as strong; almost, though. Distilled from barley, rye, maize, or other grains, it ran from thirty-five per cent to as high as forty-six per cent, in some of the imported "Scotches." Rum, you know, was made of distilled molasses and the by-products of cane sugar factories. Not as strong as whisky, it was stronger than gin, which latter had about thirty per cent alcohol. Gin was distilled from unmalted grain and flavored with juniper berries. Those were the common drinks and the base ingredients for mixed drinks.

Wine, made from the fermented juice of the grape, ran from ten per cent to twenty-five per cent alcohol. Beer, supposed to be made from the fermented malt, flavored with hops—but which it rarely was in America—contained, before the war measures, from three to nine per cent alcohol. Ale was about the same. Of course, the beer of today has only 2.75 alcohol, but alcohol there is and men drink it for the alcohol alone. It may interest you to know that before the war, when beer in Europe was condemned as being bad, we imported it along with good beer; for, unlike European countries, we had no inspection of beer.

To whisky some distillers added chemicals which gave it a desired "age." When Scotch is genuinely made, the creosote in it comes from the peat in the making; in very good Scotch this is eliminated, for it is not good for the stomach. The average "bar Scotch" was not imported. It was made in America. Also it held creosote (injurious), artificially added so it would taste "smoky" like some real Scotch, from which the creosote is not removed. Most of the Scotch sold in America was "fake." I shall never forget the day when a salesman from a distillery came into a café where I worked. My boss considered himself an expert on whisky. The salesman came over to the bar with him and called for small glasses. Into these he poured his samples for him to taste. The boss picked up the glasses, sniffed their contents, tasted them carefully, and, as he did so, said:

"That new Bourbon is very good—Brandy ten years in the cask, fine—This is a good Irish—Where did you get that Scotch?—It's O.K."

The salesman smiled. He quoted then a price per barrel on these whiskies so cheap that it made my employer gasp, "But how can you afford to sell such goods so cheap?"

The salesman grinned. "That stuff is wood alcohol. Its tastes, colors and flavors were fixed up by our head chemist—great, hey?"

And my boss gave him a big order and I quit the job. On the level, it went against the grain. I'd be serving this stuff—wood alcohol, all doped up to conceal it to my customers and they, thinking it was good booze, paying fancy prices for it. Few are the men who can tell a cleverly-faked whisky from the real stuff.

There are wine fakers too. One day, when I was tending bar in a well-known hotel, the manager sent for me. With him was a wine man who was saying, "Put in my line of wines, and every price will be so low that you'll increase your profits." That sounded like false goods to me and I asked him how they did it.

"Oh, easy," he laughed. "We've got some chemists who are wonders. They take a little cheap California wine, some water, some vinegar and potato alcohol and turn you out as nice a bottle of claret as you want to see. We make our Rhine wine and Sauterne by using a little real sherry as a base. To this add citric acid, tannic acid (for the dry flavor), alcohol and water—and there's your Sauterne. If you want a sweet wine, like Chablis, we substitute a white sugar syrup for the tannic acid. If you want your wine aged, we add a little glycerine—altho glucose does the trick, too."

I learned from that wine man that brandy was faked by using wood alcohol as a base, adding silent spirit and cenanthic ether, and coloring and sweetening with caramel. Cordials were faked too. All the mixer did was to line up his bottles of benzoic acid, benzoic ether, acetic acid and ether, cenanthic ether and glycerine. He used a little of each, added wood or potato alcohol, added a few drops of cochineal and there's your cherry brandy. Fake booze brought prohibition.

I'm going to show up most of the brewers, too; not all, for some did try to make honest beer. Honestly, though, in my experience, I drew mighty little pure beer from the tap. Beer should be made from fermented infusions of malt flavored with hops. In Europe, beer must be lagered, stored for three months. Few American breweries could keep their beer in lager for three months. It would so putrefy as to be worthless. That is because many of our brewers used a ferment which was not inspected by the government and was not always pure. So their beer fermented rottenly. To overcome the putrefaction, the brewers added arsenious acid, white arsens or salicylic acid—which latter when used a long time did more harm to kidneys and liver than booze ever did.

The alcohol gave an exhilaration that changed dullness and weariness into a false flashing feeling of being alive. Then some drink for the dreamy forgetfulness, a dangerous indifference to actualities—a poisonous and highly-prized mood for men to attain. Men liked to drink together because of the way alcohol let down the bars. I have seen timid men become bold; and men of few words, "hard boiled" fellows, become voluble talkers. Men who when stark sober could "let themselves go," men who were in dread of convention, were utterly different beings when they drank—which is why they drank. For alcohol made most men bold. Most timid men like the feeling of boldness.

You see, I have watched the effects of alcohol and I know that its first effect is on the nerves; that is the feeling of being "lifted," the "pick up," the "glow," briefly, stimulation by alcohol hurried the heart action. The stomach glowed and felt fine; that was caused by the alcohol making the blood vessels expand through increased pumping from the heart. That made a man think a drink had "warmed him up." The brain got the stimulation. It seemed easier for him to think. He glowed. That was the first effect of a drink.

When they had one drink, I noticed that men wanted to talk. When they had a number of drinks, they still wanted to talk—generally about themselves.

Such boasting as I have chanced to hear while serving customers drinks!

There were men who came into our place, who, I believe, drank simply to get up the courage to talk about themselves. I have noticed that the more they had to drink the less discrimination they showed. They would buttonhole anybody, buy drinks for anyone who would listen to them. The more they drank, the more they prattled and the more they lied. I observed that a heavy drinker was generally very selfish. His donations to Salvation Army girls, begging nuns and the like, were most often inspired not by generosity, but by a desire to show off—to give away money with everybody looking on. It was a lack of mental balance which made him throw away money he could not afford.

In watching men drink, I formed a theory. Some booze affected men worse than other booze. I decided that a bartender should prescribe for his customers. I was a dispenser of alcohol; and one customer could stand more alcohol than another. A bartender who considered the mixing and serving of drinks an art should never let a customer take something that was "dynamite" for him.

It has been my observation that young men are harder drinkers than middle aged men; and I know that this also does not tally with general opinion. Perhaps this is because young men have keener imaginations. The booze stirred them and started rosy and pleasant dreams. I have seen young men, not thirty, stand up at the bar and, after stowing away highballs at a rate that would shock a seasoned drinker, unloosen their tongues, telling in voices heard over the whole barroom the "wonderful deals" which they were going to put through. It has been my notice that younger men were particularly anxious to have themselves thought important and so, when they were drinking, they let their tongues wag.

There is one thing, though, about the ideas which came when a man was drinking—some of them were inclined to be a little shady. I have heard men, whom I knew would never be in a crooked deal, after getting some highballs under their belts, outline to their companions some of the rawest deals. I guess booze did make some people think crooked. And I know this—the fellow who was drinking heavily all the time, got to be one awful liar. I don't understand this, but I know it is true. I knew of a young fellow who made a lot of money suddenly and took to running too fast. They used to call him "one square guy." Today nobody would believe that man under oath. He became such a liar that he couldn't tell the truth to save his soul, even on the most unimportant and trivial things. Booze did that to him.

There was one kind of drinker I never could stand and every time he lined up at the bar, I felt like climbing over and throwing him out. He was the fellow that booze made a fool—the man who, when he got a few drinks, became a "wise guy" and "knocked" everybody. I always heard this kind of fellow telling how good he was and sneering at everybody else.

Then there was that man around fifty who soaked up booze and went along the bar repeating one sentence to everybody, and asking everybody to have a drink with him. A few nights after the armistice was signed, there came to the bar the advertising manager of a well-known periodical. He was that kind. All he did for a solid hour was to drink and tell everybody who would—or would not—listen to him, "Yankee Bull and Johnnie Bull rule the world. Fine! Have a drink with me. Old England and New England!"

I never heard young men get on a single track thought like that when they were full. Young men's thoughts ran in all directions when they were drinking.

And the funny part about it all was that I could never tell whether booze was going to make a man do something wrong or not. Of course in a Broadway bar all sorts of people came in. One night, for the fun of it, I listened to the talk of a couple of gamblers with two business men. They were all drinking a lot. The talk at first was very formal. The gamblers were bent on "making a good impression." Drink by drink their talk got loose, inexact; then their pronunciation got mixed up, their speech became thick. At last they fell back upon a few stock expressions like—"I'll tell the world"—"You said something, Sammy"—"You bet, Joe." Then after that, they began to be uncertain on their feet.

That set me thinking. I guess the booze hit a fellow's brain—the way those gamblers got tied up in their talk. After that, it got at your body—the way those gamblers became unsteady on their feet. I got that hunch on booze, that it worked from the head down to the feet, and I started to watch people to see how the idea checked out. I was surprised to find how after a drink or so a man's talk brightened. And I said to myself, "How does that come? It must be the effect of the booze on the brain." I remember when I was a youngster at school how they used to tell us that the brain was a pretty delicate thing. Is it good to affect the brain with booze?

What I know about booze is this. He was a rare man who was a "moderate drinker." Few men could take a few drinks and let it alone.

On Giving Up Smoking

Y.Y.

1921

In the essay "On Giving Up Smoking," a writer known only as Y.Y. chronicles his attempts to abandon a twenty-five-year tobacco habit. Although he begins with an earnest New Year's resolution, he quickly lapses into a state of bargaining that would allow possible exceptions to his forbearance. Once he embarks on his smoke-free life, he suffers from a constellation of debilitating physical symptoms of withdrawal. "My lower eyelids began to smart as though I had been several nights without sleep. My throat ached drily," he writes. "I knew that I had only to light a cigarette, and the pain in my throat and my eyes would disappear." In this essay Y.Y. reveals how he comes to terms with his intense craving.

I have only one fault to find with giving up tobacco. It makes a man boastful. I have only one fault to find with his boastfulness. It is usually premature. This time, however, I have really given up smoking. It happened at the stroke of the New Year. Not exactly at twelve o'clock midnight, for I am no precisian. I had a friend with me till two in the morning, and it would not be polite to give up tobacco in the middle of a conversation. It would be gross and inopportune, like making a scene in church. Consequently, I post-dated the entrance of the New Year till eight o'clock in the morning.

On an ordinary morning, when a man wakes at eight, he is faced by a simple enough problem. "Shall I get up," he finds himself asking, "or shall I have breakfast in bed?" It is a problem which a thoughtless man settles in five seconds, but over which a thoughtful man may well ponder for a couple of hours. On waking at eight, however, on a morning on which one has given up tobacco, one feels like a schoolboy confronted for the first time with the binomial theorem. "If I get up," you ask yourself, "what am I to do? On the other hand, if I stay in bed, what am I to do?" You know that, whether you rise or stay in bed, you will not have begun the second cup of coffee when your hand will reach out automatically in search of the cigarettes. It is as natural as blinking. Try to keep your eyelids open for twenty minutes and you will realize a part of the effort that is required to control the human hand as it reaches out for an after-breakfast cigarette. You will have to concentrate every faculty you possess on that miserable little purpose. You will not be able to read the paper without moving your eyelids. You will not be able to talk without it. You will not be able to work without it.

Seeing that it was useless for a man beginning a new life to attempt to do anything else at the same time, I remained in bed till luncheon, in the hope that I might solve my difficulties in sleep. But I could not sleep: I could only feel cross. Now, I had made a resolution not to be cross in the New Year. Neither the children nor the cat, neither the servants nor the government, were to know the rough edge of my tongue any more. Yet here I was, already fuming like a volcano, and the bell not yet gone for noon. Had I met my enemy in such a mood, I should have poured boiling lava down his neck. I am sure I should have. Here was I, an infinitely better man than I had been twenty-four hours previously, and yet in an infinitely worse temper than I had known since the last time I gave up tobacco—gave it up, I mean, genuinely.

I do not know how I could have got through the rest of the day if I had not left myself what moralists may regard as a loophole, but what I regard as a graceful concession to human nature. I am no believer in absolute virtue. That is for another world. Life is mainly a compromise, and there is a crucial difference between being a practical teetotaller and being a practising teetotaller. I myself, I may say, am a practical teetotaller. I inhabit the lower slopes of virtue, and dare not aspire to the heights. Not that I am niggard of respect to those who can clamber up the frozen brows of precipices and stand on them, elate and ungiddy. I salute them from afar. I feel that on this huge mountain of virtue we are all brothers. But nature herself teaches us that, while some may climb to the roof of Mont Blanc for pleasure, it is lower down that you must look not only for fruit and flower but for the ding-dong works of practical man.

Anyhow, in all humility, I made a compromise. I resolved that, though I would give up tobacco, I would not give it up so absolutely as to forbid myself to smoke a cigarette if I were having a meal with a friend. At first, I limited myself to two cigarettes. Then, on consideration, I said three. I admit that, when I first made my resolution about tobacco, I had not thought of humanizing it in this way. But I remembered that I had to go out to dinner on New Year's night, and I felt that it would be an act of discourtesy to my host to appear sullen and self-centred, as a man wholly given up to the attempt to lead a new life is bound to appear. My compromise was a social, not a selfish, act. It was a compliment to my host at my own expense. It had the incidental advantage of enabling me to get through Saturday without breaking my resolution.

True, I was unable to work. All the afternoon I could do nothing but think of my symptoms. My temples were as if pressed in a vice. My lower eyelids began to smart as though I had been several nights without sleep. My throat ached drily. Generally speaking, I felt all gone to pieces—the sort of person you see described in a patent-medicine advertisement. On looking in the glass, I could see that I had aged. My skin was yellow and haggard. My eyes were hollow and had dark rings under them. I knew that I had only to light a cigarette, and the pain in my throat and my eyes would disappear. But I did not light it. I sat in my chair with my mouth open, thinking of dinner.

About five, I tried a game of auction, but I found myself wanting to go sixteen no trumps, which seemed to me funny but to the others merely hysterical. Luckily, the dinner was an early one. I felt younger with every course, not because I am particularly fond of food, but because each course brought me a stage nearer my first smoke of the day. My only criticism of the meal would be that the others lingered rather long over the ices. Even this, however, worked to my advantage. It was during the ices that I boldly faced the problem whether a cigar and a cigarette are technically the same thing or technically different. It was a problem, I may say, that, though I had been a smoker for twenty-five years, I had never faced before. I have never liked cigars. Now, however, as I looked round my fellow-guests all sipping their ices as if they were going to live to be a thousand, it slowly struck me that a cigar was merely a cigarette of larger growth.

A year ago I should have said that a cigar was equal to six cigarettes. Now I realized that a cigar was essentially the same as a cigarette, and that, with a cigar and two cigarettes, I might be able not only to keep my resolution but to keep it joyfully. It was a jolly dinner. Not being a cigar-smoker, I dared not convert all three of my cigarettes into cigars, but you can suck the stump even of one cigar for quite a long time. It was like a speck of loose mould in my lips when at length I threw it away in the Tube on the way home.

Sunday was like Saturday—only worse. Abstinence from tobacco is a disease with easily recognized symptoms. Your pulse flags, your eye-sockets ache, your ankles swell. You begin to wonder whether your ankles are not thicker than your knees. You have seen the word "Phat-pheet" in an advertisement, and you think you must be suffering from it. You cannot remember whether it is a disease or a cure, but your feet are so heavy that you feel you must have it. Then aphasia sets in. You forget how to spell "accommodate." You take up a newspaper and begin an article entitled "Premiums for Babies." But what you think you are reading is "Petroleum for Babies," and before you are half through the article you would give a sovereign to know whether it is you or the writer who is mad. When you are alone in the room, life is just tolerable. You can obtain a measure of relief from your hydraulically-pressed temples and your aching throat and eyes by screwing up your features into shapes you had never before thought of, but you must take care that no one comes in on you suddenly while you are doing so. Your wife will tell you that she cannot stay in the room with a man who is practising impersonations of the Idiot Boy.

The way of transgressors is hard, but the way of non-smokers is harder. I wonder if all non-smokers habitually behave as I behaved, on the 1st and 2nd of January. If so, I am not surprised that Stevenson advised women never to marry a man who does not smoke. Not to smoke, it seems to me, is the nearest thing to being a lunatic that a sane man can achieve. On Sunday, my reason was saved by a man who called about half-past six. He had already had tea, and so had I, and it was too early for dinner. But I vehemently insisted on his having a second tea, having decided that tea was a meal within the meaning of my oath.

Then came three cigarettes, and it was not till after supper that I lost my temper again.

On Monday . . .

Now, on Monday, life is real, life is earnest. The problem immediately arose, how one was to work and not smoke at the same time. How to do two things at once? The thing is not possible save to a juggler, or a Sir Boyle Roche. I had taken my resolve, however, and I devoted the day to not smoking. With the help of luncheon with one friend, and tea with another, I contrived to get through a certain amount of routine work, but, as for attempting a book-review or even a poem, I might as well have tried to climb the moon.

On Tuesday . . .

On Tuesday I had a really important article to write. I had promised it—promised it not only to myself but to an editor. Now, my promise to give up tobacco was made only to myself. Even the people who solve breakfast-table problems in the *British Weekly* would, I think, admit that here was a nice case of conscience. Charitable reader, what would you have done in the circumstances? I will tell you what I did. I smoked. I did not smoke absolutely, however. I compromised. I resolved to find out the date of old New Year's Day, which must fall about the 12th, and to give up tobacco then. That is why—I am perfectly frank about it—I am smoking a pipe as I write. I am feeling a little better, but I have been down to the roots of the mountains.

BIG BLONDE

Dorothy Parker

1929

As a founding member of the Algonquin Round Table, Dorothy Parker soon became known as the witty purveyor of the twenties' most famous literary clique. A heavy drinker prone to acerbic remarks, Parker began her career at Vogue, *where she created photo captions for ten dollars a week. Later she worked as a theater critic for* Vanity Fair, *wrote short stories and book reviews for* The New Yorker, *and published poetry. With her second husband, Alan Campbell, she moved to Hollywood to become a screenwriter and won an Academy Award for her work on the 1937 hit* A Star Is Born. *Afterward she returned to New York, where she lived alone in an East Side hotel until her death in 1967. "Big Blonde," her story of an all-American woman's love affair with alcohol, won the O. Henry Award in 1930.*

Hazel Morse was a large, fair woman of the type that incites some men when they use the word "blonde" to click their tongues and wag their heads roguishly. She prided herself upon her small feet and suffered for her vanity, boxing them in snub-toed, high-heeled slippers of the shortest bearable size. The curious things about her were her hands, strange terminations to the flabby white arms splattered with pale tan spots—long, quivering hands with deep and convex nails. She should not have disfigured them with little jewels.

She was not a woman given to recollections. At her middle thirties, her old days were a blurred and flickering sequence, an imperfect film, dealing with the actions of strangers.

In her twenties, after the deferred death of a hazy widowed mother, she had been employed as a model in a wholesale dress establishment— it was still the day of the big woman, and she was then prettily colored and erect and high-breasted. Her job was not onerous, and she met numbers of men and spent numbers of evenings with them, laughing at their jokes and telling them she loved their neckties. Men liked her, and she took it for granted that the liking of many men was a desirable thing. Popularity seemed to her to be worth all the work that had to be put into its achievement. Men liked you because you were fun, and when they liked you they took you out, and there you were. So, and successfully, she was fun. She was a good sport. Men liked a good sport.

No other form of diversion, simpler or more complicated, drew her attention. She never pondered if she might not be better occupied doing something else. Her ideas, or, better, her acceptances, ran right along with those of the other substantially built blondes in whom she found her friends.

When she had been working in the dress establishment some years she met Herbie Morse. He was thin, quick, attractive, with shifting lines about his shiny, brown eyes and a habit of fiercely biting at the skin around his finger nails. He drank largely; she found that entertaining. Her habitual greeting to him was an allusion to his state of the previous night.

"Oh, what a peach you had," she used to say, through her easy laugh. "I thought I'd die, the way you kept asking the waiter to dance with you."

She liked him immediately upon their meeting. She was enormously amused at his fast, slurred sentences, his interpolations of apt phrases from vaudeville acts and comic strips; she thrilled at the feel of his lean arm tucked firm beneath the sleeve of her coat; she wanted to touch the wet, flat surface of his hair. He was as promptly drawn to her. They were married six weeks after they had met.

She was delighted at the idea of being a bride; coquetted with it, played upon it. Other offers of marriage she had had, and not a few of them, but it happened that they were all from stout, serious men who had visited the dress establishment as buyers; men from Des Moines and Houston and Chicago and, in her phrase, even funnier places. There was always something immensely comic to her in the thought of

living elsewhere than New York. She could not regard as serious pro-
posals that she share a western residence.

She wanted to be married. She was nearing thirty now, and she did
not take the years well. She spread and softened, and her darkening
hair turned her to inexpert dabblings with peroxide. There were times
when she had little flashes of fear about her job. And she had had a
couple of thousand evenings of being a good sport among her male acquaintances. She had come to be more conscientious than spontaneous
about it.

Herbie earned enough, and they took a little apartment far uptown.
There was a Mission-furnished dining-room with a hanging central
light globed in liver-colored glass; in the living-room were an "over-
stuffed suite," a Boston fern, and a reproduction of the Henner "Mag-
dalene" with the red hair and the blue draperies; the bedroom was
in gray enamel and old rose, with Herbie's photograph on Hazel's
dressing-table and Hazel's likeness on Herbie's chest of drawers.

She cooked—and she was a good cook—and marketed and chatted
with the delivery boys and the colored laundress. She loved the flat,
she loved her life, she loved Herbie. In the first months of their marriage, she gave him all the passion she was ever to know.

She had not realized how tired she was. It was a delight, a new game,
a holiday, to give up being a good sport. If her head ached or her arches
throbbed, she complained piteously, babyishly. If her mood was quiet,
she did not talk. If tears came to her eyes, she let them fall.

She fell readily into the habit of tears during the first year of her
marriage. Even in her good sport days, she had been known to weep
lavishly and disinterestedly on occasion. Her behavior at the theater
was a standing joke. She could weep at anything in a play—tiny gar-
ments, love both unrequited and mutual, seduction, purity, faithful
servitors, wedlock, the triangle.

"There goes Haze," her friends would say, watching her. "She's off
again."

Wedded and relaxed, she poured her tears freely. To her who had
laughed so much, crying was delicious. All sorrows became her sorrows; she was Tenderness. She would cry long and softly over newspaper accounts of kidnaped babies, deserted wives, unemployed men,
strayed cats, heroic dogs. Even when the paper was no longer before

her, her mind revolved upon these things and the drops slipped rhythmically over her plump cheeks.

"Honestly," she would say to Herbie, "all the sadness there is in the world when you stop to think about it!"

"Yeah," Herbie would say.

She missed nobody. The old crowd, the people who had brought her and Herbie together, dropped from their lives, lingeringly at first. When she thought of this at all, it was only to consider it fitting. This was marriage. This was peace.

But the thing was that Herbie was not amused.

For a time, he had enjoyed being alone with her. He found the voluntary isolation novel and sweet. Then it palled with a ferocious suddenness. It was as if one night, sitting with her in the steam-heated living-room, he would ask no more; and the next night he was through and done with the whole thing.

He became annoyed by her misty melancholies. At first, when he came home to find her softly tired and moody, he kissed her neck and patted her shoulder and begged her to tell her Herbie what was wrong. She loved that. But time slid by, and he found that there was never anything really, personally, the matter.

"Ah, for God's sake," he would say. "Crabbing again. All right, sit here and crab your head off. I'm going out."

And he would slam out of the flat and come back late and drunk.

She was completely bewildered by what happened to their marriage. First they were lovers; and then, it seemed without transition, they were enemies. She never understood it.

There were longer and longer intervals between his leaving his office and his arrival at the apartment. She went through agonies of picturing him run over and bleeding, dead and covered with a sheet. Then she lost her fears for his safety and grew sullen and wounded. When a person wanted to be with a person, he came as soon as possible. She desperately wanted him to want to be with her; her own hours only marked the time till he would come. It was often nearly nine o'clock before he came home to dinner. Always he had had many drinks, and their effect would die in him, leaving him loud and querulous and bristling for affronts.

He was too nervous, he said, to sit and do nothing for an evening.

He boasted, probably not in all truth, that he had never read a book in his life.

"What am I expected to do—sit around this dump on my tail all night?" he would ask, rhetorically. And again he would slam out.

She did not know what to do. She could not manage him. She could not meet him.

She fought him furiously. A terrific domesticity had come upon her, and she would bite and scratch to guard it. She wanted what she called "a nice home." She wanted a sober, tender husband, prompt at dinner, punctual at work. She wanted sweet, comforting evenings. The idea of intimacy with other men was terrible to her; the thought that Herbie might be seeking entertainment in other women set her frantic.

It seemed to her that almost everything she read—novels from the drug-store lending library, magazine stories, women's pages in the papers—dealt with wives who lost their husbands' love. She could bear those, at that, better than accounts of neat, companionable marriage and living happily ever after.

She was frightened. Several times when Herbie came home in the evening, he found her determinedly dressed—she had had to alter those of her clothes that were not new, to make them fasten—and rouged.

"Let's go wild tonight, what do you say?" she would hail him. "A person's got lots of time to hang around and do nothing when they're dead."

So they would go out, to chop houses and the less expensive cabarets. But it turned out badly. She could no longer find amusement in watching Herbie drink. She could not laugh at his whimsicalities, she was so tensely counting his indulgences. And she was unable to keep back her remonstrances—"Ah, come on, Herb, you've had enough, haven't you? You'll feel something terrible in the morning."

He would be immediately enraged. All right, crab; crab, crab, crab, crab, that was all she ever did. What a lousy sport *she* was! There would be scenes, and one or the other of them would rise and stalk out in fury.

She could not recall the definite day that she started drinking, herself. There was nothing separate about her days. Like drops upon a window-pane, they ran together and trickled away. She had been married six months; then a year; then three years.

She had never needed to drink, formerly. She could sit for most of a night at a table where the others were imbibing earnestly and never droop in looks or spirits, nor be bored by the doings of those about her. If she took a cocktail, it was so unusual as to cause twenty minutes or so of jocular comment. But now anguish was in her. Frequently, after a quarrel, Herbie would stay out for the night, and she could not learn from him where the time had been spent. Her heart felt tight and sore in her breast, and her mind turned like an electric fan.

She hated the taste of liquor. Gin, plain or in mixtures, made her promptly sick. After experiment, she found that Scotch whisky was best for her. She took it without water, because that was the quickest way to its effect.

Herbie pressed it on her. He was glad to see her drink. They both felt it might restore her high spirits, and their good times together might again be possible.

"'Atta girl," he would approve her. "Let's see you get boiled, baby."

But it brought them no nearer. When she drank with him, there would be a little while of gaiety and then, strangely without beginning, they would be in a wild quarrel. They would wake in the morning not sure what it had all been about, foggy as to what had been said and done, but each deeply injured and bitterly resentful. There would be days of vengeful silence.

There had been a time when they had made up their quarrels, usually in bed. There would be kisses and little names and assurances of fresh starts. . . . "Oh, it's going to be great now, Herb. We'll have swell times. I was a crab. I guess I must have been tired. But everything's going to be swell. You'll see."

Now there were no gentle reconciliations. They resumed friendly relations only in the brief magnanimity caused by liquor, before more liquor drew them into new battles. The scenes became more violent. There were shouted invectives and pushes, and sometimes sharp slaps. Once she had a black eye. Herbie was horrified next day at sight of it. He did not go to work; he followed her about, suggesting remedies and heaping dark blame on himself. But after they had had a few drinks— "to pull themselves together"—she made so many wistful references to her bruise that he shouted at her and rushed out and was gone for two days.

Each time he left the place in a rage, he threatened never to come back. She did not believe him, nor did she consider separation. Somewhere in her head or her heart was the lazy, nebulous hope that things would change and she and Herbie settle suddenly into soothing married life. Here were her home, her furniture, her husband, her station. She summoned no alternatives.

She could no longer bustle and potter. She had no more vicarious tears; the hot drops she shed were for herself. She walked ceaselessly about the rooms, her thoughts running mechanically round and round Herbie. In those days began the hatred of being alone that she was never to overcome. You could be by yourself when things were all right, but when you were blue you got the howling horrors.

She commenced drinking alone, little, short drinks all through the day. It was only with Herbie that alcohol made her nervous and quick in offense. Alone, it blurred sharp things for her. She lived in a haze of it. Her life took on a dream-like quality. Nothing was astonishing.

A Mrs. Martin moved into the flat across the hall. She was a great blonde woman of forty, a promise in looks of what Mrs. Morse was to be. They made acquaintance, quickly became inseparable. Mrs. Morse spent her days in the opposite apartment. They drank together, to brace themselves after the drinks of the nights before.

She never confided her troubles about Herbie to Mrs. Martin. The subject was too bewildering to her to find comfort in talk. She let it be assumed that her husband's business kept him much away. It was not regarded as important; husbands, as such, played but shadowy parts in Mrs. Martin's circle.

Mrs. Martin had no visible spouse; you were left to decide for yourself whether he was or was not dead. She had an admirer, Joe, who came to see her almost nightly. Often he brought several friends with him—"The Boys," they were called. The Boys were big, red, good-humored men, perhaps forty-five, perhaps fifty. Mrs. Morse was glad of invitations to join the parties—Herbie was scarcely ever at home at night now. If he did come home, she did not visit Mrs. Martin. An evening alone with Herbie meant inevitably a quarrel, yet she would stay with him. There was always her thin and wordless idea that, maybe, this night, things would begin to be all right.

The Boys brought plenty of liquor along with them whenever they came to Mrs. Martin's. Drinking with them, Mrs. Morse became lively and good-natured and audacious. She was quickly popular. When she had drunk enough to cloud her most recent battle with Herbie, she was excited by their approbation. Crab, was she? Rotten sport, was she? Well, there were some that thought different.

Ed was one of The Boys. He lived in Utica—had "his own business" there, was the awed report—but he came to New York almost every week. He was married. He showed Mrs. Morse the then current photographs of Junior and Sister, and she praised them abundantly and sincerely. Soon it was accepted by the others that Ed was her particular friend.

He staked her when they all played poker; sat next to her and occasionally rubbed his knee against hers during the game. She was rather lucky. Frequently she went home with a twenty-dollar bill or a ten-dollar bill or a handful of crumpled dollars. She was glad of them. Herbie was getting, in her words, something awful about money. To ask him for it brought an instant row.

"What the hell do you do with it?" he would say. "Shoot it all on Scotch?"

"I try to run this house half-way decent," she would retort. "Never thought of that, did you? Oh, no, his lordship couldn't be bothered with that."

Again, she could not find a definite day, to fix the beginning of Ed's proprietorship. It became his custom to kiss her on the mouth when he came in, as well as for farewell, and he gave her little quick kisses of approval all through the evening. She liked this rather more than she disliked it. She never thought of his kisses when she was not with him.

He would run his hand lingeringly over her back and shoulders.

"Some dizzy blonde, eh?" he would say. "Some doll."

One afternoon she came home from Mrs. Martin's to find Herbie in the bedroom. He had been away for several nights, evidently on a prolonged drinking bout. His face was gray, his hands jerked as if they were on wires. On the bed were two old suitcases, packed high. Only her photograph remained on his bureau, and the wide doors of his closet disclosed nothing but coat-hangers.

"I'm blowing," he said. "I'm through with the whole works. I got a job in Detroit."

She sat down on the edge of the bed. She had drunk much the night before, and the four Scotches she had had with Mrs. Martin had only increased her fogginess.

"Good job?" she said.

"Oh, yeah," he said. "Looks all right."

He closed a suitcase with difficulty, swearing at it in whispers.

"There's some dough in the bank," he said. "The bank book's in your top drawer. You can have the furniture and stuff."

He looked at her, and his forehead twitched.

"God damn it, I'm through, I'm telling you," he cried. "I'm through."

"All right, all right," she said. "I heard you, didn't I?"

She saw him as if he were at one end of a cannon and she at the other. Her head was beginning to ache bumpingly, and her voice had a dreary, tiresome tone. She could not have raised it.

"Like a drink before you go?" she asked.

Again he looked at her, and a corner of his mouth jerked up.

"Cockeyed again for a change, aren't you?" he said. "That's nice. Sure, get a couple of shots, will you?"

She went to the pantry, mixed him a stiff highball, poured herself a couple of inches of whisky and drank it. Then she gave herself another portion and brought the glasses into the bedroom. He had strapped both suitcases and had put on his hat and overcoat.

He took his highball.

"Well," he said, and he gave a sudden, uncertain laugh. "Here's mud in your eye."

"Mud in your eye," she said.

They drank. He put down his glass and took up the heavy suitcases.

"Got to get a train around six," he said.

She followed him down the hall. There was a song, a song that Mrs. Martin played doggedly on the phonograph, running loudly through her mind. She had never liked the thing.

> "Night and daytime,
> Always playtime.
> Ain't we got fun?"

At the door he put down the bags and faced her.

"Well," he said. "Well, take care of yourself. You'll be all right, will you?"

"Oh, sure," she said.

He opened the door, then came back to her, holding out his hand.

"'By, Haze," he said. "Good luck to you."

She took his hand and shook it.

"Pardon my wet glove," she said.

When the door had closed behind him, she went back to the pantry.

She was flushed and lively when she went in to Mrs. Martin's that evening. The Boys were there, Ed among them. He was glad to be in town, frisky and loud and full of jokes. But she spoke quietly to him for a minute.

"Herbie blew today," she said. "Going to live out west."

"That so?" he said. He looked at her and played with the fountain pen clipped to his waistcoat pocket.

"Think he's gone for good, do you?" he asked.

"Yeah," she said. "I know he is. I know. Yeah."

"You going to live on across the hall just the same?" he said. "Know what you're going to do?"

"Gee, I don't know," she said. "I don't give much of a damn."

"Oh, come on, that's no way to talk," he told her. "What you need—you need a little snifter. How about it?"

"Yeah," she said. "Just straight."

She won forty-three dollars at poker. When the game broke up, Ed took her back to her apartment.

"Got a little kiss for me?" he asked.

He wrapped her in his big arms and kissed her violently. She was entirely passive. He held her away and looked at her.

"Little tight, honey?" he asked, anxiously. "Not going to be sick, are you?"

"Me?" she said. "I'm swell."

II

When Ed left in the morning, he took her photograph with him. He said he wanted her picture to look at, up in Utica. "You can have that one on the bureau," she said.

She put Herbie's picture in a drawer, out of her sight. When she could look at it, she meant to tear it up. She was fairly successful in keeping her mind from racing around him. Whisky slowed it for her. She was almost peaceful, in her mist.

She accepted her relationship with Ed without question or enthusiasm. When he was away, she seldom thought definitely of him. He was good to her; he gave her frequent presents and a regular allowance. She was even able to save. She did not plan ahead of any day, but her wants were few, and you might as well put money in the bank as have it lying around.

When the lease of her apartment neared its end, it was Ed who suggested moving. His friendship with Mrs. Martin and Joe had become strained over a dispute at poker; a feud was impending.

"Let's get the hell out of here," Ed said. "What I want you to have is a place near the Grand Central. Make it easier for me."

So she took a little flat in the Forties. A colored maid came in every day to clean and to make coffee for her—she was "through with that housekeeping stuff," she said, and Ed, twenty years married to a passionately domestic woman, admired this romantic uselessness and felt doubly a man of the world in abetting it.

The coffee was all she had until she went out to dinner, but alcohol kept her fat. Prohibition she regarded only as a basis for jokes. You could always get all you wanted. She was never noticeably drunk and seldom nearly sober. It required a larger daily allowance to keep her misty-minded. Too little, and she was achingly melancholy.

Ed brought her to Jimmy's. He was proud, with the pride of the transient who would be mistaken for a native, in his knowledge of small, recent restaurants occupying the lower floors of shabby brownstone houses; places where, upon mentioning the name of an habitué friend, might be obtained strange whisky and fresh gin in many of their ramifications. Jimmy's place was the favorite of his acquaintances.

There, through Ed, Mrs. Morse met many men and women, formed quick friendships. The men often took her out when Ed was in Utica. He was proud of her popularity.

She fell into the habit of going to Jimmy's alone when she had no engagement. She was certain to meet some people she knew, and join them. It was a club for her friends, both men and women.

The women at Jimmy's looked remarkably alike, and this was curious, for, through feuds, removals, and opportunities of more profitable contacts, the personnel of the group changed constantly. Yet always the newcomers resembled those whom they replaced. They were all big women and stout, broad of shoulder and abundantly breasted, with faces thickly clothed in soft, high-colored flesh. They laughed loud and often, showing opaque and lusterless teeth like squares of crockery. There was about them the health of the big, yet a slight, unwholesome suggestion of stubborn preservation. They might have been thirty-six or forty-five or anywhere between.

They composed their titles of their own first names with their husbands' surnames—Mrs. Florence Miller, Mrs. Vera Riley, Mrs. Lilian Block. This gave at the same time the solidity of marriage and the glamour of freedom. Yet only one or two were actually divorced. Most of them never referred to their dimmed spouses; some, a shorter time separated, described them in terms of great biological interest. Several were mothers, each of an only child—a boy at school somewhere, or a girl being cared for by a grandmother. Often, well on toward morning, there would be displays of Kodak portraits and of tears.

They were comfortable women, cordial and friendly and irrepressibly matronly. Theirs was the quality of ease. Become fatalistic, especially about money matters, they unworried. Whenever their funds dropped alarmingly, a new donor appeared; this had always happened. The aim of each was to have one man, permanently, to pay all her bills, in return for which she would have immediately given up other admirers and probably would have become exceedingly fond of him; for the affections of all of them were, by now, unexacting, tranquil, and easily arranged. This end, however, grew increasingly difficult yearly. Mrs. Morse was regarded as fortunate.

Ed had a good year, increased her allowance and gave her a sealskin coat. But she had to be careful of her moods with him. He insisted upon gaiety. He would not listen to admissions of aches or weariness.

"Hey, listen," he would say, "I got worries of my own, and plenty. Nobody wants to hear other people's troubles, sweetie. What you got to do, you got to be a sport and forget it. See? Well, slip us a little smile, then. That's my girl."

She never had enough interest to quarrel with him as she had with Herbie, but she wanted the privilege of occasional admitted sadness. It was strange. The other women she saw did not have to fight their moods. There was Mrs. Florence Miller who got regular crying jags, and the men sought only to cheer and comfort her. The others spent whole evenings in grieved recitals of worries and ills; their escorts paid them deep sympathy. But she was instantly undesirable when she was low in spirits. Once, at Jimmy's, when she could not make herself lively, Ed had walked out and left her.

"Why the hell don't you stay home and not go spoiling everybody's evening?" he had roared.

Even her slightest acquaintances seemed irritated if she were not conspicuously light-hearted.

"What's the matter with you, anyway?" they would say. "Be your age, why don't you? Have a little drink and snap out of it."

When her relationship with Ed had continued nearly three years, he moved to Florida to live. He hated leaving her; he gave her a large check and some shares of a sound stock, and his pale eyes were wet when he said good-by. She did not miss him. He came to New York infrequently, perhaps two or three times a year, and hurried directly from the train to see her. She was always pleased to have him come and never sorry to see him go.

Charley, an acquaintance of Ed's that she had met at Jimmy's, had long admired her. He had always made opportunities of touching her and leaning close to talk to her. He asked repeatedly of all their friends if they had ever heard such a fine laugh as she had. After Ed left, Charley became the main figure in her life. She classified him and spoke of him as "not so bad." There was nearly a year of Charley; then she divided her time between him and Sydney, another frequenter of Jimmy's; then Charley slipped away altogether.

Sydney was a little, brightly dressed, clever Jew. She was perhaps nearest contentment with him. He amused her always; her laughter was not forced.

He admired her completely. Her softness and size delighted him. And he thought she was great, he often told her, because she kept gay and lively when she was drunk.

"Once I had a gal," he said, "used to try and throw herself out of the window every time she got a can on. Jee-*zuss*," he added, feelingly.

Then Sydney married a rich and watchful bride, and then there was Billy. No—after Sydney came Fred, then Billy. In her haze, she never recalled how men entered her life and left it. There were no surprises. She had no thrill at their advent, nor woe at their departure. She seemed to be always able to attract men. There was never another as rich as Ed, but they were all generous to her, in their means.

Once she had news of Herbie. She met Mrs. Martin dining at

Jimmy's, and the old friendship was vigorously renewed. The still admiring Joe, while on a business trip, had seen Herbie. He had settled in Chicago, he looked fine, he was living with some woman—seemed to be crazy about her. Mrs. Morse had been drinking vastly that day. She took the news with mild interest, as one hearing of the sex peccadilloes of somebody whose name is, after a moment's groping, familiar.

"Must be damn near seven years since I saw him," she commented. "Gee. Seven years."

More and more, her days lost their individuality. She never knew dates, nor was sure of the day of the week.

"My God, was that a year ago!" she would exclaim, when an event was recalled in conversation.

She was tired so much of the time. Tired and blue. Almost everything could give her the blues. Those old horses she saw on Sixth Avenue—struggling and slipping along the car-tracks, or standing at the curb, their heads dropped level with their worn knees. The tightly stored tears would squeeze from her eyes as she teetered past on her aching feet in the stubby, champagne-colored slippers.

The thought of death came and stayed with her and lent her a sort of drowsy cheer. It would be nice, nice and restful, to be dead.

There was no settled, shocked moment when she first thought of killing herself; it seemed to her as if the idea had always been with her. She pounced upon all the accounts of suicides in the newspapers. There was an epidemic of self-killings—or maybe it was just that she searched for the stories of them so eagerly that she found many. To read of them roused reassurance in her; she felt a cozy solidarity with the big company of the voluntary dead.

She slept, aided by whisky, till deep into the afternoons, then lay abed, a bottle and glass at her hand, until it was time to dress and go out for dinner. She was beginning to feel toward alcohol a little puzzled distrust, as toward an old friend who has refused a simple favor. Whisky could still soothe her for most of the time, but there were sudden, inexplicable moments when the cloud fell treacherously away from her, and she was sawed by the sorrow and bewilderment and nuisance of all living. She played voluptuously with the thought of cool, sleepy retreat. She had never been troubled by religious belief and no vision of an after-life intimidated her. She dreamed by day of never again putting on tight shoes, of never having to laugh and listen and admire, of never more being a good sport. Never.

But how would you do it? It made her sick to think of jumping from heights. She could not stand a gun. At the theater, if one of the actors drew a revolver, she crammed her fingers into her ears and could not even look at the stage until after the shot had been fired. There was no gas in her flat. She looked long at the bright blue veins in her slim wrists—a cut with a razor blade, and there you'd be. But it would hurt, hurt like hell, and there would be blood to see. Poison—something tasteless and quick and painless—was the thing. But they wouldn't sell it to you in drug-stores, because of the law.

She had few other thoughts.

There was a new man now—Art. He was short and fat and exacting and hard on her patience when he was drunk. But there had been only occasionals for some time before him, and she was glad of a little stability. Too, Art must be away for weeks at a stretch, selling silks, and that was restful. She was convincingly gay with him, though the effort shook her.

"The best sport in the world," he would murmur, deep in her neck. "The best sport in the world."

One night, when he had taken her to Jimmy's, she went into the dressing-room with Mrs. Florence Miller. There, while designing curly mouths on their faces with lip-rouge, they compared experiences of insomnia.

"Honestly," Mrs. Morse said, "I wouldn't close an eye if I didn't go to bed full of Scotch. I lie there and toss and turn and toss and turn. Blue! Does a person get blue lying awake that way!"

"Say, listen, Hazel," Mrs. Miller said, impressively, "I'm telling you I'd be awake for a year if I didn't take veronal. That stuff makes you sleep like a fool."

"Isn't it poison, or something?" Mrs. Morse asked.

"Oh, you take too much and you're out for the count," said Mrs. Miller. "I just take five grains—they come in tablets. I'd be scared to fool around with it. But five grains, and you cork off pretty."

"Can you get it anywhere?" Mrs. Morse felt superbly Machiavellian.

"Get all you want in Jersey," said Mrs. Miller. "They won't give it to you here without you have a doctor's prescription. Finished? We'd better go back and see what the boys are doing."

That night, Art left Mrs. Morse at the door of her apartment; his mother was in town. Mrs. Morse was still sober, and it happened that there was no whisky left in her cupboard. She lay in bed, looking up at the black ceiling.

She rose early, for her, and went to New Jersey. She had never taken the tube, and did not understand it. So she went to the Pennsylvania Station and bought a railroad ticket to Newark. She thought of nothing in particular on the trip out. She looked at the uninspired hats of the women about her and gazed through the smeared window at the flat, gritty scene.

In Newark, in the first drug-store she came to, she asked for a tin of talcum powder, a nailbrush, and a box of veronal tablets. The powder and the brush were to make the hypnotic seem also a casual need. The clerk was entirely unconcerned. "We only keep them in bottles," he said, and wrapped up for her a little glass vial containing ten white tablets, stacked one on another.

She went to another drug-store and bought a face-cloth, an orange-wood stick, and a bottle of veronal tablets. The clerk was also uninterested.

"Well, I guess I got enough to kill an ox," she thought, and went back to the station.

At home, she put the little vials in the drawer of her dressing-table and stood looking at them with a dreamy tenderness.

"There they are, God bless them," she said, and she kissed her finger-tip and touched each bottle.

The colored maid was busy in the living-room.

"Hey, Nettie," Mrs. Morse called. "Be an angel, will you? Run around to Jimmy's and get me a quart of Scotch."

She hummed while she awaited the girl's return.

During the next few days, whisky ministered to her as tenderly as it had done when she first turned to its aid. Alone, she was soothed and vague, at Jimmy's she was the gayest of the groups. Art was delighted with her.

Then, one night, she had an appointment to meet Art at Jimmy's for an early dinner. He was to leave afterward on a business excursion, to be away for a week. Mrs. Morse had been drinking all the afternoon;

while she dressed to go out, she felt herself rising pleasurably from drowsiness to high spirits. But as she came out into the street the effects of the whisky deserted her completely, and she was filled with a slow, grinding wretchedness so horrible that she stood swaying on the pavement, unable for a moment to move forward. It was a gray night with spurts of mean, thin snow, and the streets shone with dark ice. As she slowly crossed Sixth Avenue, consciously dragging one foot past the other, a big, scarred horse pulling a rickety express-wagon crashed to his knees before her. The driver swore and screamed and lashed the beast insanely, bringing the whip back over his shoulder for every blow, while the horse struggled to get a footing on the slippery asphalt. A group gathered and watched with interest.

Art was waiting, when Mrs. Morse reached Jimmy's.

"What's the matter with you, for God's sake?" was his greeting to her.

"I saw a horse," she said. "Gee, I—a person feels sorry for horses. I—it isn't just horses. Everything's kind of terrible, isn't it? I can't help getting sunk."

"Ah, sunk, me eye," he said. "What's the idea of all the bellyaching? What have you got to be sunk about?"

"I can't help it," she said.

"Ah, help it, me eye," he said. "Pull yourself together, will you? Come on and sit down, and take that face off you."

She drank industriously and she tried hard, but she could not overcome her melancholy. Others joined them and commented on her gloom, and she could do no more for them than smile weakly. She made little dabs at her eyes with her handkerchief, trying to time her movements so they would be unnoticed, but several times Art caught her and scowled and shifted impatiently in his chair.

When it was time for him to go to his train, she said she would leave, too, and go home.

"And not a bad idea, either," he said. "See if you can't sleep yourself out of it. I'll see you Thursday. For God's sake, try and cheer up by then, will you?"

"Yeah," she said. "I will."

In her bedroom, she undressed with a tense speed wholly unlike her usual slow uncertainty. She put on her nightgown, took off her hair-net and passed the comb quickly through her dry, vari-colored hair.

Then she took the two little vials from the drawer and carried them into the bathroom. The splintering misery had gone from her, and she felt the quick excitement of one who is about to receive an anticipated gift.

She uncorked the vials, filled a glass with water and stood before the mirror, a tablet between her fingers. Suddenly she bowed graciously to her reflection, and raised the glass to it.

"Well, here's mud in your eye," she said.

The tablets were unpleasant to take, dry and powdery and sticking obstinately half-way down her throat. It took her a long time to swallow all twenty of them. She stood watching her reflection with deep, impersonal interest, studying the movements of the gulping throat. Once more she spoke aloud.

"For God's sake, try and cheer up by Thursday, will you?" she said. "Well, you know what he can do. He and the whole lot of them."

She had no idea how quickly to expect effect from the veronal. When she had taken the last tablet, she stood uncertainly, wondering, still with a courteous, vicarious interest, if death would strike her down then and there. She felt in no way strange, save for a slight stirring of sickness from the effort of swallowing the tablets, nor did her reflected face look at all different. It would not be immediate, then; it might even take an hour or so.

She stretched her arms high and gave a vast yawn.

"Guess I'll go to bed," she said. "Gee, I'm nearly dead."

That struck her as comic, and she turned out the bathroom light and went in and laid herself down in her bed, chuckling softly all the time.

"Gee, I'm nearly dead," she quoted. "That's a hot one!"

III

Nettie, the colored maid, came in late the next afternoon to clean the apartment, and found Mrs. Morse in her bed. But then, that was not unusual. Usually, though, the sounds of cleaning waked her, and she did not like to wake up. Nettie, an agreeable girl, had learned to move softly about her work.

But when she had done the living-room and stolen in to tidy the little square bedroom, she could not avoid a tiny clatter as she arranged the objects on the dressing-table. Instinctively, she glanced over her shoulder at the sleeper, and without warning a sickly uneasiness crept over her. She came to the bed and stared down at the woman lying there.

Mrs. Morse lay on her back, one flabby, white arm flung up, the wrist against her forehead. Her stiff hair hung untenderly along her face. The bed covers were pushed down, exposing a deep square of soft neck and a pink nightgown, its fabric worn uneven by many launderings; her great breasts, freed from their tight confiner, sagged beneath her arm-pits. Now and then she made knotted, snoring sounds, and from the corner of her opened mouth to the blurred turn of her jaw ran a lane of crusted spittle.

"Mis' Morse," Nettie called. "Oh, Mis' Morse! It's terrible late."

Mrs. Morse made no move.

"Mis' Morse," said Nettie. "Look, Mis' Morse. How'm I goin' get this bed made?"

Panic sprang upon the girl. She shook the woman's hot shoulder.

"Ah, wake up, will yuh?" she whined. "Ah, please wake up."

Suddenly the girl turned and ran out in the hall to the elevator door, keeping her thumb firm on the black, shiny button until the elderly car and its Negro attendant stood before her. She poured a jumble of words over the boy, and led him back to the apartment. He tiptoed creakingly in to the bedside; first gingerly, then so lustily that he left marks in the soft flesh, he prodded the unconscious woman.

"Hey, there!" he cried, and listened intently, as for an echo.

"Jeez. Out like a light," he commented.

At his interest in the spectacle, Nettie's panic left her. Importance was big in both of them. They talked in quick, unfinished whispers, and it was the boy's suggestion that he fetch the young doctor who lived on the ground floor. Nettie hurried along with him. They looked forward to the limelit moment of breaking their news of something untoward, something pleasurably unpleasant. Mrs. Morse had become the medium of drama. With no ill wish to her, they hoped that her state was serious, that she would not let them down by being awake and normal on their return. A little fear of this determined them to make the most, to the doctor, of her present condition. "Matter of life and death," returned to Nettie from her thin store of reading. She considered startling the doctor with the phrase.

The doctor was in and none too pleased at interruption. He wore a yellow and blue striped dressing-gown, and he was lying on his sofa, laughing with a dark girl, her face scaly with inexpensive powder, who perched on the arm. Half-emptied highball glasses stood beside them, and her coat and hat were neatly hung up with the comfortable implication of a long stay. Always something, the doctor grumbled. Couldn't let anybody alone after a hard day. But he put some bottles and instruments into a case, changed his dressing-gown for his coat and started out with the Negroes.

"Snap it up there, big boy," the girl called after him. "Don't be all night."

The doctor strode loudly into Mrs. Morse's flat and on to the bedroom, Nettie and the boy right behind him. Mrs. Morse had not moved; her sleep was as deep, but soundless, now. The doctor looked sharply at her, then plunged his thumbs into the lidded pits above her eyeballs and threw his weight upon them. A high, sickened cry broke from Nettie.

"Look like he tryin' to push her right on th'ough the bed," said the boy. He chuckled.

Mrs. Morse gave no sign under the pressure. Abruptly the doctor abandoned it, and with one quick movement swept the covers down to the foot of the bed. With another he flung her nightgown back and lifted the thick, white legs, cross-hatched with blocks of tiny, iris-colored veins. He pinched them repeatedly, with long, cruel nips, back of the knees. She did not awaken.

"What's she been drinking?" he asked Nettie, over his shoulder.

With the certain celerity of one who knows just where to lay hands on a thing, Nettie went into the bathroom, bound for the cupboard where Mrs. Morse kept her whisky. But she stopped at the sight of the two vials, with their red and white labels, lying before the mirror. She brought them to the doctor.

"Oh, for the Lord Almighty's sweet sake!" he said. He dropped Mrs. Morse's legs, and pushed them impatiently across the bed. "What did she want to go taking that tripe for? Rotten yellow trick, that's what a thing like that is. Now we'll have to pump her out, and all that stuff. Nuisance, a thing like that is; that's what it amounts to. Here, George, take me down in the elevator. You wait here, maid. She won't do anything."

"She won't die on me, will she?" cried Nettie.

"No," said the doctor. "God, no. You couldn't kill her with an ax."

IV

After two days, Mrs. Morse came back to consciousness, dazed at first, then with a comprehension that brought with it the slow, saturating wretchedness.

"Oh, Lord, oh, Lord," she moaned, and tears for herself and for life striped her cheeks.

Nettie came in at the sound. For two days she had done the ugly, incessant tasks in the nursing of the unconscious, for two nights she had caught broken bits of sleep on the living-room couch. She looked coldly at the big, blown woman in the bed.

"What you been tryin' to do, Mis' Morse?" she said. "What kine o' work is that, takin' all that stuff?"

"Oh, Lord," moaned Mrs. Morse, again, and she tried to cover her eyes with her arms. But the joints felt stiff and brittle, and she cried out at their ache.

"Tha's no way to ack, takin' them pills," said Nettie. "You can thank you' stars you heah at all. How you feel now?"

"Oh, I feel great," said Mrs. Morse. "Swell, I feel."

Her hot, painful tears fell as if they would never stop.

"Tha's no way to take on, cryin' like that," Nettie said. "After what you done. The doctor, he says he could have you arrested, doin' a thing like that. He was fit to be tied, here."

"Why couldn't he let me alone?" wailed Mrs. Morse. "Why the hell couldn't he have?"

"Tha's terr'ble, Mis' Morse, swearin' an' talkin' like that," said Nettie, "after what people done for you. Here I ain' had no sleep at all for two nights, an' had to give up goin' out to my other ladies!"

"Oh, I'm sorry, Nettie," she said. "You're a peach. I'm sorry I've given you so much trouble. I couldn't help it. I just got sunk. Didn't you ever feel like doing it? When everything looks just lousy to you?"

"I wouldn' think o' no such thing," declared Nettie. "You got to cheer up. Tha's what you got to do. Everybody's got their troubles."

"Yeah," said Mrs. Morse. "I know."

"Come a pretty picture card for you," Nettie said. "Maybe that will cheer you up."

She handed Mrs. Morse a post-card. Mrs. Morse had to cover one eye with her hand, in order to read the message; her eyes were not yet focusing correctly.

It was from Art. On the back of a view of the Detroit Athletic Club he had written: "Greeting and salutations. Hope you have lost that gloom. Cheer up and don't take any rubber nickels. See you on Thursday."

She dropped the card to the floor. Misery crushed her as if she were between great smooth stones. There passed before her a slow, slow pageant of days spent lying in her flat, of evenings at Jimmy's being a good sport, making herself laugh and coo at Art and other Arts; she saw a long parade of weary horses and shivering beggars and all beaten, driven, stumbling things. Her feet throbbed as if she had crammed them into the stubby champagne-colored slippers. Her heart seemed to swell and harden.

"Nettie," she cried, "for heaven's sake pour me a drink, will you?"

The maid looked doubtful.

"Now you know, Mis' Morse," she said, "you been near daid. I don' know if the doctor he let you drink nothin' yet."

"Oh, never mind him," she said. "You get me one, and bring in the bottle. Take one yourself."

"Well," said Nettie.

She poured them each a drink, deferentially leaving hers in the bathroom to be taken in solitude, and brought Mrs. Morse's glass in to her.

Mrs. Morse looked into the liquor and shuddered back from its odor. Maybe it would help. Maybe, when you had been knocked cold for a few days, your very first drink would give you a lift. Maybe whisky would be her friend again. She prayed without addressing a God, without knowing a God. Oh, please, please, let her be able to get drunk, please keep her always drunk.

She lifted the glass.

"Thanks, Nettie," she said. "Here's mud in your eye."

The maid giggled. "That's the way, Mis' Morse," she said. "You cheer up, now."

"Yeah," said Mrs. Morse. "Sure."

THE SORROWS OF GIN

John Cheever

1953

A meticulous observer of suburban life, John Cheever quickly won an admiring audience as a frequent contributor to The New Yorker. *His novel* The Wapshot Chronicle *won the National Book Award in 1958, and his short story collection,* The Stories of John Cheever, *won the 1979 Pulitzer Prize. An alcoholic, Cheever often tried to control his drinking by forcing himself to stay at his desk until noon—or, in some cases, 11 A.M.—before taking his first drink of the day. After completing a twenty-eight-day detoxification program in New York, he encouraged other writers, such as Truman Capote, to seek help for their alcoholism. Cheever died of cancer at the age of seventy. "The Sorrows of Gin" focuses on the life of a young girl who grows up in a world consumed by drinking.*

It was Sunday afternoon, and from her bedroom Amy could hear the Beardens coming in, followed a little while later by the Farquarsons and the Parminters. She went on reading *Black Beauty* until she felt in her bones that they might be eating something good. Then she closed her book and went down the stairs. The living-room door was shut, but through it she could hear the noise of loud talk and laughter. They must have been gossiping or worse, because they all stopped talking when she entered the room.

"Hi, Amy," Mr. Farquarson said.

"Mr. Farquarson spoke to you, Amy," her father said.

"Hello, Mr. Farquarson," she said. By standing outside the group for a minute, until they had resumed their conversation, and then by slipping past Mrs. Farquarson, she was able to swoop down on the nut dish and take a handful.

"Amy!" Mr. Lawton said.

"I'm sorry, Daddy," she said, retreating out of the circle, toward the piano.

"Put those nuts back," he said.

"I've handled them, Daddy," she said.

"Well, pass the nuts, dear," her mother said sweetly. "Perhaps someone else would like nuts."

Amy filled her mouth with the nuts she had taken, returned to the coffee table, and passed the nut dish.

"Thank you, Amy," they said, taking a peanut or two.

"How do you like your new school, Amy?" Mrs. Bearden asked.

"I like it," Amy said. "I like private schools better than public schools. It isn't so much like a factory."

"What grade are you in?" Mrs. Bearden asked.

"Fourth," she said.

Her father took Mr. Parminter's glass and his own, and got up to go into the dining room and refill them. She fell into the chair he had left vacant.

"Don't sit in your father's chair, Amy," her mother said, not realizing that Amy's legs were worn out from riding a bicycle, while her father had done nothing but sit down all day.

As she walked toward the French doors, she heard her mother beginning to talk about the new cook. It was a good example of the interesting things they found to talk about.

"You'd better put your bicycle in the garage," her father said, returning with the fresh drinks. "It looks like rain."

Amy went out onto the terrace and looked at the sky, but it was not very cloudy, it wouldn't rain, and his advice, like all the advice he gave her, was superfluous. They were always at her. "Put your bicycle away." "Open the door for Grandmother, Amy." "Feed the cat." "Do your homework." "Pass the nuts." "Help Mrs. Bearden with her parcels." "Amy, please try and take more pains with your appearance."

They all stood, and her father came to the door and called her. "We're going over to the Parminters' for supper," he said. "Cook's here, so you won't be alone. Be sure and go to bed at eight like a good girl. And come and kiss me good night."

After their cars had driven off, Amy wandered through the kitchen to the cook's bedroom beyond it and knocked on the door. "Come in," a voice said, and when Amy entered, she found the cook, whose name was Rosemary, in her bathrobe, reading the Bible. Rosemary smiled at Amy. Her smile was sweet and her old eyes were blue. "Your parents have gone out again?" she asked. Amy said that they had, and the old woman invited her to sit down. "They do seem to enjoy themselves, don't they? During the four days I've been here, they've been out every night, or had people in." She put the Bible face down on her lap and smiled, but not at Amy. "Of course, the drinking that goes on here is all sociable, and what your parents do is none of my business, is it? I worry about drink more than most people, because of my poor sister. My poor sister drank too much. For ten years, I went to visit her on Sunday afternoons, and most of the time she was *non compos mentis.* Sometimes I'd find her huddled up on the floor with one or two sherry bottles empty beside her. Sometimes she'd seem sober enough to a stranger, but I could tell in a second by the way she spoke her words that she'd drunk enough not to be herself any more. Now my poor sister is gone, I don't have anyone to visit at all."

"What happened to your sister?" Amy asked.

"She was a lovely person, with a peaches-and-cream complexion and fair hair," Rosemary said. "Gin makes some people gay—it makes them laugh and cry—but with my sister it only made her sullen and withdrawn. When she was drinking, she would retreat into herself. Drink made her contrary. If I'd say the weather was fine, she'd tell me I was wrong. If I'd say it was raining, she'd say it was clearing. She'd correct me about everything I said, however small it was. She died in Bellevue Hospital one summer while I was working in Maine. She was the only family I had."

The directness with which Rosemary spoke had the effect on Amy of making her feel grown, and for once politeness came to her easily. "You must miss your sister a great deal," she said.

"I was just sitting here now thinking about her. She was in service, like me, and it's lonely work. You're always surrounded by a family, and yet you're never a part of it. Your pride is often hurt. The Madams seem condescending and inconsiderate. I'm not blaming the ladies I've worked for. It's just the nature of the relationship. They order chicken salad, and you get up before dawn to get ahead of yourself, and just as you've finished the chicken salad, they change their minds and want crab-meat soup."

"My mother changes her mind all the time," Amy said.

"Sometimes you're in a country place with nobody else in help. You're tired, but not too tired to feel lonely. You go out onto the servants' porch when the pots and pans are done, planning to enjoy God's creation, and although the front of the house may have a fine view of the lake or the mountains, the view from the back is never much. But there is the sky and the trees and the stars and the birds singing and the pleasure of resting your feet. But then you hear them in the front of the house, laughing and talking with their guests and their sons and daughters. If you're new and they whisper, you can be sure they're talking about you. That takes all the pleasure out of the evening."

"Oh," Amy said.

"I've worked all kinds of places—places where there were eight or nine in help and places where I was expected to burn the rubbish myself, on winter nights, and shovel the snow. In a house where there's a lot of help, there's usually some devil among them—some old butler or parlormaid—who tries to make your life miserable from the beginning. 'The Madam doesn't like it this way,' and 'The Madam doesn't like it that way,' and 'I've been with the Madam for twenty years,' they tell you. It takes a diplomat to get along. Then there is the rooms they give you, and every one of them I've ever seen is cheerless. If you have a bottle in your suitcase, it's a terrible temptation in the beginning not to take a drink to raise your spirits. But I have a strong character. It was different with my poor sister. She used to complain about nervousness, but, sitting here thinking about her tonight, I wonder if she suffered from nervousness at all. I wonder if she didn't make it all up. I wonder if she just wasn't meant to be in service. Toward the end, the only work she could get was out in the country, where nobody else would go, and she never lasted much more than a week or two. She'd take a little gin for her nervousness, then a little for her tiredness, and when she'd drunk her own bottle and everything she could steal, they'd hear about it in the front part of the house. There was usually a scene, and my poor sister always liked to have the last word. Oh, if I had had my way,

they'd be a law against it! It's not my business to advise you to take anything from your father, but I'd be proud of you if you'd empty his gin
bottle into the sink now and then—the filthy stuff! But it's made me
feel better to talk with you, sweetheart. It's made me not miss my poor
sister so much. Now I'll read a little more in my Bible, and then I'll get
you some supper."

———

The Lawtons had had a bad year with cooks—there had been five of
them. The arrival of Rosemary had made Marcia Lawton think back to
a vague theory of dispensations; she had suffered, and now she was
being rewarded. Rosemary was clean, industrious, and cheerful, and
her table—as the Lawtons said—was just like the Chambord. On
Wednesday night after dinner, she took the train to New York, promising to return on the evening train Thursday. Thursday morning,
Marcia went into the cook's room. It was a distasteful but a habitual
precaution. The absence of anything personal in the room—a package
of cigarettes, a fountain pen, an alarm clock, a radio, or anything else
that could tie the old woman to the place—gave her the uneasy feeling that she was being deceived, as she had so often been deceived by
cooks in the past. She opened the closet door and saw a single uniform
hanging there and, on the closet floor, Rosemary's old suitcase and the
white shoes she wore in the kitchen. The suitcase was locked, but when
Marcia lifted it, it seemed to be nearly empty.

Mr. Lawton and Amy drove to the station after dinner on Thursday
to meet the eight-sixteen train. The top of the car was down, and the
brisk air, the starlight, and the company of her father made the little
girl feel kindly toward the world. The railroad station in Shady Hill
resembled the railroad stations in old movies she had seen on television, where detectives and spies, bluebeards and their trusting victims,
were met to be driven off to remote country estates. Amy liked the station, particularly toward dark. She imagined that the people who traveled on the locals were engaged on errands that were more urgent and
sinister than commuting. Except when there was a heavy fog or a
snowstorm, the club car that her father traveled on seemed to have the
gloss and the monotony of the rest of his life. The locals that ran at
odd hours belonged to a world of deeper contrasts, where she would
like to live.

They were a few minutes early, and Amy got out of the car and stood on the platform. She wondered what the fringe of string that hung above the tracks at either end of the station was for, but she knew enough not to ask her father, because he wouldn't be able to tell her. She could hear the train before it came into view, and the noise excited her and made her happy. When the train drew in to the station and stopped, she looked in the lighted windows for Rosemary and didn't see her. Mr. Lawton got out of the car and joined Amy on the platform. They could see the conductor bending over someone in a seat, and finally the cook arose. She clung to the conductor as he led her out to the platform of the car, and she was crying. "Like peaches and cream," Amy heard her sob. "A lovely, lovely person." The conductor spoke to her kindly, put his arm around her shoulders, and eased her down the steps. Then the train pulled out, and she stood there drying her tears. "Don't say a word, Mr. Lawton," she said, "and I won't say anything." She held out a small paper bag. "Here's a present for you, little girl."

"Thank you, Rosemary," Amy said. She looked into the paper bag and saw that it contained several packets of Japanese water flowers.

Rosemary walked toward the car with the caution of someone who can hardly find her way in the dim light. A sour smell came from her. Her best coat was spotted with mud and ripped in the back. Mr. Lawton told Amy to get in the back seat of the car, and made the cook sit in front, beside him. He slammed the car door shut after her angrily, and then went around to the driver's seat and drove home. Rosemary reached into her handbag and took out a Coca-Cola bottle with a cork stopper and took a drink. Amy could tell by the smell that the Coca-Cola bottle was filled with gin.

"Rosemary!" Mr. Lawton said.

"I'm lonely," the cook said. "I'm lonely, and I'm afraid, and it's all I've got."

He said nothing more until he had turned into their drive and brought the car around to the back door. "Go and get your suitcase, Rosemary," he said. "I'll wait here in the car."

As soon as the cook had staggered into the house, he told Amy to go in by the front door. "Go upstairs to your room and get ready for bed."

Her mother called down the stairs when Amy came in, to ask if Rosemary had returned. Amy didn't answer. She went to the bar, took an open gin bottle, and emptied it into the pantry sink. She was nearly crying when she encountered her mother in the living room, and told her that her father was taking the cook back to the station.

When Amy came home from school the next day, she found a heavy, black-haired woman cleaning the living room. The car Mr. Lawton usually drove to the station was at the garage for a checkup, and Amy drove to the station with her mother to meet him. As he came across the station platform, she could tell by the lack of color in his face that he had had a hard day. He kissed her mother, touched Amy on the head, and got behind the wheel.

"You know," her mother said, "there's something terribly wrong with the guest-room shower."

"Damn it, Marcia," he said, "I wish you wouldn't always greet me with bad news!"

His grating voice oppressed Amy, and she began to fiddle with the button that raised and lowered the window.

"Stop that, Amy!" he said.

"Oh, well, the shower isn't important," her mother said. She laughed weakly.

"When I got back from San Francisco last week," he said, "you couldn't wait to tell me that we need a new oil burner."

"Well, I've got a part-time cook. That's good news."

"Is she a lush?" her father asked.

"Don't be disagreeable, dear. She'll get us some dinner and wash the dishes and take the bus home. We're going to the Farquarsons'."

"I'm really too tired to go anywhere," he said.

"Who's going to take care of me?" Amy asked.

"You always have a good time at the Farquarsons'," her mother said.

"Well, let's leave early," he said.

"Who's going to take care of me?" Amy asked.

"Mrs. Henlein," her mother said.

When they got home, Amy went over to the piano.

Her father washed his hands in the bathroom off the hall and then went to the bar. He came into the living room holding the empty gin bottle. "What's her name?" he asked.

"Ruby," her mother said.

"She's exceptional. She's drunk a quart of gin on her first day."

"Oh dear!" her mother said. "Well, let's not make any trouble now."

"Everybody is drinking my liquor," her father shouted, "and I am God-damned sick and tired of it!"

"There's plenty of gin in the closet," her mother said. "Open another bottle."

"We paid that gardener three dollars an hour and all he did was sneak in here and drink up my Scotch. The sitter we had before we got Mrs. Henlein used to water my bourbon, and I don't have to remind you about Rosemary. The cook before Rosemary not only drank everything in my liquor cabinet but she drank all the rum, kirsch, sherry, and wine that we had in the kitchen for cooking. Then, there's that Polish woman we had last summer. Even that old laundress. *And* the painters. I think they must have put some kind of a mark on my door. I think the agency must have checked me off as an easy touch."

"Well, let's get through dinner, and then you can speak to her."

"The hell with that!" he said. "I'm not going to encourage people to rob me. *Ruby!*" He shouted her name several times, but she didn't answer. Then she appeared in the dining-room doorway anyway, wearing her hat and coat.

"I'm sick," she said. Amy could see that she was frightened.

"I should think that you would be," her father said.

"I'm sick," the cook mumbled, "and I can't find anything around here, and I'm going home."

"Good," he said. "Good! I'm through with paying people to come in here and drink my liquor."

The cook started out the front way, and Marcia Lawton followed her into the front hall to pay her something. Amy had watched this scene from the piano bench, a position that was withdrawn but that still gave her a good view. She saw her father get a fresh bottle of gin and make a shaker of Martinis. He looked very unhappy.

"Well," her mother said when she came back into the room. "You know, she didn't look drunk."

"Please don't argue with me, Marcia," her father said. He poured two cocktails, said "Cheers," and drank a little. "We can get some dinner at Orpheo's," he said.

"I suppose so," her mother said. "I'll rustle up something for Amy." She went into the kitchen, and Amy opened her music to "Reflets d'Automne." "COUNT," her music teacher had written. "COUNT and lightly, lightly . . ." Amy began to play. Whenever she made a mistake, she said "Darn it!" and started at the beginning again. In the middle of "Reflets d'Automne" it struck her that *she* was the one who had emptied the gin bottle. Her perplexity was so intense that she stopped playing, but her feelings did not go beyond perplexity, although she did not have the strength to continue playing the piano. Her mother relieved her. "Your supper's in the kitchen, dear," she said. "And you can take a popsicle out of the deep freeze for dessert. Just one."

Marcia Lawton held her empty glass toward her husband, who filled it from the shaker. Then she went upstairs. Mr. Lawton remained in the room, and, studying her father closely, Amy saw that his tense look had begun to soften. He did not seem so unhappy any more, and as she passed him on her way to the kitchen, he smiled at her tenderly and patted her on the top of the head.

When Amy had finished her supper, eaten her popsicle, and exploded the bag it came in, she returned to the piano and played "Chopsticks" for a while. Her father came downstairs in his evening clothes, put his drink on the mantelpiece, and went to the French doors to look at his terrace and his garden. Amy noticed that the transformation that had begun with a softening of his features was even more advanced. At last, he seemed happy. Amy wondered if he was drunk, although his walk was not unsteady. If anything, it was more steady.

Her parents never achieved the kind of rolling, swinging gait that she saw impersonated by a tightrope walker in the circus each year while the band struck up "Show Me the Way to Go Home" and that she liked to imitate herself sometimes. She liked to turn round and round and round on the lawn, until, staggering and a little sick, she would whoop, "I'm drunk! I'm a drunken man!" and reel over the grass, righting herself as she was about to fall and finding herself not unhappy at having lost for a second her ability to see the world. But she had never seen her parents like that. She had never seen them hanging on to a lamppost and singing and reeling, but she had seen them fall down. They were never indecorous—they seemed to get more decorous and formal the more they drank—but sometimes her father would get up to fill everybody's glass and he would walk straight enough but his shoes would seem to stick to the carpet. And sometimes, when he got to the dining-room door, he would miss it by a foot or more. Once, she had seen him walk into the wall with such force that he collapsed onto the floor and broke most of the glasses he was carrying. One or two people laughed, but the laughter was not general or hearty, and most of them pretended that he had not fallen down at all. When her father got to his feet, he went right on to the bar as if nothing had happened. Amy had once seen Mrs. Farquarson miss the chair she was about to sit in, by a foot, and thump down onto the floor, but nobody laughed then, and they pretended that Mrs. Farquarson hadn't fallen down at all. They seemed like actors in a play. In the school play, when you knocked over a paper tree you were supposed to pick it up without showing what you were doing, so that you would not spoil the illusion of being in a deep forest, and that was the way *they* were when somebody fell down.

Now her father had that stiff, funny walk that was so different from the way he tramped up and down the station platform in the morning, and she could see that he was looking for something. He was looking for his drink. It was right on the mantelpiece, but he didn't look there. He looked on all the tables in the living room. Then he went out onto the terrace and looked there, and then he came back into the living room and looked on all the tables again. Then he went back onto the terrace, and then back over the living-room tables, looking three times in the same place, although he was always telling her to look intelligently when she lost her sneakers or her raincoat. "Look for it, Amy," he was always saying. "Try and remember where you left it. I can't buy you a new raincoat every time it rains." Finally he gave up and poured himself a cocktail in another glass. "I'm going to get Mrs. Henlein," he told Amy, as if this were an important piece of information.

Amy's only feeling for Mrs. Henlein was indifference, and when her father returned with the sitter, Amy thought of the nights, stretching into weeks—the years, almost—when she had been cooped up with Mrs. Henlein. Mrs. Henlein was very polite and was always telling Amy what was ladylike and what was not. Mrs. Henlein also wanted to know where Amy's parents were going and what kind of party it was, although it was none of her business. She always sat down on the sofa as if she owned the place, and talked about people she had never even been introduced to, and asked Amy to bring her the newspaper, although she had no authority at all.

When Marcia Lawton came down, Mrs. Henlein wished her good evening. "Have a lovely party," she called after the Lawtons as they went out the door. Then she turned to Amy. "Where are your parents going, sweetheart?

"But you must know, sweetheart. Put on your thinking cap and try and remember. Are they going to the club?"

"No," Amy said.

"I wonder if they could be going to the Trenchers'," Mrs. Henlein said. "The Trenchers' house was lighted up when we came by."

"They're not going to the Trenchers'," Amy said. "They hate the Trenchers."

"Well, where are they going, sweetheart?" Mrs. Henlein asked.

"They're going to the Farquarsons'," Amy said.

"Well, that's all I wanted to know, sweetheart," Mrs. Henlein said. "Now get me the newspaper and hand it to me politely. *Politely,*" she said, as Amy approached her with the paper. "It doesn't mean anything when you do things for your elders unless you do them politely." She put on her glasses and began to read the paper.

Amy went upstairs to her room. In a glass on her table were the Japanese flowers that Rosemary had brought her, blooming stalely in water that was colored pink from the dyes. Amy went down the back stairs and through the kitchen into the dining room. Her father's cocktail things were spread over the bar. She emptied the gin bottle into the pantry sink and then put it back where she had found it. It was too late to ride her bicycle and too early to go to bed, and she knew that if she got anything interesting on the television, like a murder, Mrs. Henlein would make her turn it off. Then she remembered that her father had brought her home from his trip West a book about horses, and she ran cheerfully up the back stairs to read her new book.

It was after two when the Lawtons returned. Mrs. Henlein, asleep on the living-room sofa dreaming about a dusty attic, was awakened by their voices in the hall. Marcia Lawton paid her, and thanked her, and asked if anyone had called, and then went upstairs. Mr. Lawton was in the dining room, rattling the bottles around. Mrs. Henlein, anxious to get into her own bed and back to sleep, prayed that he wasn't going to pour himself another drink, as they so often did. She was driven home night after night by drunken gentlemen. He stood in the door of the dining room, holding an empty bottle in his hand. "You must be stinking, Mrs. Henlein," he said.

"Hmm," she said. She didn't understand.

"You drank a full quart of gin," he said.

The lackluster old woman—half between wakefulness and sleep—gathered together her bones and groped for her gray hair. It was in her nature to collect stray cats, pile the bathroom up to the ceiling with interesting and valuable newspapers, rouge, talk to herself, sleep in her underwear in case of fire, quarrel over the price of soup bones, and have it circulated around the neighborhood that when she finally died in her dusty junk heap, the mattress would be full of bankbooks and the pillow stuffed with hundred-dollar bills. She had resisted all these rich temptations in order to appear a lady, and she was repaid by being called a common thief. She began to scream at him.

"You take that back, Mr. Lawton! You take back every one of those words you just said! I never stole anything in my whole life, and nobody in my family ever stole anything, and I don't have to stand here and be insulted by a drunk man. Why, as for drinking, I haven't drunk enough to fill an eyeglass for twenty-five years. Mr. Henlein took me to a place of refreshment twenty-five years ago, and I drank two Manhattan cocktails that made me so sick and dizzy that I've never liked the stuff ever since. How dare you speak to me like this! Calling me a thief and a drunken woman! Oh, you disgust me—you disgust me in your ignorance of all the trouble I've had. Do you know what I had for Christmas dinner last year? I had a bacon sandwich. Son of a bitch!" She began to weep. "I'm glad I said it!" she screamed. "It's the first time I've used a dirty word in my whole life and I'm glad I said it. Son of a bitch!" A sense of liberation, as if she stood at the bow of a great ship, came over her. "I lived in this neighborhood my whole life. I can remember when it was full of good farming people and there was fish in the rivers. My father had four acres of sweet meadowland and a name that was known far and wide, and on my mother's side I'm descended from patroons, Dutch nobility. My mother was the spit and image of Queen Wilhelmina. You think you can get away with insulting me, but you're very, very, very much mistaken." She went to the telephone and, picking up the receiver, screamed, "Police! Police! Police! This is Mrs. Henlein, and I'm over at the Lawtons'. He's drunk, and he's calling me insulting names, and I want you to come over here and arrest him!"

The voices woke Amy, and, lying in her bed, she perceived vaguely the pitiful corruption of the adult world; how crude and frail it was, like a piece of worn burlap, patched with stupidities and mistakes, useless and ugly, and yet they never saw its worthlessness, and when you pointed it out to them, they were indignant. But as the voices went on and she heard the cry "Police! Police!" she was frightened. She did not see how they could arrest her, although they could find her fingerprints on the empty bottle, but it was not her own danger that frightened her but the collapse, in the middle of the night, of her father's house. It was all her fault, and when she heard her father speaking into the extension telephone in the library, she felt sunk in guilt. Her father tried to be good and kind—and, remembering the expensive illustrated book about horses that he had brought her from the West, she had to set her teeth to keep from crying. She covered her head with a pillow and realized miserably that she would have to go away. She had plenty of friends from the time when they used to live in New York, or she could spend the night in the Park or hide in a museum. She would have to go away.

———

"Good morning," her father said at breakfast. "Ready for a good day!" Cheered by the swelling light in the sky, by the recollection of the manner in which he had handled Mrs. Henlein and kept the police from coming, refreshed by his sleep, and pleased at the thought of playing golf, Mr. Lawton spoke with feeling, but the words seemed to Amy offensive and fatuous; they took away her appetite, and she slumped over her cereal bowl, stirring it with a spoon. "Don't slump, Amy," he said. Then she remembered the night, the screaming, the resolve to go. His cheerfulness refreshed her memory. Her decision was settled. She had a ballet lesson at ten, and she was going to have lunch with Lillian Towele. Then she would leave.

Children prepare for a sea voyage with a toothbrush and a Teddy bear; they equip themselves for a trip around the world with a pair of odd socks, a conch shell, and a thermometer; books and stones and peacock feathers, candy bars, tennis balls, soiled handkerchiefs, and skeins of old string appear to them to be the necessities of travel, and Amy packed, that afternoon, with the impulsiveness of her kind. She was late coming home from lunch, and her getaway was delayed, but she didn't mind. She could catch one of the late-afternoon locals; one of the cooks' trains. Her father was playing golf and her mother was off somewhere. A part-time worker was cleaning the living room. When Amy had finished packing, she went into her parents' bedroom and flushed the toilet. While the water murmured, she took a twenty-dollar bill from her mother's desk. Then she went downstairs and left the house and walked around Blenhollow Circle and down Alewives Lane to the station. No regrets or goodbyes formed in her mind. She went over the names of the friends she had in the city, in case she decided not to spend the night in a museum. When she opened the door of the waiting room, Mr. Flanagan, the stationmaster, was poking his coal fire.

"I want to buy a ticket to New York," Amy said.

"One-way or round-trip?"

"One-way, please."

Mr. Flanagan went through the door into the ticket office and raised the glass window. "I'm afraid I haven't got a half-fare ticket for you, Amy," he said. "I'll have to write one."

"That's all right," she said. She put the twenty-dollar bill on the counter.

"And in order to change that," he said, "I'll have to go over to the other side. Here's the four-thirty-two coming in now, but you'll be able to get the five-ten." She didn't protest, and went and sat beside her cardboard suitcase, which was printed with European hotel and place names. When the local had come and gone, Mr. Flanagan shut his glass window and walked over the footbridge to the northbound platform and called the Lawtons'. Mr. Lawton had just come in from his game and was mixing himself a cocktail. "I think your daughter's planning to take some kind of a trip," Mr. Flanagan said.

It was dark by the time Mr. Lawton got down to the station. He saw his daughter through the station window. The girl sitting on the bench, the rich names on her paper suitcase, touched him as it was in her power to touch him only when she seemed helpless or when she was very sick. Someone had walked over his grave! He shivered with longing, he felt his skin coarsen as when, driving home late and alone, a shower of leaves on the wind crossed the beam of his headlights, liberating him for a second at the most from the literal symbols of his life—the buttonless shirts, the vouchers and bank statements, the order blanks, and the empty glasses. He seemed to listen—God knows for what. Commands, drums, the crackle of signal fires, the music of the glockenspiel—how sweet it sounds on the Alpine air—singing from a tavern in the pass, the honking of wild swans; he seemed to smell the salt air in the churches of Venice. Then, as it was with the leaves, the power of her figure to trouble him was ended; his gooseflesh vanished. He was himself. Oh, why should she want to run away? Travel—and who knew better than a man who spent three days of every fortnight on the road—was a world of overheated plane cabins and repetitious magazines, where even the coffee, even the champagne, tasted of plastics. How could he teach her that home sweet home was the best place of all?

FROM

THE DOORS OF PERCEPTION

Aldous Huxley

1954

In the spring of 1953—two decades after the release of his satirical novel Brave New World—*the English novelist and critic Aldous Huxley embarked on a systematic study of drug use. Mescaline—a potent hallucinogen derived from peyote—had already captured the attention of famed psychologists, such as Weir Mitchell and Havelock Ellis. Offering himself up as a research subject, Huxley began his project by consuming almost half a gram of mescaline dissolved in water. His observations are recorded in his philosophical treatise* The Doors of Perception.

I took my pill at eleven. An hour and a half later, I was sitting in my study, looking intently at a small glass vase. The vase contained only three flowers—a full-blown Belle of Portugal rose, shell pink with a hint at every petal's base of a hotter, flamier hue; a large magenta and cream-colored carnation; and, pale purple at the end of its broken stalk, the bold heraldic blossom of an iris. Fortuitous and provisional, the little nosegay broke all the rules of traditional good taste. At breakfast that morning I had been struck by the lively dissonance of its colors. But that was no longer the point. I was not looking now at an unusual flower arrangement. I was seeing what Adam had seen on the morning of his creation—the miracle, moment by moment, of naked existence.

"Is it agreeable?" somebody asked. (During this part of the experiment, all conversations were recorded on a dictating machine, and it has been possible for me to refresh my memory of what was said.)

"Neither agreeable nor disagreeable," I answered. "It just *is*."

Istigkeit—wasn't that the word Meister Eckhart liked to use? "Isness." The Being of Platonic philosophy—except that Plato seems to have made the enormous, the grotesque mistake of separating Being from becoming and identifying it with the mathematical abstraction of the Idea. He could never, poor fellow, have seen a bunch of flowers shining with their own inner light and all but quivering under the pressure of the significance with which they were charged; could never have perceived that what rose and iris and carnation so intensely signified was nothing more, and nothing less, than what they were—a transience that was yet eternal life, a perpetual perishing that was at the same time pure Being, a bundle of minute, unique particulars in which, by some unspeakable and yet self-evident paradox, was to be seen the divine source of all existence.

I continued to look at the flowers, and in their living light I seemed to detect the qualitative equivalent of breathing—but of a breathing without returns to a starting point, with no recurrent ebbs but only a repeated flow from beauty to heightened beauty, from deeper to ever deeper meaning. Words like "grace" and "transfiguration" came to my mind, and this, of course, was what, among other things, they stood for. My eyes traveled from the rose to the carnation, and from that feathery incandescence to the smooth scrolls of sentient amethyst which were the iris. The Beatific Vision, *Sat Chit Ananda*, Being-Awareness-Bliss—for the first time I understood, not on the verbal level, not by inchoate hints or at a distance, but precisely and completely what those prodigious syllables referred to. And then I remembered a passage I had read in one of Suzuki's essays. "What is the Dharma-Body of the Buddha?" ("The Dharma-Body of the Buddha" is another way of saying Mind, Suchness, the Void, the Godhead.) The question is asked in a Zen monastery by an earnest and bewildered novice. And with the prompt irrelevance of one of the Marx Brothers, the Master answers, "The hedge at the bottom of the garden." "And the man who realizes this truth," the novice dubiously inquires, "what, may I ask, is he?" Groucho gives him a whack over the shoulders with his staff and answers, "A golden-haired lion."

It had been, when I read it, only a vaguely pregnant piece of non-sense. Now it was all as clear as day, as evident as Euclid. Of course the Dharma-Body of the Buddha was the hedge at the bottom of the garden. At the same time, and no less obviously, it was these flowers, it was anything that I—or rather the blessed Not-I, released for a moment from my throttling embrace—cared to look at. The books, for example, with which my study walls were lined. Like the flowers, they glowed, when I looked at them, with brighter colors, a profounder significance. Red books, like rubies; emerald books; books bound in white jade; books of agate; of aquamarine, of yellow topaz; lapis lazuli books whose color was so intense, so intrinsically meaningful, that they seemed to be on the point of leaving the shelves to thrust themselves more insistently on my attention.

"What about spatial relationships?" the investigator inquired, as I was looking at the books.

It was difficult to answer. True, the perspective looked rather odd, and the walls of the room no longer seemed to meet in right angles. But these were not the really important facts. The really important facts were that spatial relationships had ceased to matter very much and that my mind was perceiving the world in terms of other than spatial categories. At ordinary times the eye concerns itself with such problems as *Where?—How far?—How situated in relation to what?* In the mescalin experience the implied questions to which the eye responds are of another order. Place and distance cease to be of much interest. The mind does its perceiving in terms of intensity of existence, profundity of significance, relationships within a pattern. I saw the books, but was not at all concerned with their positions in space. What I noticed, what impressed itself upon my mind was the fact that all of them glowed with living light and that in some the glory was more manifest than in others. In this context position and the three dimensions were beside the point. Not, of course, that the category of space had been abolished. When I got up and walked about, I could do so quite normally, without misjudging the whereabouts of objects. Space was still there; but it had lost its predominance. The mind was primarily concerned, not with measures and locations, but with being and meaning.

And along with indifference to space there went an even more complete indifference to time.

"There seems to be plenty of it," was all I would answer, when the investigator asked me to say what I felt about time.

Plenty of it, but exactly how much was entirely irrelevant. I could, of course, have looked at my watch; but my watch, I knew, was in another universe. My actual experience had been, was still, of an indefinite duration or alternatively of a perpetual present made up of one continually changing apocalypse.

From the books the investigator directed my attention to the furniture. A small typing table stood in the center of the room; beyond it, from my point of view, was a wicker chair and beyond that a desk. The three pieces formed an intricate pattern of horizontals, uprights and diagonals—a pattern all the more interesting for not being interpreted in terms of spatial relationships. Table, chair and desk came together in a composition that was like something by Braque or Juan Gris, a still life recognizably related to the objective world, but rendered without depth, without any attempt at photographic realism. I was looking at my furniture, not as the utilitarian who has to sit on chairs, to write at desks and tables, and not as the cameraman or scientific recorder, but as the pure aesthete whose concern is only with forms and their relationships within the field of vision or the picture space. But as I looked, this purely aesthetic, Cubist's-eye view gave place to what I can only describe as the sacramental vision of reality. I was back where I had been when I was looking at the flowers—back in a world where everything shone with the Inner Light, and was infinite in its significance. The legs, for example, of that chair—how miraculous their tubularity, how supernatural their polished smoothness! I spent several minutes— or was it several centuries?—not merely gazing at those bamboo legs, but actually *being* them—or rather being myself in them; or, to be still more accurate (for "I" was not involved in the case, nor in a certain sense were "they") being my Not-self in the Not-self which was the chair.

Reflecting on my experience, I find myself agreeing with the eminent Cambridge philosopher, Dr. C. D. Broad, "that we should do well to consider much more seriously than we have hitherto been inclined to do the type of theory which Bergson put forward in connection with memory and sense perception. The suggestion is that the function of the brain and nervous system and sense organs is in the main *eliminative* and not productive. Each person is at each moment capable of remembering all that has ever happened to him and of perceiving everything that is happening everywhere in the universe. The function of the brain and nervous system is to protect us from being overwhelmed and confused by this mass of largely useless and irrelevant knowledge, by shutting out most of what we should otherwise perceive or remember at any moment, and leaving only that very small and special selection which is likely to be practically useful." According to such a theory, each one of us is potentially Mind at Large. But in so far as we are animals, our business is at all costs to survive. To make biological survival possible, Mind at Large has to be funneled through the reducing valve of the brain and nervous system. What comes out at the other end is a measly trickle of the kind of consciousness which will help us to stay alive on the surface of this particular planet. To formulate and express the contents of this reduced awareness, man has invented and endlessly elaborated those symbol-systems and implicit philosophies which we call languages. Every individual is at once the beneficiary and the victim of the linguistic tradition into which he has been born—the beneficiary inasmuch as language gives access to the accumulated records of other people's experience, the victim in so far as it confirms him in the belief that reduced awareness is the only awareness and as it bedevils his sense of reality, so that he is all too apt to take his concepts for data, his words for actual things. That which, in the language of religion, is called "this world" is the universe of reduced awareness, expressed, and, as it were, petrified by language. The various "other worlds," with which human beings erratically make contact are so many elements in the totality of the awareness belonging to Mind at Large. Most people, most of the time, know only what comes through the reducing valve and is consecrated as genuinely real by the local language. Certain persons, however, seem to be born with a kind of by-pass that circumvents the reducing valve. In others temporary by-passes may be acquired either spontaneously, or as the result of deliberate "spiritual exercises," or through hypnosis, or by means of drugs. Through these permanent or temporary by-passes there flows, not indeed the perception "of everything that is happening everywhere in the universe" (for the by-pass does not abolish the reducing valve, which still excludes the total content of Mind at Large), but something more than, and above all something different from, the carefully selected utilitarian material which our narrowed, individual minds regard as a complete, or at least sufficient, picture of reality.

The brain is provided with a number of enzyme systems which serve to co-ordinate its workings. Some of these enzymes regulate the supply of glucose to the brain cells. Mescalin inhibits the production of these enzymes and thus lowers the amount of glucose available to an organ that is in constant need of sugar. When mescalin reduces the brain's normal ration of sugar what happens? Too few cases have been observed, and therefore a comprehensive answer cannot yet be given. But what happens to the majority of the few who have taken mescalin under supervision can be summarized as follows.

(1) The ability to remember and to "think straight" is little if at all reduced. (Listening to the recordings of my conversation under the influence of the drug, I cannot discover that I was then any stupider than I am at ordinary times.)

(2) Visual impressions are greatly intensified and the eye recovers some of the perceptual innocence of childhood, when the sensum was not immediately and automatically subordinated to the concept. Interest in space is diminished and interest in time falls almost to zero.

(3) Though the intellect remains unimpaired and though perception is enormously improved, the will suffers a profound change for the worse. The mescalin taker sees no reason for doing anything in particular and finds most of the causes for which, at ordinary times, he was prepared to act and suffer, profoundly uninteresting. He can't be bothered with them, for the good reason that he has better things to think about.

(4) These better things may be experienced (as I experienced them) "out there," or "in here," or in both worlds, the inner and the outer, simultaneously or successively. That they *are* better seems to be self-evident to all mescalin takers who come to the drug with a sound liver and an untroubled mind.

FROM

NAKED LUNCH

William S. Burroughs

1959

A self-proclaimed addict for fifteen years, the American writer William S. Burroughs used a variety of drugs, including morphine, heroin, Dilaudid, opium, and Demerol. "I have smoked junk, eaten it, sniffed it, injected it in vein-skin-muscle, inserted it in rectal suppositories," he writes in the introduction to his classic drug odyssey, Naked Lunch. *"The needle is not important. Whether you sniff it smoke it eat it or shove it up your ass the result is the same: addiction." In this excerpt from* Naked Lunch, *Burroughs chronicles the street life of an addict.*

I can feel the heat closing in, feel them out there making their moves, setting up their devil doll stool pigeons, crooning over my spoon and dropper I throw away at Washington Square Station, vault a turnstile and two flights down the iron stairs, catch an uptown A train ... Young, good looking, crew cut, Ivy League, advertising exec type fruit holds the door back for me. I am evidently his idea of a character. You know the type comes on with bartenders and cab drivers, talking about right hooks and the Dodgers, call the counterman in Nedick's by his first name. A real asshole. And right on time this narcotics dick in a white trench coat (imagine tailing somebody in a white trench coat—trying to pass as a fag I guess) hit the platform. I can hear the way he would say it holding my outfit in his left hand, right hand on his piece: "I think you dropped something, fella."

But the subway is moving.

"So long flatfoot!" I yell, giving the fruit his B production. I look into the fruit's eyes, take in the white teeth, the Florida tan, the two hundred dollar sharkskin suit, the button-down Brooks Brothers shirt and carrying *The News* as a prop. "Only thing I read is Little Abner."

A square wants to come on hip. . . . Talks about "pod," and smoke it now and then, and keeps some around to offer the fast Hollywood types.

"Thanks, kid," I say, "I can see you're one of our own." His face lights up like a pinball machine, with stupid, pink effect.

"Grassed on me he did," I said morosely. (Note: Grass is English thief slang for inform.) I drew closer and laid my dirty junky fingers on his sharkskin sleeve. "And us blood brothers in the same dirty needle. I can tell you in confidence he is due for a hot shot." (Note: This is a cap of poison junk sold to addict for liquidation purposes. Often given to informers. Usually the hot shot is strychnine since it tastes and looks like junk.)

"Ever see a hot shot hit, kid? I saw the Gimp catch one in Philly. We rigged his room with a one-way whorehouse mirror and charged a sawski to watch it. He never got the needle out of his arm. They don't if the shot is right. That's the way they find them, dropper full of clotted blood hanging out of a blue arm. The look in his eyes when it hit— Kid, it was tasty. . . .

"Recollect when I am traveling with the Vigilante, best Shake Man in the industry. Out in Chi . . . We is working the fags in Lincoln Park. So one night the Vigilante turns up for work in cowboy boots and a black vest with a hunka tin on it and a lariat slung over his shoulder.

"So I says: 'What's with you? You wig already?'

"He just looks at me and says: 'Fill your hand stranger' and hauls out an old rusty six shooter and I take off across Lincoln Park, bullets cutting all around me. And he hangs three fags before the fuzz nail him. I mean the Vigilante earned his moniker. . . .

"Ever notice how many expressions carry over from queers to con men? Like 'raise,' letting someone know you are in the same line?

"'Get her!'

"'Get the Paregoric Kid giving that mark the build up!'

"'Eager Beaver wooing him much too fast.'

"The Shoe Store Kid (he got that moniker shaking down fetishists in shoe stores) say: 'Give it to a mark with K.Y. and he will come back moaning for more.' And when the Kid spots a mark he begin to breathe heavy. His face swells and his lips turn purple like an Eskimo in heat. Then slow, slow he comes on the mark, feeling for him, palpating him with fingers of rotten ectoplasm.

———

"The Rube has a sincere little boy look, burns through him like blue neon. That one stepped right off a *Saturday Evening Post* cover with a string of bullheads, and preserved himself in junk. His marks never beef and the Bunko people are really carrying a needle for the Rube. One day Little Boy Blue starts to slip, and what crawls out would make an ambulance attendant puke. The Rube flips in the end, running through empty automats and subway stations, screaming: 'Come back, kid!! Come back!!' and follows his boy right into the East River, down through condoms and orange peels, mosaic of floating newspapers, down into the silent black ooze with gangsters in concrete, and pistols pounded flat to avoid the probing finger of prurient ballistic experts."

And the fruit is thinking: "What a character!! Wait till I tell the boys in Clark's about this one." He's a character collector, would stand still for Joe Gould's seagull act. So I put it on him for a sawski and make a meet to sell him some "pod" as he calls it, thinking, "I'll catnip the jerk." (Note: Catnip smells like marijuana when it burns. Frequently passed on the incautious or uninstructed.)

"Well," I said, tapping my arm, "duty calls. As one judge said to another: 'Be just and if you can't be just, be arbitrary.'"

I cut into the automat and there is Bill Gains huddled in someone else's overcoat looking like a 1910 banker with paresis, and Old Bart, shabby and inconspicuous, dunking pound cake with his dirty fingers, shiny over the dirt.

I had some uptown customers Bill took care of, and Bart knew a few old relics from hop smoking times, spectral janitors, grey as ashes, phantom porters sweeping out dusty halls with a slow old man's hand, coughing and spitting in the junk-sick dawn, retired asthmatic fences in theatrical hotels, Pantopon Rose the old madam from Peoria, stoical Chinese waiters never show sickness. Bart sought them out with his old junky walk, patient and cautious and slow, dropped into their bloodless hands a few hours of warmth.

I made the round with him once for kicks. You know how old people lose all shame about eating, and it makes you puke to watch them?

Old junkies are the same about junk. They gibber and squeal at sight of it. The spit hangs off their chin, and their stomach rumbles and all their guts grind in peristalsis while they cook up, dissolving the body's decent skin, you expect any moment a great blob of protoplasm will flop right out and surround the junk. Really disgust you to see it.

"Well, my boys will be like that one day," I thought philosophically. "Isn't life peculiar?"

So back downtown by the Sheridan Square Station in case the dick is lurking in a broom closet.

Like I say it couldn't last. I knew they were out there powowing and making their evil fuzz magic, putting dolls of me in Leavenworth. "No use sticking needles in that one, Mike."

I hear they got Chapin with a doll. This old eunuch dick just sat in the precinct basement hanging a doll of him day and night, year in year out. And when Chapin hanged in Connecticut, they find this old creep with his neck broken.

"He fell downstairs," they say. You know the old cop bullshit.

Junk is surrounded by magic and taboos, curses and amulets. I could find my Mexico City connection by radar. "Not this street, the next, right . . . now left. Now right again," and there he is, toothless old woman face and cancelled eyes.

I know this one pusher walks around humming a tune and everybody he passes takes it up. He is so grey and spectral and anonymous they don't see him and think it is their own mind humming the tune. So the customers come in on *Smiles,* or *I'm in the Mood for Love,* or *They Say We're Too Young to Go Steady,* or whatever the song is for that day. Sometime you can see maybe fifty ratty-looking junkies squealing sick, running along behind a boy with a harmonica, and there is The Man on a cane seat throwing bread to the swans, a fat queen drag walking his Afghan hound through the East Fifties, an old wino pissing against an El post, a radical Jewish student giving out leaflets in Washington Square, a tree surgeon, an exterminator, an advertising fruit in Nedick's where he calls the counterman by his first name. The world network of junkies, tuned on a cord of rancid jissom, tying up in furnished rooms, shivering in the junk-sick morning. (Old Pete men suck the black smoke in the Chink laundry back room and Melancholy Baby dies from an overdose of time or cold turkey withdrawal of breath.) In Yemen, Paris, New Orleans, Mexico City and Istanbul—shivering under the air hammers and the steam shovels, shrieked junky curses at one another neither of us heard, and The Man leaned out of a passing steam roller and I coped in a bucket of tar. (Note: Istanbul is being torn down and rebuilt, especially shabby junk quarters. Istanbul has more heroin junkies than NYC.) The living and the dead, in sickness or on the nod, hooked or kicked or hooked again, come in on the junk beam and the Connection is eating Chop Suey on Dolores Street, Mexico D.F., dunking pound cake in the automat, chased up Exchange Place by a baying pack of People. (Note: People is New Orleans slang for narcotic fuzz.)

The old Chinaman dips river water into a rusty tin can, washes down a yen pox hard and black as a cinder. (Note: Yen pox is the ash of smoked opium.)

Well, the fuzz has my spoon and dropper, and I know they are coming in on my frequency led by this blind pigeon known as Willy the Disk. Willy has a round, disk mouth lined with sensitive, erectile black hairs. He is blind from shooting in the eyeball, his nose and palate eaten away sniffing H, his body a mass of scar tissue hard and dry as wood. He can only eat the shit now with that mouth, sometimes sways out on a long tube of ectoplasm, feeling for the silent frequency of junk. He follows my trail all over the city into rooms I move out already, and the fuzz walks in some newlyweds from Sioux Falls.

"All right, Lee!! Come out from behind that strap-on! We know you" and pull the man's prick off straightaway.

Now Willy is getting hot and you can hear him always out there in darkness (he only functions at night) whimpering, and feel the terrible urgency of that blind, seeking mouth. When they move in for the bust, Willy goes all out of control, and his mouth eats a hole right through the door. If the cops weren't there to restrain him with a stock probe, he would suck the juice right out of every junky he ran down.

I knew, and everybody else knew they had the Disk on me. And if my kid customers ever hit the stand: "He force me to commit all kinda awful sex acts in return for junk" I could kiss the street goodbye.

So we stock up on H, buy a second-hand Studebaker, and start West.

———

The Vigilante copped out as a schizo possession case:

"I was standing outside myself trying to stop those hangings with

ghost fingers. . . . I am a ghost wanting what every ghost wants—a
body—after the Long Time moving through odorless alleys of space
where no life is only the colorless no smell of death. . . . Nobody can
breathe and smell it through pink convolutions of gristle laced with
crystal snot, time shit and black blood filters of flesh."

He stood there in elongated court room shadow, his face torn like a
broken film by lusts and hungers of larval organs stirring in the tenta-
tive ectoplasmic flesh of junk kick (ten days on ice at time of the First
Hearing) flesh that fades at the first silent touch of junk.

I saw it happen. Ten pounds lost in ten minutes standing with
the syringe in one hand holding his pants up with the other, his abdi-
cated flesh burning in a cold yellow halo, there in the New York hotel
room . . . night table litter of candy boxes, cigarette butts cascading out
of three ashtrays, mosaic of sleepless nights and sudden food needs of
the kicking addict nursing his baby flesh. . . .

The Vigilante is prosecuted in Federal Court under a lynch bill and
winds up in a Federal Nut House specially designed for the contain-
ment of ghosts: precise, prosaic impact of objects . . . washstand . . .
door . . . toilet . . . bars . . . there they are . . . this is it . . . all lines cut . . .
nothing beyond . . . Dead End . . . And the Dead End in every face. . . .

The physical changes were slow at first, then jumped forward in
black klunks, falling through his slack tissue, washing away the human
lines. . . . In his place of total darkness mouth and eyes are one organ
that leaps forward to snap with transparent teeth . . . but no organ is
constant as regards either function or position . . . sex organs sprout
anywhere . . . rectums open, defecate and close . . . the entire organism
changes color and consistency in split-second adjustments. . . .

———

The Rube is a social liability with his attacks as he calls them. The
Mark Inside was coming up on him and that's a rumble nobody can
cool; outside Philly he jumps out to con a prowl car and the fuzz takes
one look at his face and bust all of us.

Seventy-two hours and five sick junkies in the cell with us. Now not
wishing to break out my stash in front of these hungry coolies, it takes
maneuvering and laying of gold on the turnkey before we are in a
separate cell.

Provident junkies, known as squirrels, keep stashes against a bust.
Every time I take a shot I let a few drops fall into my vest pocket, the

lining is stiff with stuff. I had a plastic dropper in my shoe and a safety-pin stuck in my belt. You know how this pin and dropper routine is put down: "She seized a safety pin caked with blood and rust, gouged a great hole in her leg which seemed to hang open like an obscene, festering mouth waiting for unspeakable congress with the dropper which she now plunged out of sight into the gaping wound. But her hideous galvanized need (hunger of insects in dry places) has broken the dropper off deep in the flesh of her ravaged thigh (looking rather like a poster on soil erosion). But what does she care? She does not even bother to remove the splintered glass, looking down at her bloody haunch with the cold blank eyes of a meat trader. What does she care for the atom bomb, the bed bugs, the cancer rent, Friendly Finance waiting to repossess her delinquent flesh. . . . Sweet dreams, Pantopon Rose."

The real scene you pinch up some leg flesh and make a quick stab hole with a pin. Then fit the dropper *over, not in* the hole and feed the solution slow and careful so it doesn't squirt out the sides. . . . When I grabbed the Rube's thigh the flesh came up like wax and stayed there, and a slow drop of pus oozed out the hole. And I never touched a living body cold as the Rube there in Philly. . . .

I decided to lop him off if it meant a smother party. (This is a rural English custom designed to eliminate aged and bedfast dependents. A family so afflicted throws a "smother party" where the guests pile mattresses on the old liability, climb up on top of the mattresses and lush themselves out.) The Rube is a drag on the industry and should be led out into the skid rows of the world. (This is an African practice. Official known as the "Leader Out" has the function of taking old characters out into the jungle and leaving them there.)

The Rube's attacks become an habitual condition. Cops, doormen, dogs, secretaries snarl at his approach. The blond God has fallen to untouchable vileness. Con men don't change, they break, shatter—explosions of matter in cold interstellar space, drift away in cosmic dust, leave the empty body behind. Hustlers of the world, there is one Mark you cannot beat: The Mark Inside. . . .

I left the Rube standing on a corner, red brick slums to the sky, under a steady rain of soot. "Going to hit this croaker I know. Right back with that good pure drugstore M. . . . No, you wait here—don't want him to rumble you." No matter how long, Rube, wait for me right on that corner. Goodbye, Rube, goodbye kid. . . . Where do they go when they walk out and leave the body behind?

Chicago: invisible hierarchy of decorticated wops, smell of atrophied gangsters, earthbound ghost hits you at North and Halstead, Cicero, Lincoln Park, panhandler of dreams, past invading the present, rancid magic of slot machines and roadhouses.

Into the Interior: a vast subdivision, antennae of television to the meaningless sky. In lifeproof houses they hover over the young, sop up a little of what they shut out. Only the young bring anything in, and they are not young very long. (Through the bars of East St. Louis lies the dead frontier, riverboat days.) Illinois and Missouri, miasma of mound-building peoples, groveling worship of the Food Source, cruel and ugly festivals, dead-end horror of the Centipede God reaches from Moundville to the lunar deserts of coastal Peru.

America is not a young land: it is old and dirty and evil before the settlers, before the Indians. The evil is there waiting.

And always cops: smooth college-trained state cops, practiced, apologetic patter, electronic eyes weigh your car and luggage, clothes and face; snarling big city dicks, soft-spoken country sheriffs with something black and menacing in old eyes color of a faded grey flannel shirt. . . .

And always car trouble: in St. Louis traded the 1942 Studebaker in (it has a built-in engineering flaw like the Rube) on an old Packard limousine heated up and barely made Kansas City, and bought a Ford turned out to be an oil burner, packed it in on a jeep we push too hard (they are no good for highway driving)—and burn something out inside, rattling around, went back to the old Ford V-8. Can't beat that engine for getting there, oil burner or no.

And the U.S. drag closes around us like no other drag in the world, worse than the Andes, high mountain towns, cold wind down from postcard mountains, thin air like death in the throat, river towns of Ecuador, malaria grey as junk under black Stetson, muzzle loading shotguns, vultures pecking through the mud streets—and what hits you when you get off the Malmo Ferry in (no juice tax on the ferry) Sweden knocks all that cheap, tax free juice right out of you and brings you all the way down: averted eyes and the cemetery in the middle of town (every town in Sweden seems to be built around a cemetery), and nothing to do in the afternoon, not a bar not a movie and I blasted my last stick of Tangier tea and I said, "K.E. let's get right back on that ferry."

But there is no drag like U.S. drag. You can't see it, you don't know where it comes from. Take one of those cocktail lounges at the end of a subdivision street—every block of houses has its own bar and drugstore and market and liquorstore. You walk in and it hits you. But where does it come from?

Not the bartender, not the customers, nor the cream-colored plastic rounding the bar stools, nor the dim neon. Not even the TV.

And our habits build up with the drag, like cocaine will build you up staying ahead of the C bring-down. And the junk was running low. So there we are in this no-horse town strictly from cough syrup. And vomited up the syrup and drove on and on, cold spring wind whistling through that old heap around our shivering sick sweating bodies and the cold you always come down with when the junk runs out of you. . . . On through the peeled landscape, dead armadillos in the road and vultures over the swamp and cypress stumps. Motels with beaverboard walls, gas heater, thin pink blankets.

Itinerant short con and carny hyp men have burned down the croakers of Texas. . . .

And no one in his right mind would hit a Louisiana croaker. State Junk Law.

Came at last to Houston where I know a druggist. I haven't been there in five years but he looks up and makes me with one quick look and just nods and says: "Wait over at the counter. . . ."

So I sit down and drink a cup of coffee and after a while he comes and sits beside me and says, "What do you want?"

"A quart of PG and a hundred nembies."

He nods, "Come back in half an hour."

So when I come back he hands me a package and says, "That's fifteen dollars. . . . Be careful."

Shooting PG is a terrible hassle, you have to burn out the alcohol first, then freeze out the camphor and draw this brown liquid off with a dropper—have to shoot it in the vein or you get an abscess, and usually end up with an abscess no matter where you shoot it. Best deal is to drink it with goof balls. . . . So we pour it in a Pernod bottle and start for New Orleans past iridescent lakes and orange gas flares, and swamps and garbage heaps, alligators crawling around in broken bottles and tin cans, neon arabesques of motels, marooned pimps scream obscenities at passing cars from islands of rubbish. . . .

New Orleans is a dead museum. We walk around Exchange Place breathing PG and find The Man right away. It's a small place and the fuzz always knows who is pushing so he figures what the hell does it matter and sells to anybody. We stock up on H and backtrack for Mexico.

Back through Lake Charles and the dead slot-machine country, south end of Texas, nigger-killing sheriffs look us over and check the car papers. Something falls off you when you cross the border into Mexico, and suddenly the landscape hits you straight with nothing between you and it, desert and mountains and vultures; little wheeling specks and others so close you can hear wings cut the air (a dry husking sound), and when they spot something they pour out of the blue sky, that shattering bloody blue sky of Mexico, down in a black funnel. . . . Drove all night, came at dawn to a warm misty place, barking dogs and the sound of running water.

"Thomas and Charlie," I said.

"What?"

"That's the name of this town. Sea level. We climb straight up from here ten thousand feet." I took a fix and went to sleep in the back seat. She was a good driver. You can tell as soon as someone touches the wheel.

Mexico City where Lupita sits like an Aztec Earth Goddess doling out her little papers of lousy shit.

"Selling is more of a habit than using," Lupita says. Nonusing pushers have a contact habit, and that's one you can't kick. Agents get it too. Take Bradley the Buyer. Best narcotics agent in the industry. Anyone would make him for junk. (Note: Make in the sense of dig or size up.) I mean he can walk up to a pusher and score direct. He is so anonymous, grey and spectral the pusher don't remember him afterwards. So he twists one after the other. . . .

Well the Buyer comes to look more and more like a junky. He can't drink. He can't get it up. His teeth fall out. (Like pregnant women lose their teeth feeding the stranger, junkies lose their yellow fangs feeding the monkey.) He is all the time sucking on a candy bar. Baby Ruths he digs special. "It really disgust you to see the Buyer sucking on them candy bars so nasty," a cop says.

The Buyer takes on an ominous grey-green color. Fact is his body is making its own junk or equivalent. The Buyer has a steady connection. A Man Within you might say. Or so he thinks. "I'll just set in my room," he says. "Fuck 'em all. Squares on both sides. I am the only complete man in the industry."

But a yen comes on him like a great black wind through the bones. So the Buyer hunts up a young junky and gives him a paper to make it.

"Oh all right," the boy says. "So what you want to make?"

"I just want to rub up against you and get fixed."

"Ugh ... Well all right. . . . But why cancha just get physical like a human?"

Later the boy is sitting in a Waldorf with two colleagues dunking pound cake. "Most distasteful thing I ever stand still for," he says. "Some way he make himself all soft like a blob of jelly and surround me so nasty. Then he gets wet all over like with green slime. So I guess he come to some kinda awful climax. . . . I come near wigging with that green stuff all over me, and he stink like a old rotten cantaloupe."

"Well it's still an easy score."

The boy sighed resignedly; "Yes, I guess you can get used to anything. I've got a meet with him again tomorrow."

The Buyer's habit keeps getting heavier. He needs a recharge every half hour. Sometimes he cruises the precincts and bribes the turnkey to let him in with a cell of junkies. It gets to where no amount of contact will fix him. At this point he receives a summons from the District Supervisor:

"Bradley, your conduct has given rise to rumors—and I hope for your sake they are no more than that—so unspeakably distasteful that ... I mean Caesar's wife ... hrump ... that is, the Department must be above suspicion . . . certainly above such suspicions as you have seemingly aroused. You are lowering the entire tone of the industry. We are prepared to accept your immediate resignation."

The Buyer throws himself on the ground and crawls over to the D.S. "No, Boss Man, no . . . The Department is my very lifeline."

He kisses the D.S.'s hand thrusting his fingers into his mouth (the D.S. must feel his toothless gums) complaining he has lost his teeth "inna thervith." "Please Boss Man. I'll wipe your ass, I'll wash out your dirty condoms, I'll polish your shoes with the oil on my nose. . . ."

"Really, this is most distasteful! Have you no pride? I must tell you I

feel a distinct revulsion. I mean there is something, well, rotten about
you, and you smell like a compost heap." He put a scented handkerchief in front of his face. "I must ask you to leave this office at
once."

"I'll do anything, Boss, *anything*." His ravaged green face splits in a
horrible smile. "I'm still young, Boss, and I'm pretty strong when I get
my blood up."

The D.S. retches into his handkerchief and points to the door with
a limp hand. The Buyer stands up looking at the D.S. dreamily. His
body begins to dip like a dowser's wand. He flows forward. . . .

"No! No!" screams the D.S.

"Schlup . . . schlup schlup." An hour later they find the Buyer on the
nod in the D.S.'s chair. The D.S. has disappeared without a trace.

The Judge: "Everything indicates that you have, in some unspeakable manner uh . . . assimilated the District Supervisor. Unfortunately
there is no proof. I would recommend that you be confined or more
accurately contained in some institution, but I know of no place suitable for a man of your caliber. I must reluctantly order your release."

"That one should stand in an aquarium," says the arresting officer.

The Buyer spreads terror throughout the industry. Junkies and
agents disappear. Like a vampire bat he gives off a narcotic effluvium,
a dank green mist that anesthetizes his victims and renders them helpless in his enveloping presence. And once he has scored he holes up for
several days like a gorged boa constrictor. Finally he is caught in the
act of digesting the Narcotics Commissioner and destroyed with a
flame thrower—the court of inquiry ruling that such means were justified in that the Buyer had lost his human citizenship and was, in consequence, a creature without species and a menace to the narcotics
industry on all levels.

———

In Mexico the gimmick is to find a local junky with a government
script whereby they are allowed a certain quantity every month. Our
Man was Old Ike who had spent most of his life in the States.

"I was travelling with Irene Kelly and her was a sporting woman. In
Butte, state of Montany, she gets the coke horrors and run through the
hotel screaming Chinese coppers chase her with meat cleavers. I knew
this cop in Chicago sniff coke used to come in form of crystals, blue
crystals. So he go nuts and start screaming the Federals is after him and

run down this alley and stick his head in the garbage can. And I said, 'What you think you are doing?' and he say, 'Get away or I shoot you. I got myself hid good.'"

We are getting some C on RX at this time. Shoot it in the mainline, son. You can smell it going in, clean and cold in your nose and throat then a rush of pure pleasure right through the brain lighting up those C connections. Your head shatters in white explosions. Ten minutes later you want another shot . . . you will walk across town for another shot. But if you can't score for C you eat, sleep and forget about it.

This is a yen of the brain alone, a need without feeling and without body, earthbound ghost need, rancid ectoplasm swept out by an old junky coughing and spitting in the sick morning.

One morning you wake up and take a speed ball, and feel bugs under your skin. 1890 cops with black mustaches block the doors and lean in through the windows snarling their lips back from blue and bold embossed badges. Junkies march through the room singing the Moslem Funeral Song, bear the body of Bill Gains, stigmata of his needle wounds glow with a soft blue flame. Purposeful schizophrenic detectives sniff at your chamber pot.

It's the coke horrors. . . . Sit back and play it cool and shoot in plenty of that GI M.

Day of the Dead: I got the chucks and ate my little Willy's sugar skull. He cried and I had to go out for another. Walked past the cocktail lounge where they blasted the Jai Lai bookie.

———

In Cuernavaca or was it Taxco? Jane meets a pimp trombone player and disappears in a cloud of tea smoke. The pimp is one of these vibration and dietary artists—which is a means he degrades the female sex by forcing his chicks to swallow all this shit. He was continually enlarging his theories . . . he would quiz a chick and threaten to walk out if she hadn't memorized every nuance of his latest assault on logic and the human image.

"Now, baby. I got it here to give. But if you won't receive it there's just nothing I can do."

He was a ritual tea smoker and very puritanical about junk the way some teaheads are. He claimed tea put him in touch with supra blue gravitational fields. He had ideas on every subject: what kind of underwear was healthy, when to drink water, and how to wipe your ass. He had a shiny red face and great spreading smooth nose, little red eyes that lit up when he looked at a chick and went out when he looked at anything else. His shoulders were very broad and suggested deformity. He acted as if other men did not exist, conveying his restaurant and store orders to male personnel through a female intermediary. And no Man ever invaded his blighted, secret place.

So he is putting down junk and coming on with tea. I take three drags, Jane looked at him and her flesh crystallized. I leaped up screaming "I got the fear!" and ran out of the house. Drank a beer in a little restaurant—mosaic bar and soccer scores and bullfight posters—and waited for the bus to town.

A year later in Tangier I heard she was dead.

THE BLOOD OF A WIG

Terry Southern

1967

*As a screenwriter, novelist, and short-story writer, Terry Southern
earned an enthusiastic audience for his hard-edged accounts of the
1960s drug culture. Best known as coauthor of the screenplays* Dr.
Strangelove or: How I Learned to Stop Worrying and Love
the Bomb *(1964) and* Easy Rider *(1969), Southern later worked
as a writer for* Saturday Night Live. *"The Blood of a Wig,"
from the collection* Red Dirt Marijuana and Other Tastes, *is
a young New Yorker's tale of drug use during his brief stint as a
magazine editor.*

My most outlandish drug experience, now that I think about it, didn't
occur with beat Village or Harlem weirdos, but during a brief run with
the ten-to-four Mad Ave crowd.

How it happened, this friend of mine who was working at *Lance*
("The Mag for Men") phoned me one morning—he knew I was
strapped.

"One of the fiction editors is out with syph or something," he said.
"You want to take his place for a while?"

I was still mostly asleep, so I tried to cool it by shooting a few inci-
sive queries as to the nature of the gig—which he couldn't seem to follow.

"Well," he said finally, "you won't have to *do* anything, if that's what
you mean." He had a sort of blunt and sullen way about him—John
Fox his name was, an ex-Yalie and would-be writer who was constantly
having to "put it back on the shelf," as he expressed it (blunt, sullen),

and take one of these hot-shot Mad Ave jobs, and always for some odd reason—like at present, paying for his mom's analysis.

Anyway, I accepted the post, and now I had been working there about three weeks. It wasn't true, of course, what he'd said about not having to do anything—I mean the way he had talked I wouldn't even have to get out of bed—but after three weeks my routine was fairly smooth: up at ten, wash face, brush teeth, fresh shirt, dex, and make it. I had this transistor-shaver I'd copped for five off a junky-booster, so I would shave with it in the cab, and walk into the office at ten-thirty or so, dapper as Dan and hip as Harry. Then into my own small office, lock the door, and start stashing the return postage from the unsolicited mss. We would get an incredible amount of mss.—about two hundred a day—and these were divided into two categories: (1) those from agents, and (2) those that came in cold, straight from the author. The ratio was about 30 to 1, in favor of the latter—which formed a gigantic heap called "the shit pile," or (by the girl-readers) "the garbage dump." These always contained a lot of return postage—so right away I was able to supplement my weekly wage by seven or eight dollars a day in postage stamps. Everyone else considered the "shit pile" as something heinously repugnant, especially the sensitive girl ("garbage") readers, so it was a source of irritation and chagrin to my secretary when I first told her I wished to read "*all* unsolicited manuscripts and *no* manuscripts from agents."

John Fox found it quite incomprehensible.

"You must be out of your nut!" he said. "Ha! Wait until you try to read some of that crap in the shit pile!"

I explained however (and it was actually true in the beginning) that I had this theory about the existence of a *pure, primitive, folklike* literature—which, if it did exist, could only turn up among the unsolicited mss. Or *weird,* something really *weird,* even insane, might turn up there—whereas I knew the stuff from the agents would be the same old predictably competent tripe. So, aside from stashing the stamps, I would read each of these shit-pile mss. Very carefully—reading subtleties, insinuations, multilevel *entendre* into what was actually just a sort of flat, straightforward simplemindedness. I would think each was a put-on—a fresh and curious parody of some kind, and I would read on, and on, all the way to the end, waiting for the payoff . . . but, of course, that never happened, and I gradually began to revise my theory and to refine my method. By the second week, I was able to reject a ms. after reading the opening sentence, and by the third I could often reject on the basis of *title* alone—the principle being if an author would allow a blatantly dumbbell title, he was incapable of writing a story worth reading. (This was thoroughly tested and proved before adopting.) Then instead of actually *reading* mss., I would spend hours, days really, just thinking, trying to refine and extend my method of blitz-rejection. I was able to take it a little farther, but not much. For example, any woman author who used "Mrs." in her name could be rejected out of hand—*unless* it was used with only one name, like "by Mrs. Carter," then it might be a weirdie. And again, any author using a middle initial or a "Jr." in his name, shoot it right back to him! I knew I was taking a chance with that one (because of Connell and Selby), but I figured what the hell, I could hardly afford to gear the sort of fast-moving synchro-mesh operation I had in mind to a couple of exceptions—which, after all, only went to prove the consarn rule, so to speak. Anyway, there it was, the end of the third week and the old job going smoothly enough, except that I had developed quite a little dexie habit by then—not actually a *habit*, of course, but a sort of very real dependence . . . having by nature a nocturnal metabolism whereby my day (pre-*Lance*) would ordinarily begin at three or four in the afternoon and finish at eight or nine in the morning. As a top staffer at *Lance,* however, I had to make other arrangements. Early on I had actually asked John Fox if it would be possible for me to come in at four and work until midnight.

"Are you out of your *nut?*" (That was his standard comeback.) "Don't you know what's happening here? This is a *social* scene, man—these guys want to *see* you, they want to get to *know* you!"

"What are they, faggots?"

"No, they're not *faggots,*" he said stoutly, but then seemed hard pressed to explain, and shrugged it off. "It's just that they don't have very much, you know, *to do.*"

It was true in a way that no one seemed to actually *do* anything—except for the typists, of course, always typing away. But the guys just sort of hung out, or around, buzzing each other, sounding the chicks, that sort of thing.

The point is though that I had to make it in by ten, or thereabouts. One reason for this was the "prelunch conference," which Hacker, or the "Old Man" (as, sure enough, the publisher was called), might decide to have on any given day. And so it came to pass that on this particular—Monday it was—morning, up promptly at nine-three-oh, wash face, brush teeth, fresh shirt, all as per usual, and reach for the dex . . . no dex, out of dex. This was especially inopportune because it was on top of two straight white and active nights, and it was somewhat as though an 800-pound bag, of loosely packed sand, began to settle slowly on the head. No panic, just immediate death from fatigue.

At Sheridan Square, where I usually got the taxi, I went into the drugstore. The first-shift pharmacist, naturally a guy I had never seen before, was on duty. He looked like an aging efficiency expert.

"Uh, I'd like to get some Dexamyl, please."

The pharmacist didn't say anything, just raised one hand to adjust his steel-rimmed glasses, and put the other one out for the prescription.

"It's on file here," I said, nodding toward the back.

"What name?" he wanted to know, then disappeared behind the glass partition, but very briefly indeed.

"Nope," he said, coming back, and was already looking over my shoulder to the next customer.

"Could you call Mr. Robbins?" I asked. "He can tell you about it." Of course this was simply whistling in the dark, since I was pretty sure Robbins, the night-shift man, didn't know me by name, but I had to keep the ball rolling.

"I'm not gonna wake Robbins at this hour—he'd blow his stack. Who's next?"

"Well, listen, can't you just *give* me a couple—I've, uh, got a long drive ahead."

"You can't get dexies without a script," he said, rather reproachfully, wrapping a box of Tampax for a teenybopper nifty behind me, "*you* know that."

"Okay, how about if I get the doctor to phone you?"

"Phone's up front," he said, and to the nifty: "That's seventy-nine."

The phone was under siege—one person using it, and about five waiting—all, for some weird reason, spade fags and prancing gay. Not that I give a damn about who uses the phone, it was just one of those absurd incongruities that seem so often to conspire to undo sanity in times of crisis. What the hell was going on? They were obviously together, very excited, chattering like magpies. Was it the Katherine Dunham contingent of male dancers? Stranded? Lost? Why out so early? One guy had a list of numbers in his hand the size of a small flag. I stood there for a moment, confused in pointless speculation, then left abruptly and hurried down West Fourth to the dinette. This was doubly to purpose, since not only is there a phone, but the place is frequented by all manner of heads, and a casual score might well be in order—though it was a bit early for the latter, granted.

And this did, in fact, prove to be the case. There was no one there whom I knew—and, worse still, halfway to the phone, I suddenly remembered my so-called doctor (Dr. Friedman, his name was) had gone to California on vacation a few days ago. Christ almighty! I sat down at the counter. This called for a quick think-through. Should I actually call him in California? Have him phone the drugstore from there? Quite a production for a couple of dex. I looked at my watch, it was just after ten. That meant just after seven in Los Angeles—Friedman would blow his stack. I decided to hell with it and ordered a cup of coffee. Then a remarkable thing happened. I had sat down next to a young man who now quite casually removed a small transparent silo-shaped vial from his pocket, and without so much as a glance in any direction, calmly tapped a couple of the belovedly familiar green-hearted darlings into his cupped hand, and tossed them off like two salted peanuts. *Deus ex machina!*

"Uh, excuse me," I said, in the friendliest sort of way, "I just happened to notice you taking a couple of, ha ha, Dexamyl." And I proceeded to lay my story on him—while he, after one brief look of appraisal, sat listening, his eyes straight ahead, hands still on the counter, one of them half covering the magic vial. Finally he just nodded and shook out two more on the counter. "Have a ball," he said.

———

I reached the office about five minutes late for the big prelunch confab. John Fox made a face of mild disgust when I came in the conference room. He always seemed to consider my flaws as his responsibility since it was he who had recommended me for the post. Now he glanced uneasily at old Hacker, who was the publisher, editor-in-chief, etc. etc. A man of about fifty-five, he bore a striking resemblance to Edward G. Robinson—an image to which he gave further credence by frequently sitting in a squatlike manner, chewing an unlit cigar butt, and mouthing coarse expressions. He liked to characterize himself as a "tough old bastard," one of his favorite prefaces being: "I know most of you guys think I'm a *tough old bastard,* right? Well, maybe I am. In the quality-Lit game you *gotta* be tough!" And bla-bla-bla.

Anyway as I took my usual seat between Fox and Bert Katz, the feature editor, Old Hack looked at his watch, then back at me.

"Sorry," I mumbled.

"We're running a *magazine* here, young man, not a *whorehouse.*"

"Right and double right," I parried crisply. Somehow Old Hack always brought out the schoolboy in me.

"If you want to be *late,*" he continued, "be late at the *whorehouse*—and do it on your own time!"

Part of his design in remarks of this sort was to get a reaction from the two girls present—Maxine, his cutiepie private sec, and Miss Rogers, assistant to the art director—both of whom managed, as usual, a polite blush and half-lowered eyes for his benefit.

The next ten minutes were spent talking about whether to send our own exclusive third-rate photographer to Viet Nam or to use the rejects of a second-rate one who had just come back.

"Even with the rejects we could still run our *E.L. trade,*" said Katz, referring to an italicized phrase *Exclusively Lance* which appeared under photographs and meant they were not being published elsewhere—though less through exclusivity, in my view, than general crappiness.

Without really resolving this, we went on to the subject of "Twiggy," the British fashion-model who had just arrived in New York and about whose boyish hair and bust-line raged a storm of controversy. What did it mean philosophically? Aesthetically? Did it signal a new trend? Should we adjust our center-spread requirements (traditionally 42-24-38) to meet current taste? Or was it simply a flash fad?

"Come next issue," said Hack, "we don't want to find ourselves holding the wrong end of the shit-stick, now do we?"

Everyone was quick to agree.

"Well, *I* think she's absolutely *delightful,*" exclaimed Ronnie Rondell, the art director (prancing gay and proud of it), "she's so much more ... sensitive-looking and ... *delicate* than those awful ... *milk-factories*!" He gave a little shiver of revulsion and looked around excitedly for corroboration.

Hack, who had a deep-rooted antifag streak, stared at him for a moment like he was some kind of weird lizard, and he seemed about to say something cruel and uncalled for to Ron, but then he suddenly turned on me instead.

"Well, Mister Whorehouse man, isn't it about time we heard from you? Got any ideas that might conceivably keep this operation out of the shithouse for another issue or two?"

"Yeah, well I've been thinking," I said, winging it completely, "I mean, Fox here and I had an idea for a series of interviews with unusual persons. . . ."

"Unusual *persons?*" he growled, "what the hell does that mean?"

"Well, you know, a whole new department, like a regular feature. Maybe call it, uh, 'Lance Visits. . . .'"

He was scowling, but he was also nodding vigorously. "'Lance Visits. . . .' Yeh, yeh, you wantta gimme a fer instance?"

"Well, you know, like, uh, . . . 'Lance Visits a Typical Teenybopper'—cute teenybopper tells about cute teen-use of Saran Wrap as a contraceptive, etcetera . . . and uh, let's see . . . 'Lance Visits a Giant Spade Commie Bull-Dike' . . . 'Lance Visits the Author of *Masturbation Now!*', a really fun-guy."

Now that I was getting warmed up, I was aware that Fox, on my left, had raised a hand to his face and was slowly massaging it, mouth open, eyes closed. I didn't look at Hack, but I knew he had stopped nodding. I pressed on . . . "You see, it could become a sort of regular department, we could do a 'T.L.' on it . . . *'Another Exclusive Lance Visit.'* How about this one: 'Lance Visits a Cute Junkie Hooker' . . . 'Lance Visits a Zany Ex-Nun Nympho' . . . 'Lance Visits the Fabulous Rose Chan, beautiful research and development technician for the so-called French Tickler . . ."

"Okay," said Hack, "how about *this* one: 'Lance Visits Lance,'—know where? Up shit-creek without a paddle! Because that's where we'd be if we tried any of that stuff." He shook his head in a lament of disgust and pity. "Jeez, that's some sense of humor you got, boy." Then he turned to Fox. "What rock you say you found him under? Jeez."

Fox, as per usual, made no discernible effort to defend me, simply pretended to suppress a yawn, eyes averted, continuing to doodle on his "Think Pad," as it was called, one of which lay by each of our ashtrays.

"Okay," said Hack, lighting a new cigar, "suppose *I* come up with an

idea? I mean, I don't wantta *surprise* you guys, cause any *heart attacks*...
by *me* coming up with an *idea*," he saying this with a benign serpent
smile, then adding in grim significance, "*after twenty-seven years in this
goddam game!*" He took a sip of water, as though trying to cool his irritation at being (as per usual) "the only slob around here who delivers."
"Now let's just stroke this one for a while," he said, "and see if it gets
stiff. Okay, lemme ask you a question: what's the hottest thing in mags
at this time? What's raising all the stink and hullabaloo? The *Manchester* book, right? The suppressed passages, right?" He was referring, of
course, to a highly publicized account of the assassination of President
Kennedy—certain passages of which had allegedly been deleted. "Okay,
now all this stink and hullabaloo—*I* don't like it, *you* don't like it. In the
first place, it's infringement on freedom of the press. In the second,
they've exaggerated it all out of proportion. I mean, what the hell was
in those passages? See what I mean? All right, suppose we do a *takeoff*
on those same passages?"

He gave me a slow look, eyes narrowed—ostensibly to protect them
from his cigar smoke, but with a Mephistophelian effect. *He* knew that
I knew that his "idea" was actually an idea I had gotten from Paul
Krassner, editor of *The Realist*, a few evenings earlier, and had mentioned, *en passant* so to speak, at the last prelunch confab. He seemed to
be wondering if I would crack. A test, like. I avoided his eyes, doodled
on the "Think Pad." He exhaled in my direction, and continued:

"Know what I mean? Something *light*, something *zany*, kid the pants
off the guys who suppressed it in the first place. A satire like. Get the
slant?"

No one at the table seemed to. Except for Hack we were all in our
thirties or early forties, and each had been hurt in some way by the
President's death. It was not easy to imagine any particular "zaniness"
in that regard.

Fox was the first to speak, somewhat painfully it seemed. "I'm, uh,
not quite sure I follow," he said. "You mean it would be done in the
style of the book?"

"Right," said Hack, "but get this, we don't say it *is* the real thing, we
say it *purports* to be the real thing. And editorially we *challenge* the *au-
thenticity* of it! Am I getting through to you?"

"Well, uh, yeah," said Fox, "but I'm not sure it can be, you know, uh,
funny."

Hack shrugged. "So? *You're* not sure, *I'm* not sure. Nobody's sure it can be funny. We all take a crack at it—just stroke it a while and see if we get any jism—right?"

Right.

———

After work that evening I picked up a new Dexamyl prescription and stopped off at Sheridan Square to get it filled. Coming out of the drug-store, I paused momentarily to take in the scene. It was a fantastic evening—late spring evening, warm breeze promise of great summer evenings imminent—and teenies in minies floating by like ballerinas, young thighs flashing. Summer, I thought, will be the acid test for minies when it gets too warm for tights, body-stockings, that sort of thing. It should be quite an interesting phenomenon. On a surge of sex-dope impulse I decided to fall by the dinette and see if anything of special import was shaking, so to speak.

Curious that the first person I should see there, hunched over his coffee, frozen saintlike, black shades around his head as though a hippy crown of thorns, should be the young man who had given me the dex that very morning. I had the feeling he hadn't moved all day. But this wasn't true because he now had on a white linen suit and was sitting in a booth. He nodded in that brief formal way it is possible to nod and mean more than just hello. I sat down opposite him.

"I see you got yourself all straightened out," he said with a wan smile, nodding again, this time at my little paper bag with the pharmacy label on it.

I took out the vial of dex and popped a quick one, thinking to do a bit of the old creative Lit later on. Then I shook out four or five and gave them to the young man.

"Here's some interest."

"Anytime," he said, dropping them in his top pocket, and after a pause, "You ever in the mood for something beside dexies?"

"Like what?"

He shrugged, "Oh, you know," he said, raising a vague limp hand, then added with a smile, "I mean you know your moods better than I do."

During the next five minutes he proved to be the most acquisi-tive pusher, despite his tender years, I have ever encountered. His range was extensive—beginning with New Jersey pot, and ending with something called a "Frisco Speedball," a concoction of heroin and co-caine, with a touch of acid ("gives it a little color"). While we were sit-ting there, a veritable parade of his far-flung connections commenced, sauntering over, or past the booth, pausing just long enough to inquire if he wanted to score—for sleepers, leapers, creepers . . . acid in cubes, vials, capsules, tablets, powder . . . "hash, baby, it's black as O" . . . mush-rooms, mescalin, buttons . . . cosanyl, codeine, coke . . . coke in crystals, coke in powder, coke that looked like karo syrup . . . red birds, yellow jackets, purple hearts . . . "liquid-O, it comes straight from Indochina, stamped right on the can" . . . and from time to time the young man ("Trick" he was called) would turn to me and say: "Got eyes?"

After committing to a modest (thirty dollars) score for crystals, and again for two ounces of what was purported to be "Panamanian Green" ("It's 'one-poke pot,' baby."), I declined further inducement. Then an extremely down-and-out type, a guy I had known before whose actual name was Rattman, but who was known with simple familiarity as "Rat," and even more familiarly, though somehow obscurely, as "The Rat-Prick Man," half staggered past the booth, clocked the acquisitive Trick, paused, moved uncertainly towards the booth, took a crumpled brown paper bag out of his coat pocket, and opened it to show.

"Trick," he muttered, almost without moving his lips, ". . . Trick, can you use any Lights? Two-bits for the bunch." We both looked in, on some commodity quite unrecognizable—tiny, dark cylinder-shaped capsules, sticky with a brown-black guk, flat on each end, and appar-ently made of plastic. There was about a handful of them. The young man made a weary face of distaste and annoyance.

"Man," he asked softly, plaintively, looking up at Rattman, "*when* are you going to get buried?"

But the latter, impervious, gave a soundless guffaw, and shuffled on.

"What," I wanted to know, "were those things?" asking this of the young man half in genuine interest, half in annoyance at not know-ing. He shrugged, raised a vague wave of dismissal. "Lights they're called . . . they're used nicotine-filters. You know, those nicotine-filters you put in a certain kind of cigarette holder."

"*Used* nicotine-filters? What do you do with them?"

"Well, you know, drop two or three in a cup of coffee—gives you a little buzz."

"A little *buzz*?" I said, "are you kidding? How about a little *cancer*? That's all tar and nicotine in there, isn't it?"

"Yeah, well, you know . . ." he chuckled dryly, "anything for kicks. Right?"

Right, right, right.

And it was just about then he sprung it—first giving me his look of odd appraisal, then the sigh, the tired smile, the haltering deference: "Listen, man . . . you ever made red-split?"

"I beg your pardon?"

"Yeah, you know—*the blood of a wig.*"

"No," I said, not really understanding, "I don't believe I have."

"Well, it's something else, baby, I can tell you that."

"Uh, well, *what* did you call it—I'm not sure I understood. . . ."

"'Red-split,' man, it's called 'red-split'—it's schizo-juice . . . *blood* . . . the blood of a wig."

"Oh, I see." I had, in fact, read about it in a recent article in the *Times*—how they had shot up a bunch of volunteer prisoners (very normal, healthy guys, of course) with the blood of schizophrenia patients—and the effect had been quite pronounced . . . in some cases, manic; in other cases, depressive—about 50/50 as I recalled.

"But that can be a big bring-down, can't it?"

He shook his head somberly. "Not with *this* juice it can't. You know who this is out of?" Then he revealed the source—Chin Lee, it was, a famous East Village resident, a Chinese symbolist poet, who was presently residing at Bellevue in a straightjacket. "Nobody," he said, "and I mean *nobody*, baby, has gone anywhere but *up, up, up* on *this* taste!"

I thought that it might be an interesting experience, but using caution as my watchword (the *Times* article had been very sketchy) I had to know more about this so-called red-split, blood of a wig. "Well, how long does it, uh, you know, *last*?"

He seemed a little vague about that—almost to the point of resenting the question. "It's a *trip,* man—four hours, six if you're lucky. It all depends. It's a question of *combination*—how your blood makes it with his, you dig?" He paused and gave me a very straight look. "I'll tell you this much, baby, it *cuts acid and STP* . . ." He nodded vigorously. "That's right, cuts both them. *Back, down,* and *sideways.*"

"Really?"

He must have felt he was getting a bit too loquacious, a bit too much on the old hard-sell side, because then he just cooled it, and nodded. "That's right," he said, so soft and serious that it wasn't really audible.

"How much?" I asked, finally, uncertain of any other approach.

"I'll level with you," he said, "I've got this connection—a ward attendant . . . you know, a male nurse . . . has, what you might call *access* to the hospital pharmacy . . . does a little trading with the guards on the fifth floor—that's where the *monstro*-wigs are—'High Five' it's called. That's where Chin Lee's at. Anyway, he's operating at cost right now— I mean, he'll cop as much M, or whatever other hard-shit he can, from the pharmacy, then he'll go up to High Five and trade for the juice— you know, just fresh, straight, uncut wig-juice—90 c.c.'s, that's the regular hit, about an ounce, I guess . . . I mean, that's what they hit the wigs for, a 90 c.c. syringeful, then they cap the spike and put the whole outfit in an insulated wrapper. Like it's supposed to stay at body temperature, you dig? They're very strict about that—about how much they tap the wig for, and about keeping it fresh and warm, that sort of thing. Which is okay, because that's the trip—90 c.c.'s, 'piping hot,' as they say." He gave a tired little laugh at the curious image. "Anyway the point is, he never knows in front what the *price* will be, my friend doesn't, because he never knows what kind of M score he'll make. I mean like if he scores for half-a-bill of M, then that's what he charges for the split, you dig?"

To me, with my Mad Ave savvy, this seemed fairly illogical.

"Can't he hold out on the High Five guys?" I asked, ". . . you know, tell them he only got half what he really got, and save it for later?"

He shrugged, almost unhappily. "He's a very ethical guy," he said, "I mean like he's pretty weird. He's not really interested in narcotics, just *changes*. I mean, like he lets *them* do the count on the M—they tell him how much it's worth and that's what he charges for the split."

"That *is* weird," I agreed.

"Yeah, well it's like a new market, you know. I mean there's no established price yet, he's trying to develop a clientele—can you make half-a-bill?"

While I pondered, he smiled his brave tired smile, and said: "There's one thing about the cat, being so ethical and all—he'll never burn you."

So in the end it was agreed, and he went off to complete the arrangements.

The effect of red-split was "as advertised" so to speak—in this case, quite gleeful. Sense-derangementwise, it was unlike acid in that it was not a question of the "Essential I" having new insights, but of becoming a different person entirely. So that in a way there was nothing very scary about it, just extremely weird, and as it turned out, somewhat mischievous (Chin Lee, incidentally, was not merely a great wig, but also a great wag). At about six in the morning I started to work on the alleged "Manchester passages." Krassner might be cross, I thought, but what the hell, you can't copyright an idea. Also I intended to give him full and ample credit. "Darn good exposure for Paul" I mused benignly, taking up the old magic quill.

The first few passages were fairly innocuous, the emphasis being on a style identical to that of the work in question. Towards the end of Chapter Six, however, I really started cooking: ". . . wan, and wholly bereft, she steals away from the others, moving trancelike towards the darkened rear-compartment where the casket rests. She enters, and a whispery circle of light shrouds her bowed head as she closes the door behind her and leans against it. Slowly she raises her eyes and takes a solemn step forward. She gasps, and is literally slammed back against the door by the sheer impact of the outrageous horror confronting her: i.e., the hulking Texan silhouette at the casket, its lid half raised, and he hunching bestially, his coarse animal member thrusting into the casket, and indeed into the neck-wound itself.

"Great God," she cries, "how heinous! It must be a case of . . . of . . . *NECK*-ROPHILIA!"

I finished at about ten, dexed, and made it to the office. I went directly into Fox's cubicle (the "Lair" it was called).

"You know," I began, lending the inflection a childlike candor, "I could be wrong but I think I've *got* it," and I handed him the ms.

"Got what?" he countered dryly, "the clap?"

"You know, that Manchester thing we discussed at the last prelunch confab." While he read, I paced about, flapped my arms in a gesture of uncertainty and humble doubt. "Oh, it may need a little tightening up, brightening up, granted, but I hope you'll agree that the *essence* is there."

For a while he didn't speak, just sat with his head resting on one hand staring down at the last page. Finally he raised his eyes; his eyes were always somehow sad.

"You really *are* out of your nut, aren't you?"

"Sorry, John," I said. "Don't follow."

He looked back at the ms., moved his hands a little away from it as though it were a poisonous thing. Then he spoke with great seriousness:

"I think you ought to have your head examined."

"My *head* is swell," I said, and wished to elaborate, "my *head*..." but suddenly I felt very weary. I had evidently hit on a cow sacred even to the cynical Fox.

"Look," he said, "I'm not a *prude* or anything like that, but this..."—he touched the ms. with a cough which seemed to stifle a retch—..."I mean, *this* is the most... *grotesque*... *obscene*... well, I'd rather not even discuss it. Frankly, I think you're in very real need of psychiatric attention."

"Do you think Hack will go for it?" I asked in perfect frankness.

Fox averted his eyes and began to drum his fingers on the desk.

"Look, uh, I've got quite a bit of work to do this morning, so, you know, if you don't mind...."

"Gone too far, have I, Fox? Is that it? Maybe you're missing the point of the thing—ever consider that?"

"Listen," said Fox stoutly, lips tightened, one finger raised in accusation, "you show this... *this thing* to anybody else, you're liable to get a *big smack in the kisser!*" There was an unmistakable heat and resentment in his tone—a sort of controlled hysteria.

"How do you know I'm not from the C.I.A.?" I asked quietly. "How do *you* know this isn't a *test?*" I gave him a shrewd narrow look of appraisal. "Isn't it just possible, Fox, that this quasi-indignation of yours is, in point of fact, simply an *act?* A *farce?* A *charade?* An *act,* in short, to *save your own skin!?!*"

He had succeeded in putting me on the defensive. But now, steeped in Chink poet cunning, I had decided that an offense was the best defense, and so plunged ahead. "Isn't it true, Fox, that in this parable you see certain underlying homosexual tendencies which you unhappily recognize in yourself? Tendencies, I say, which to confront would bring you to the very brink of, 'fear and trembling,' so to speak." I was counting on the Kierkegaard allusion to bring him to his senses.

"You crazy son of a bitch," he said flatly, rising behind his desk, hands clenching and unclenching. He actually seemed to be moving towards me in some weird menacing way. It was then I changed my tack. "Well listen," I said, "what would you say if I told you that it wasn't actually *me* who did that, but a Chinese poet? Probably a Commie . . . an insane Commie-fag-spade-Chinese poet. Then we could view it objectively, right?"

Fox, now crazed with his own righteous adrenalin, and somewhat encouraged by my lolling helplessly in the chair, played his indignation to the hilt.

"Okay, Buster," he said, towering above me, "keep talking, but make it good."

"Well, uh, let's see now. . . ." So I begin to tell him about my experience with the red-split. And speaking in a slow, deliberate, very serious way, I managed to cool him. And then I told him about an insight I had gained into Viet Nam, Cassius Clay, Chessman, the Rosenbergs, and all sorts of interesting things. He couldn't believe it. But, of course, no one ever really does—do they?

FROM

THE STORY OF JUNK

Linda Yablonsky

1997

In a downtown New York City apartment, a woman who grew up believing she was a "nice girl" from the suburbs embarks on an entirely different type of existence—that of a streetwise drug dealer. In The Story of Junk, *a coolheaded—yet ultimately unsettling—fictional account of the 1980s junk scene, Linda Yablonsky's narrator supplies heroin to an assortment of regular customers, including ragged downtown artists, flashy trans-sexuals, and uptight overachievers. In due time she finds a drug-enforcement agent at her door and is forced to examine the question of who among her closest friends has betrayed her.*

It doesn't take a lot of know-how to know how to deal drugs. You learn as you go along. You buy, you mix, you weigh and measure; you bag, trade, and sell. It's a business, like any other religion: same dependence on faith and ritual, same promise of deliverance, same foundation in fear. Same flow of tax-free cash.

But this is not an easy business to profit by; the product can tempt more than the proceeds. It's all about turnover and control, same as restaurants. Restaurants can't depend on serving food alone. They have to have personalities. That's how it is in drugs: a dealer can't be too honest or too devious; attitude counts the most. It might be nice to have a patient, kind, and understanding nature, to be close-mouthed and mature, but none of that is really very useful. It takes a bitch to be a dealer.

Advertising is out, except by word of mouth, and that's a double-edged sword. The word can easily reach the wrong ears. I can't let myself sell to just anyone; that's the business of the street.

Besides, I'm no kind of pusher. Pushers are the "nifty Louie" types you see in movies, extortionists with an evil glint in their eyes and the monkey on a taut, stinking leash. Private dealers like me do not remotely resemble these Hollywood lowlifes. We're respectable, and selective. When I drop hints around Sticky's, it's all very furtive, very hush-hush. Kit does the same at her gigs. And before long, people start calling.

The needleheads come first. That's natural, I can't complain. They're the steady customers. *Knock-knock, ring-ring, beep-beep: Are you in now? Are you in? Okay to stop by now? Got anything to drink? How is this stuff? How much should I do?* This is the usual drill. *Can I pay you later? tomorrow? next week?*

I prefer the less regular customers, chippers and partyheads, over-achievers, friends—filmmakers, poets, painters, musician friends of Kit's. Not all of them are into drugs, but the ones who aren't have husbands or girlfriends or sisters who are, and they all come together and hang out. It's not a big scene but I enjoy it. I was always such a loner. I have a community now.

On nights I have to work, I deal the way I did for Big Guy, weighing out tenths and half-tenths of a gram from a green plastic miniscale that fits in the pocket of my grill jacket. The walk-in refrigerator is my place of business. Pedro calls it the Food and Drug Administration. Everything coming out of Sticky's, he says, is FDA-tested and approved.

At home I deal from the living room, salon-style. If they're very good friends, Honey and Magna, or Big Guy and Mr. Leather (Belle comes by only when no one will know), I work out of the bedroom, where Kit and I actually live. It's the one comfortable room in the apartment: a carpet and two armchairs, a small table and the bed, a raised platform. Kit and Betty had been sleeping on the floor, but I couldn't put up with that. Too slummy.

Dean's all right, though. He delivers, but he's slow, a little slow. He teaches shop in a high school downtown. Every day after class he comes by to pick up money, then he goes to his source while I wait. I wait and so do all my friends, outside on the benches, at home by the phone, in bars. I don't like to keep them waiting, but what can I do?

When Dean finally arrives, he lays out a taste, then he wants to stay and talk and I have to listen.

It's the biggest part of my job, listening, or pretending to. Having a private dealership is like sitting in a confessional—that religious aspect again. Sometimes it's more like therapy. People are supposed to tell a shrink everything on their minds, but who ever actually does that? No one I know, not when they can spill to a dealer. A dealer has to keep mum.

I don't know what Dean thinks about besides drugs and money. Every now and then he mentions an ex-girlfriend, emphasizing the "ex," but mostly all I hear are vague references to his supplier, and Rico.

Was it Rico who set him up with this connection, I wonder? Maybe it's someone Rico owes a favor and Dean is someone he promised a favor and now they're all making out, through me. They make the money and I do all the work. I work just as hard at this as I ever have in a kitchen. Then how can I be serving so many people and not come out ahead? I keep strict control of Kit's intake, am even harder on my own. The problem is the cost to me: I must not be close enough to the source. Yet the dope is pure, not stepped-on, not cut to shit by having passed through too many hands. Nobody's touching it but me, a little, I don't want to spoil anyone. This might not last.

I ask Dean to cut me a better deal. Impossible, he says. Why? I'm turning it over fast enough, building a regular clientele. "It is what it is," he says. This is the way we talk now, the language of self-evidence: it is what it is, truth is truth, Ruth is Ruth. When you're looking to get high, when you're looking to get over, you don't waste time looking for words.

I have to find a way to keep our expenses down. If we didn't indulge ourselves, this would be a piece of cake, but if we didn't indulge, I wouldn't be dealing in the first place. I'll have to work harder. I can't work any harder. I'm taking in more money in a day than I do in a week at my job, but it all goes back into buying more. Kit complains about this; half our investment is her money. What's the point of dealing dope, she says, if you can't get it when you want? We get it when we need, I say. Sometimes when we want.

Finally, when the winter is nearly over, I make enough profit to buy a warm coat, which I don't already happen to own. It's a gangster-style thick navy wool with deep pockets and subtle red stripes in a window-pane pattern—sixty dollars at an East Side thrift store. Some profit. Now I really look like a dealer—good thing I have a job. But I don't want to depend on drugs for a living. Dealing is just a sideline.

———

"Listen," Rico confides one night. We're hanging out on his office couch. "Be nice to Sticky," he says. "Okay? He's having trouble at home. His wife is threatening to leave him and he's really depressed. So be nice."

He lays a line of coke on my belly and snorts it. It tickles but it doesn't turn me on. Rico doesn't do much for me anymore, not since I've been with Kit. She does it all, and then some.

"Nice?" I say. "I'm always nice, especially to Sticky. I love that guy." And I do. We've never touched, not a hug, not a handshake, but for six years our lives have been lived in each other's faces. He hasn't just been tolerant. He's been swell. Forget about the dealing. When I was sick, when I broke my foot on the job, when a former cook in a drug-induced rage punched me bloody in the face, Sticky was always there, paying the expenses, covering my ass. Unlike the grumpy Flint, Sticky never got temperamental, not with me. Fuck his wife—Angie is her name. She's his second, and not much older than his oldest child. I'll be nice to him, of course.

Rico puts some coke on my tongue and sucks it. In spite of myself, this turns me on. "I don't like Sticky doing dope," he says. "Man his age, with his bad colon—he's not up to it. But you know how it is. He says a little goes a long way."

"How long?" I say, reaching into his drawers. "In inches?"

———

The next night business is very bad, nothing doing in the kitchen. Pedro and I amuse ourselves by creating new dishes no one is there to eat. Then I see Sticky by the coffee machine, glumly pouring himself a cup. His head is bowed, his shoulders slump. I follow him to the office, where I find him at his desk, a shot of brandy in front of him and a bag of dope in his hand.

"Can I come in?" I ask.

"Sure," he says. "Have a seat."

"Sticky," I say. "I don't mean to get personal, but are you all right?"

"I'm just bored," he says. "If I could, I'd close this place and move on. Once I get bored with a joint, it's time to go."

"It's just boredom?"

He picks up the brandy, looks through the glass. "You really want to hear this?"

Not really. But I love this guy. I'll listen to whatever he has to say.

He hesitates. "I'm terribly shy around women," he murmurs. Well, I knew that. In all the years I've known Sticky, this is the first time he's ever looked at me.

"How'd you manage two marriages?" I ask.

"I don't know. The wives—they helped. I was always kind of a nerd." He strokes his hawklike nose and gives a smile. "It's funny," he snorts. Sticky's asthmatic. "My restaurants have always attracted the crazies, the drunks, and the drug addicts, and I was never into any of it myself. But drug addicts are some of the best people I know. Sure, they've got problems, who doesn't? They don't take life the way it's handed to them. They put on a show and the town comes to watch. And I make all the money. Or I did." He flips through the receipts on his desk with a sigh.

I wonder what's happened to the money. "Oh, you know, two wives, four kids, alimony . . ." He lifts the glass of brandy. "I never expected to go into this business," he goes on. "I have a law degree, but I never practiced. I tried it for about six months, and hated it." He smiles as his eyes fall on the bag of dope still in his hand. I offer him a line of mine. He takes it.

"I was always more interested in art," he says then, "but I wasn't much good at making it. I already had a wife and two of my kids—I had to do something. We were living in a small apartment on East Tenth. A lot of artists had studios there, they were my neighbors. They wanted a place to hang out. There was an empty storefront on the block. The rent was cheap, so I took it. I built the place myself, poured the drinks, did the cooking. Hamburgers mostly. Peanuts on the bar. When it was busy, one of the artists or their girlfriends would come in and help out. A couple of them hung their paintings on the wall, so I gave them tabs. I wasn't making any money anyway. But the word got around, and it drew people in. Good people. Nice paintings." Now he's smiling. He puts down his glass, lights a smoke.

Soon, he says, he moved to a bigger space on the other side of town, a steak house in the Village, taking the artists and the peanuts with him. This place was a mess. The floor was bad so he threw sawdust and peanut shells all over it and they became a symbol, somehow, of the good life. When he got restless, he moved again, this time to an even bigger place, three glass-fronted stories on lower Park Avenue.

It was at this place I first set eyes on Sticky. I was still in school, but his bar offered a better education, not to mention a higher life. Pop artists, poets, rockers, flaming queens and macho cowboys, black, white, gay, straight—you didn't see that at the malls. I was dazzled. Reporters were always writing about the faces they saw there, the things people said other people had done. It had glamour—good bodies, big hair, wet lips. Especially on the waitresses. Half the guys in the bar came in just to pick up waitresses. Sticky got one, too. Angie.

I offer him another line. He takes it.

A week later Rico disappears. No one knows where he is for days. Then, suddenly, there's a commotion by the coffee stand in the kitchen, where he's yelling at a waitress for neglecting to freshen a pot. He stands there, one arm shaking behind him, as he waits for the liquid to drip in his cup. I almost duck when I see him turn in my direction.

"I'm really worried about Sticky now," he tells me from the other side of my prep table. He doesn't speak so much as puff. The dark circles under his eyes are black as coal, his face a mass of competing sharp planes. I can hardly make out his form beneath his clothes. He's wasted.

"Well, I'm worried about you," I say, though I don't entirely mean it. "Where you been?"

"I'm fine," he says, swaying. I reach out to catch him but because I've been boning chickens, I'm holding a knife. It clatters to the table as he steadies himself, grips my arm.

"I'm all right," he assures me. "It's that Agent Orange shit, comes and goes. I can deal with it."

Rico thinks he's been affected by wartime exposure to toxic chemicals, but the stuff caked around his nose looks more like cocaine. He's been in a blackout, he says, but he's okay now. Woke up sitting in his car at a stoplight in a strange town in upstate New York. Doesn't know how he got there. Isn't sure how he got back. Drugs weren't the only reason I ever climbed into bed with him, but right now I can't remember what other reason there was.

Next thing we know, Sticky ends up in the hospital. He's got intestinal trouble complicated by a liver thing, don't know what. He needs an operation. A pall falls over the dining room. Crowds keep coming, but they're thinner. "How's Sticky?" they say. "Is Sticky back yet?" The room's the same, the food's the same, or better, but the customers seem lost without him. Even after he recoups, slow nights run equal to busy ones. The art world's not that big. New clubs are opening, new bistros. The same people are no longer in the same place at the same time. They come, they go. They go. *Where the artists go, the world follows.* And Sticky's is no longer the only game in town.

In April, with spring in the air, I ask Flint for a raise. He fires me. I'll collect unemployment, I don't care. Rico's upset about it, though. He cares. After some discussion, back and forth, I agree to go back part-time, prepping on the day shift, doing lunches. I'm working with Big Guy again, but it's not the same. I have a business of my own now. Drugs are no sideline. Mainline.

THE PATHOLOGY OF SEX

Abraham Verghese

1998

Through his friendship with a medical student, the physician Abraham Verghese learned about the cunning power of an addiction that can be just as deadly as alcohol or heroin. Originally published in The New Yorker, *"The Pathology of Sex" details the life of David. A onetime professional tennis player, he develops an IV cocaine habit. But what ultimately proves to be more destructive is his addiction to sex. Medical authorities have long debated the clinical terminology to categorize the pathology of compulsive sexual behavior; here the addiction itself unravels a promising future with remarkable precision.*

Had you seen my best friend, David, who was also my tennis partner and a medical student on rounds with me six years ago, nothing about his pixieish face, his ready smile, or the half-swallowed laugh that punctuated his speech would have led you to imagine that at one time he had had a terrible intravenous-cocaine habit. You might have guessed from his accent that he was an Australian. His hips, which seemed too narrow for his broad shoulders, and his light, swaying tread might have led you to think that he was a tennis player. (He had, in fact, come to America on a tennis scholarship and had played briefly on the pro tour before starting medical school.) His grace on the court—a flowing slice backhand, a compact forehand, no grip change between the two, and an unerring instinct to take to the net—was difficult to reconcile with his past habit of mainlining up to twenty times a day. Nor did it fit with his story of having had daily seizures from cocaine excess, or of biting through his tongue so many times that it became three-fourths its original size.

Had you stood with me two years later, looking down at his body as it lay on a gurney in the mortuary, though, you might have assumed that a relapse and a cardiotoxic dose of cocaine had caused his death. He did relapse, but death came from a self-inflicted shotgun wound. It would have surprised you to know that to the end David was convinced that his undoing was not cocaine. He blamed another addiction—an addiction to sex.

———

I met David shortly after I arrived in El Paso, in 1991, at about the time he was beginning his fourth year of medical school. He had spent the previous year working as a phlebotomist, regularly attending Alcoholics Anonymous and Narcotics Anonymous meetings, maintaining sobriety, and proving the sobriety with frequent urine tests—all to fulfill the conditions that the medical school had imposed in order for him to return. I take credit for reintroducing him to the simple pleasure of hitting a ball back and forth across a net. The mantra of that exchange was a soothing one for both of us, and a ritual that years of cutthroat competitive tennis had made him forget.

Our friendship was an unlikely one: a senior professor and a fourth-year medical student. On the tennis court, our roles were reversed: he was the teacher and I the student. In a sense, we were both in recovery. I was coming out of a marriage, and was living in self-imposed exile in a walkup apartment in west El Paso, while he lived in a rooming house in east El Paso—the best housing either of us could afford.

A year and a half into our friendship, on a weekend when his girlfriend was out of town, he bought cocaine, shot up, and immediately went out and got more. He was by then an intern, working very long hours. There were other reasons one could invoke: his mother had died; his ex-girlfriend had moved back to El Paso; his current girlfriend had read in his journals that he was still sexually obsessed with his ex-girlfriend, and she was furious. To anyone looking back, it was apparent that his mood had soured months before his actual use of cocaine. In recovery-speak, he had climbed back on his "pity pot," retreated to "stinking thinking," and forgotten the "attitude of gratitude." When he relapsed, he was immediately discovered and whisked away, this time to one of the best treatment facilities in the country.

When David returned, after six months of in-patient rehab, he looked healthy and muscular. He was bursting with enthusiasm, and was convinced that, finally, his real problem had been addressed: not cocaine addiction but sexual addiction. I remember how carefully he pronounced those words, as if their sound was still new and exotic. When I gently teased him about the term—it sounded like an oxymoron—he became agitated, and his eyes shone like a zealot's. My jocularity about sex was precisely the problem, he said. Sex was so all-American—the great come-on in the merchandising of everything from cars to soap, the measure of robust health, the key to all entertainment, the major focus of every talk show, the subtext of our Western materialism, and the yardstick of success. For him, though, sex was just like cocaine: he would become preoccupied with an image in a magazine or with pornography and then go into a trancelike, heightened state of sexual tension. He would try to pick up women in bars, or at work, or even at the laundromat. For the sake of a quickie, he had risked arrest, physical assault by a jealous other, and venereal disease. And, as soon as he had his sexual purging, tremendous remorse and guilt would wash over him. Then he had to make an entreaty for secrecy, and live with the fear of discovery. He would feel shame, which he could diminish, temporarily, only by beginning the cycle again. Or by using cocaine.

The passion of his argument silenced me. I was well aware that his foreignness and his politeness got him looks of interest from women at the hospital. They seemed to want to mother him and to shepherd him around town, as if he had just descended from a coolibah tree and knew nothing about the ways of West Texas. We had joked about this, but now I realized that there was much more to those flirtatious glances than I had imagined.

"I didn't know," I said.

"How would you? Those are our deepest, darkest secrets."

———

I had come to believe, as an internist and an infectious-diseases clinician, that one out of every ten patients I saw in my county hospital was there for some problem directly related to alcohol and other drug addictions: heart-valve infection, overdose, seizures, abscessed veins, hepatitis B, hepatitis C, cirrhosis, H.I.V. infection, alcohol-related cardiomyopathy, bleeding from the stomach, dementia, hepatic encephalopathy. And this estimate didn't include patients whose problems—bullet and knife wounds, motor-vehicle injuries, strokes, chronic lung disease, major depression—were indirectly related to drugs. In my fifteen years or so as a clinician, however, I had never made a diagnosis of sexual addiction.

To someone used to reading about, say, typhoid or cholera, where a discrete clinical syndrome had a single and reproducible cause—"a single switch at the center of things," as the physician Lewis Thomas has put it—the literature on sexual disorders resembled a shifting terrain. I had always thought that psychiatric diagnosis, by its very nature, was subjective: there were no simple blood tests or X-ray abnormalities to confirm a clinical suspicion. The need for psychiatrists from Bangor to Biloxi to be certain that they were referring to the same disease in their discourses spawned the *Diagnostic and Statistical Manual of Mental Disorders.* Published in 1952, and generally referred to as *DSM-I,* it listed homosexuality and nymphomania as forms of mental illness. By 1980, when *DSM-III* came out, the "disease" of homosexuality had disappeared.

Undoubtedly, this shift had much to do with the radical change that took place in the American sexual landscape in the sixties and seventies. Sex was demythologized and stripped of its puritan coat. There was a new vocabulary—"wife swapping," "one-night stands," and "cruising." The Pill, the legalization of abortion, potent cures for gonorrhea and syphilis contributed to this outpouring of societal libido. The new diseases listed in *DSM-III*—as Martin Levine and Richard Troiden have pointed out—were those of "not enough sex": anorgasmia, ejaculatory incompetence, erectile insufficiency. But sexual mores were changing once more. Herpes had dampened free love. Awareness of hepatitis B and then of AIDS made body fluids a hazard. There were clearly risks to sexual overgrazing. It was time for the emergence of a new ethic, that of "too much sex," with its associated new diseases.

In 1983, Patrick Carnes, a former prison psychologist, published "The Sexual Addiction," a book that put this term on the professional map and also generated great interest in the lay press. Carnes had first observed sexual addicts in the seventies, but did not publish his book on sexual addiction until the eighties, because it was "an idea whose time had not come." Carnes was not the first, however, to see sexuality through the lens of addiction. Bill Wilson, in the A.A. bible—the Big

Book, written in 1939—alludes to it: "Now about sex. Many of us needed an overhauling there. It's so easy to get way off the track.... We all have sex problems. We'd hardly be human if we didn't." His suggestion was that each relationship be subjected to the test of whether it was selfish or not, and that the alcoholic pray for guidance and strength to do the right thing.

In the mid-seventies, a member of a Boston A.A. group began to practice "sexual sobriety," modifying the traditional A.A. twelve steps to focus on his compulsive sexual need. He formed Sex and Love Addicts Anonymous, and their Big Book equivalent appeared in 1986. Its first two chapters tell a compelling personal story that is not dissimilar to David's. (When I met David, he had already been married and divorced twice.)

Given the universality of sex, much rests on the definition of what constitutes sexual addiction. Carnes described it as a "pathological relationship with a mood altering experience"—the emphasis resting on the experience or on a behavior rather than on a drug or a chemical. Sexual addicts were those whose sexual behavior had become unstoppable, despite serious consequences: job loss, breakdown of the family, sexually transmitted diseases, unwanted pregnancy.

Patrick Carnes developed a twenty-five-question sexual-addiction screening test. In it, a response in the affirmative to thirteen questions or more suggests addiction. Some of the questions are clear-cut: Have you had sex with minors? Were you abused as a child? Do your parents have a history of trouble with sexual behavior? But others are disturbing in their generality: Have you subscribed to or regularly purchased sexually explicit magazines? Have you ever worried about people finding out about your sexual activities? Has sex been a way to escape your problems?

David's behavior, if viewed through the Carnes model of sexual addiction, stemmed from a "personal belief system" (the programming about sex and relationships which one receives from parents and society) that was very "sex negative." When coupled with low self-esteem, such a belief system resulted in a lasting shamefulness. Then, according to Carnes, an individual could enter an obsessive cycle of sexual behavior. Carnes posited a progression of untreated addiction. The initiation phase was characterized by pivotal sexual acts or experiences that were seared into the memory. In the establishment phase, there was a repetition of an addictive cycle of preoccupation, ritualization, and sexual acting out, followed by shame and guilt. The behavior could then escalate, or, at times, deëscalate, or be subsumed into another addictive behavior, or it could progress to an acute phase. Carnes's model certainly seemed to fit what David had told me about his own behavior.

The use of the word "addiction" in the context of sex generated intense controversy. Psychiatrists, psychologists, sexologists, and addictionists stepped in: some felt that the disorder was best characterized as sexual compulsivity; others thought it to be sexual impulsivity; and still others proposed it to be a variant of obsessive-compulsive disorder. Perhaps because of the lack of consensus, the term "sexual addiction" does not appear in *DSM-III* or *DSM-IV,* which was published in 1994. Yet what Carnes would call sexual addiction is listed under "Sexual Disorder Not Otherwise Specified," with one of three cited examples being "Distress about a pattern of repeated sexual relationships involving a succession of lovers who are experienced by the individual only as things to be used."

If the American Psychiatric Association chose to be coy or conservative about whether sexual addiction exists or not, this wasn't the case with the public. It was a catchy new phrase, bringing new life to the topic of sex just when it appeared that there was little more to say about it. Soon it was trotted out by well-known people, such as Dick Morris and the late Michael Kennedy, who had been caught in embarrassing situations. The phrase brought with it a certain protective mantle.

———

One of the more vocal critics of the idea of sexual addiction is Marty Klein, a California marriage counsellor and sex therapist whose home page on the Web is entitled "Ask Me Anything." In his published work Dr. Klein has expressed concern that people are diagnosing their conditions as sexual addiction, and that the sexual-addiction movement is aggressively training non-sexologists in the treatment of sexual problems. Sex addicts now have a cachet as sex experts: Ted Bundy, on the basis of his statements before he was put to death for his serial killings, is viewed as both the proof of and the expert on the deleterious effects of pornography. Implicit in the sexual-addiction model, Klein thinks, are unstated beliefs that the "goal" of sex is intimacy, that sex outside a monogamous, loving, heterosexual relationship is less healthy, and that there should be limits to sexual expression—seen notably, for example, in the theory that masturbating more than once a day isn't healthy. But these beliefs are far from universal, even in our own society. "Many people who are labelled sexual addicts feel out of control," Klein said when I spoke with him recently. "But they confuse *feeling* out of control with *being* out of control. I happen to love chocolates, and if there's a box of chocolates in the room I feel out of control and I make a choice to eat chocolate, because I like it. That's not the same as being out of control."

Klein sees the sexual-addiction model as moralistic, arbitrary, misinformed, and narrow. "There is no sense of healthy pornography, healthy sadomasochism, healthy non-monogamy. It's not a question of right and wrong. The sexual-addiction model is a very limited one."

A concern of critics of the sexual-addiction model is how easily it plays into the hands of the right wing. In the mid-eighties, the climate created by the Meese Commission on Pornography and the activities of organizations such as the National Federation for Decency and Citizens Against Pornography, whose head claimed that "smut causes sex addiction," prompted 7-Eleven to stop selling *Playboy* and *Penthouse* in its stores. Klein fears that sexual addiction appears to provide a scientific basis for the intuitive belief that sex is dangerous. In his view, many of us feel some kind of shame about our sexuality—either about our overt behavior or about the more primitive urges and images left over from childhood. It is a shame that we seek to rid ourselves of. The behavioral symptoms that we are supposedly addicted to are just a symbol of that shame. We have walked this path before: sexual behavior seen as sin, and then sin being called a sickness; one has only to look at early psychiatry's work with homosexuality. "When you have a disease, the metaphor is different," Klein said to me. "The moral issues are less. We look down on a drunkard, but we have sympathy for the alcoholic. And when you have a disease, then the insurance industry gets in."

David undertook group and individual therapy in order to treat his sexual addiction. The goal of his treatment, he said, was thirty to ninety days of abstinence from all sexual activities, including masturbation, and then a gradual return to "normal" sex. When David returned to El Paso, he told me that he now tried to avoid all sexually explicit material. He said that he also had a "three-second" rule—that was the longest he allowed himself to focus on a sexual thought. Central to his recovery were local group meetings of fellow sex addicts. The new David was preoccupied with meetings and recovery in the same way that I imagine he had previously been preoccupied with sex. His meetings followed the A.A. format, with the substitution of the words "sex and love addiction" for "alcohol." His first step was therefore to admit that he was powerless over his sex and love addiction. We had been able to talk about everything, but it soon became awkward for us to talk about sex, or even joke about it. When I brought up the subject, I felt as if I were waving a whiskey flask under the nose of a recovering dipsomaniac.

Dr. Eli Coleman, in his thoughtful writings on the subject of compulsive sexual behavior—the term he prefers to "sexual addiction"—points out that restrictive or conservative attitudes toward sexuality may be a precursor to compulsive sexual behavior. If the traditional proscriptive treatment of a twelve-step program—abstinence—merely reinforces these attitudes, it may actually contribute to the compulsive behavior. Coleman is a professor and the director of the Program in Human Sexuality at the University of Minnesota Medical School, and is also a member of the Society for the Scientific Study of Sexuality. "It's interesting that we use the term 'compulsive gambling,' but when it comes to sex we speak of 'sexual addiction,'" Dr. Coleman said when I talked to him recently. "I think it's because of our tendency to take anything that is out of the ordinary sexually and give it a heavily laden label. 'Addiction' is an oversimplification of a complex phenomenon. The historical vestige of an addiction approach to sexual disorders is unfortunate. It helps, but in the approach is an implication that it is *the* way, as opposed to *a* way." Coleman points out that even if an individual's behavior is in conflict with the prevailing value system he may have a problem but not necessarily a compulsion.

Once, I told David that hitting on one of his fellow medical students was something that his girlfriend, whose patience was wearing thin, could not possibly approve of, and he blamed his sexual addiction. He could admit his addiction—but he believed that he had no power over his behavior. Klein and Coleman both think that the feeling of "powerlessness" is manageable, and that it can respond to psychological therapy or intervention. They believe that one's sexual behavior—unless the problem is compounded by a true obsessive-compulsive disorder or a mood disorder—is under one's control.

———

To find the "single switch at the center of things" would eliminate much of the controversy surrounding sexual disorders. If the billions of neutrons in the brain are viewed as the "hardware" of the brain, then the "software" consists of the learning or memories that we accumulate. Behavior, or the software, has in this century been viewed as the territory of the psychiatrist or the psychologist. The discovery, in 1978, of naturally occurring chemicals—known as neurotransmitters—with morphinelike (or opioid) activity, was a remarkable development. These opioids (enkephalins and endorphins) are released from the tips of neurons to act on specific receptors on other neurons. The finding suggested that even psychological disorders must arise through chemical changes.

The prime target area for research is a teleologically older part of the brain, the medial forebrain bundle. This area is, in effect, a pathway for both reward and, possibly, punishment, and is acted on by natural opioids. The balance between opposing opioids probably determines one's state of mind, signalling "good," for example, when hunger and thirst are satisfied, or after a long, pleasurable run, or when a sexual act is consummated, and signalling "bad" when pain is experienced or when risky behavior is engaged in. Drugs such as Prozac act by altering the levels of discrete neurotransmitters, as do cocaine and LSD. But the precise biological substrate for compulsive sexual disorders—something that would distinguish them from non-compulsive behavior—has still to be defined. Yet, as Dr. Avram Goldstein, a pioneer in the discovery of neurotransmitters, has written, "it is not a question of psychology *versus* biology; on the contrary, in the final analysis (but our present knowledge falls far short) psychology *is* biology."

———

The prospect of a biological model—a twisted molecule behind every form of twisted behavior—is seductive. Eventually, perhaps, *DSM-V*, or one of its descendants, will categorize sexual disorders at the neurotransmitter level, in the same way that we now speak of "good" and "bad" cholesterol. But such a classification might merely reflect new attitudes in society: abnormal sexuality as a form of Prozac deficiency and a pill taking the place of a twelve-step program.

Such a questionable advance is many years away. Meanwhile, it seems to me dangerous to isolate someone's sexual behavior and to regard it as somehow apart from the rest of him. If another young doctor with as much promise as David were to tell me the same tale that David told me, I would find no satisfaction in applying the sexual-addiction label. At best, it would be an allegory rather than an explanation.

I remember how extraordinary it was to see David in full flow on the tennis court, how his impeccable timing on the backhand allowed him to take the ball on the rise and send it back on a laser path. It appeared to me, then and now, that no mere coming together of brain and muscle could fully explain this beauty. Is it an act of hubris to think that we can ever fully fathom human behavior? The tension between our old "reptilian" brain and our new brain, between our limbic system and our neocortex, between our primitive urges and our cognitive mind—all metaphors of our own invention—is at the essence of being human. Perhaps this is why we watch with such interest the behavior of others around us. We realize that in everyone we see ourselves.

They Take a Photograph of You When You First Get Here

Kate Braverman

1998

During the 1960s the writer Kate Braverman discovered drugs while she was a student at the University of California at Berkeley. At the time she considered drug use an experiment to test the bounds of creativity—a revolutionary act in keeping with the rising tide of feminism and the political movement against racism and the Vietnam War. Since that time she has written four novels about addiction, including the 1979 cult classic Lithium for Medea, *and numerous short stories that detail the lives of addicts. "They Take a Photograph of You When You First Get Here" depicts a young woman's journey through the rigors of drug rehab.*

They take a photograph of you when you first get here. They say study it. Take a good look. This is the before. Call it early sobriety.

I examine my photograph. I'm curled on my side on a cot. I don't have a clock. I don't know what month it is. I don't know what season it is. I don't know where I am. None of this bothers me.

I chain-smoke. I wear sunglasses at all times. I feel coated in a thick whitish film, like I've been painted with cornstarch or glue. I feel laminated. I feel like I'm stuck inside of a photograph of myself. I've been taped between pages of cellophane. I'm an inanimate object, a stylized representation, and I'm trying to break out. I've somehow coalesced in only two dimensions. I don't even know how or why I manage to keep breathing.

It's a stalled afternoon, and it feels permanent. The earth keeps spinning but the buildings don't fall. It's about gravity and axis and space. It's about inventing and memorizing hierarchies and pretending the debris matters. It's about some eighteen-year-old man walking through ice to his job selling shoes in downtown Boston. He walks because he doesn't have train fare. This has nothing to do with me.

—

A woman enters. Soft floral-print dress with more flowers stitched on the collar and cuffs. Pink sweater. Pastel shoes. Trying not to threaten. Fake pearl earrings. She's got gingham curtains in her kitchen. She believes in ruffles. She makes pancakes and waffles.

"I'm Susan. I interviewed you yesterday." Big smile. Blue eyes. I wonder how she'd look with a matching blue bruise on her cheek. Something the size of a robin's egg.

I examine my photograph. I am wearing a yellowish hospital pants suit. I'm barefoot and look like I smell rancid. And I wonder what Susan and I could have spoken about? Mozart and God? Women in Congress? The triumph of global capitalism as the millennial statement, its currency and philosophy? Or perhaps we talked about taxing crack and supplying addicts with clean needles?

This Susan exudes that Girl Scout troop leader enthusiasm that AA matrons get in their forties, instead of sex or power. "You're in Villa de Palma, Chemical Detox Unit," she explains. "You'll be here six weeks. Then you move to the halfway house."

I'm imagining Susan's face with a split lip. I'm considering the slope of her chin with a wired jaw. Could she still offer that mile-long, just-polished corridor of smile? I'm wondering how her face would look with one eye gouged out and an asymmetrical glass replacement. I decide to roll up in a small ball with the pillow on top of my head. I will, of course, never speak again.

—

I dream about Sapphire. Or perhaps it is not a dream but the reconstruction of events that only trapped images know. The photo in the album can dream at will. And the inmate in a locked ward. There are no comas, only invisible stairways into landscape. The maple in fall, burning red and yellow, loves you. Night is not a requirement.

Sapphire and I are running, crossing miniature square parks like gullies, grassy arroyos. We dart across boulevards, we jog down side streets. The dogs know us and keep back. The neon turns shy when we pass. The city is a body with crevices, places to nestle and curl. The Los Angeles night is like an ocean with currents and ports. I am a vessel and I don't need wind, don't need charts. Night is filled with the sounds of bells above waves, a seared harbor. It's always the eve of a fiesta, and there are too many sails.

"What is it?" Sapphire asks, sensing something. He listens to the darkness, tests the waters. He has his denim-blue notebook with his poems written in calligraphy in a special cobalt pen. He also has a flashlight and a semiautomatic Beretta with nine hydroshock hollowpoint bullets. He's got a handful of syringes wrapped in a cotton bandanna.

"It's the laments of abandoned women. It's a night for mourning, for counting up the drownings," I tell him.

"You need a calculator for that," Sapphire laughs.

Moon glitters on his one gold earring. The urban night is intimate and specific. Sapphire knows darkness is dense with unusual currents. He's an alchemist. He mixes potions. He knows the proportions and how much powder and fluid are necessary to temporarily restrain evil. This is the impulse that made science begin.

We are winding down a narrow alley overgrown on the edges with bougainvillea and oleander. We are aiming west and we breathe easily. On balconies women water geraniums and dwarf roses, and I realize they have recently been betrayed or widowed. That's why they're howling.

We reach the pier, we know where the wire siding has been cut and we slide in. We have candles there, a mattress, blankets, silk sheets, a battery powered CD player and books. We have bags of cans we collected at the food bank. We have salmon and caviar and herring in white cream sauce. We have cherries in thick syrup and hearts of palm. This is what rich people give to food drives.

Sapphire offers me caviar. He extends a curled finger encrusted with black eggs and I crawl to him and lick it off. If I bark, he will stroke my neck and call me good dog, good dog.

I am trying to frame a thought about harbors and wharves, how they all smell of ruined canvas and shells with the crusts of edible things dried, dead, like so many gutted black peaches. Nobody thinks about pearls anymore, or placing a shell to your ear. Everyone knows there are no answers.

Later Sapphire melts the tiny brown pebbles in a spoon. He fills the syringe. I offer my arm. This is how you make time and space stop. This is how they collide, lie down side by side and make love. It is the only conjunction that matters.

When the universe curves into itself it is a grave gesture, elegant with restraint and grief. It makes me think of thunderstorms and what I imagine Paris must be. There are boulevards where people stumble uncertain between lightning and premonitions. It is a festival of forgetting. It is a time of only cobalt and aqua and a burning rain. Rivers blister your hands. Well water makes you puke. There are no more lullabies, no more orchids, no more names for daughters.

"If we had a daughter, I would name her Ariel or Annabell," I say. "I could name her Amethyst."

"No way." Sapphire uses the bad dog, bad dog voice. It's a warning.

Farther up and down the beach are tiny fires from other night dwellers. They are cooking potatoes and heroin. I imagine history has always looked like this. An ocean where candles burn by corpses laid randomly on sand. It is a season of hallucination and drunkenness and too many reeds and guitars. Taverns are crowded with veiled women and convicts. It's a time of consecutive full moons. Orbs loiter in the skies. They seem superimposed, radioactive, multiplying. There is too much polluted silver. Its shine could make you blind. It is best to hide your face.

But you cannot look down, either. The tide drags in strange sea mammals. They are bloated, the blue of fantastic rocks or flowers or stars. They wear the skin of waves. They are tattooed in the only manner that matters. This is what you cannot laser off. This is the sacrifice that lingers and defines you. This is the point of no return. This is how you know the world loves you.

"Do you love me?" I ask Jimmy Sapphire.

"Love is an inadequate coordinate," he says.

"Who am I?" I try, not certain whether I am thinking or talking. It is often raining inside my head. I am an oval filled with fluids. I am Prague and Lisbon. I have plazas and pigeons and bridges. Barges float heavy behind my eyes. They carry piles of silver haddock and sacks of mangoes. There are always bells.

"Who are you?" Sapphire repeats. "You're a gypsy and a time traveler, and I've given you a home."

"Is that significant?" I'm not sure I want this answer.

Sapphire considers the implications. It's a turquoise gully. It's a soft lavender gap. Everything about Sapphire is a form of blue. The bay he lives beside, the night he lives in, the way he distills fluid essences from powders and transports them into your blue veins. After this liquid pause in which ships sail and return, in this pale violet that could be a communion but isn't, he says, "No."

I listen to the waves. I think about stars and how Sapphire has a capacity for illicit alliances and what they may be worth. He has a gift for bargaining. He carries foreign coins that he claims are antiques smuggled from royal tombs. I have seen them, and they are ordinary bits of European change, disks of tin you'd give a bus driver in Amsterdam or Madrid.

He's a liar. His sequin shawls come from secondhand stores and thrift shops. They are not stolen tapestries. He can't read palms, either. He hasn't memorized the tarot. And he cannot predict death.

"It's not about truth," Sapphire would say. "DNA made truth obsolete."

"Then what's it about?" I would feel compelled to continue. I would be removing my sweat shirt. I would be offering him my swan arm. He can penetrate it with metal. He can saw it off.

"It's about amusement," Sapphire would say. "The dance of synapses. A few images. A metaphor between drownings. Admit it. You're never bored."

I have to concur. Nothing is dull anymore. My heart beats so fast I feel it's going to break through my chest. My organs are projectiles. I have learned certain things. I know the chant of fishermen. It is the secret of navigation and how to tame and seduce what swims. This is the litany that fills the nets. This is the method by which one masters the intricacies of breathing violet.

I have come to recognize that sounds combine in darkness, find other elements, transmute, become a fragrance, a pathway and a resolution. This is how one learns to trap stars and sculpt faces from clay. This is the sound rivers make and why women cover their heads and wear veils.

Sapphire has no comprehension of how much I've deciphered and remembered. In my dream, in my recreation of things as they almost were, in my subtle variations, I know I will soon confront him. This is inevitable. One twilight the color of crushed iris I will tell him he's a fraud. I will give him my evidence, assembled stem by stem, like a spring bouquet. My lines of revelation will be unassailable, the way calla lilies are, tulips and sweet william. I'm not a time traveler. I remember my address. I know where I live. But now there is only a sudden desire to sleep.

———

I toss and drift in forms of blue. I'm a swimmer, a virgin, a flame of water. I offer my arm.

"Beg me," Sapphire says.

"You are all things. You are why I pray. You are why I read poems and rob. You are a jewel. I place bouquets at your feet. I kiss your feet. I order schoolgirls to kneel before you. You will live forever," I say. I hold my arm out into the unsolid night.

"Convince me," Sapphire urges. He is staring into the bay. There are no lines, only gradations of violet. This is the color for penning love letters. It's a night for a tattoo.

"You are all kisses beneath palms. I wish you clairvoyant lovers who will promise you a calm world," I say. I will say anything. I am breathless. My arm is beginning to tremble.

"You're running out of stories," Sapphire says. He sounds resigned. He touches my arm with his index finger. "Let me tell you one. In Vietnam, the army medics inoculated village children. When they came back, they found a field of tiny amputated arms. They looked like doll arms. That's what the parents did. Sawed off the demon spots. Do you have marks of demonic visitation?"

I hold out my arm. My bruises are dark purple in the crushed iris night. They are tangled like grapevines. I say, "Yes."

"Do you think evil can be removed?" Sapphire is philosophical. Dawn is when he thinks he's lucid.

I say, "Yes."

Sapphire laughs. He keeps laughing. I am not worth answering, not with words or gestures. The water laps. The water beats. I shake and sweat and weep. I am lying on sand, but I feel underwater, like I'm drifting, partially submerged. There are equations of blue, there are geometries you can sail to and fluid architectures. They have their forces and properties. They have mouths but they refuse to speak.

———

In this place, they take your photograph when you first get here. I wear sunglasses when I sleep. They press into my face, sealing off my eyes. They were portals once, but I've cleverly soldered them shut. Everyone thinks I'm deformed now. But I'm camouflaged, preparing for secret actions.

This is how all discovery is made. First we see the interiors, what is most pure in objects, in a handful of wild oats, one white candle, the inexorable tide. Our voices are waves, and when we open our mouths to speak, the ocean flows in. These are not syllables or words but a sequence of broken amethyst. We learn to distill such waters and walk beside them, in a breeze composed of a subtle mesh, pale as a memory of larkspur. Then we hear foghorns and music from boats.

"You look better today," my counselor, Susan, says.

"How can you tell?" I decide to ask.

"You're not having convulsions," she replies. "You've stopped vomiting. And your color is better. You looked mottled last week, like marble."

Susan presents me with a paper bag containing a hairbrush, a toothbrush, and a bar of soap. I will not use these implements under any circumstances. Personal hygiene is irrelevant to a woman who doesn't know what year it is.

"Are you ready to tell me your name?" Susan asks, optimistically.

"Margarite," I say. I like the way it fills the air, like a woman donning a complicated antique opera dress, something with silk layers and rows of concealed buttons. It's a vivid name, a Matisse name, somehow tropical and magenta, but restrained. You could sweep down a corridor in such a name and there would be nothing improper about it.

"That's not true," Susan sighs, disappointed. She's an umpire for law and order. She keeps track while God is busy.

I have given her a different name every time she asks. Barbara. Maureen. Sylvia. Denise. Laura. Colleen. I glance at Susan, imagining her with a thick red scar running from below her left eye to her neck. Not a single scar line, like a knife makes, but rather something with branches like a river. The sort of scar a mountain lion or a jaguar might etch.

In a room nearby, someone is listening to Peruvian flute music. I heard it yesterday, too. I almost like it. I like what it isn't, namely Chopin and Mozart. Classical music makes me sick. My mother watched me practice my piano. She timed me. I would play badly, deliberately, thinking about rain and how my mother was pacing just behind my shoulder with a stopwatch. My mother never saw a house that contained a piano until she was twenty-six. That was the year she graduated from her first college. She attended the university in alternative years. In between, she was a grocery store checker. It took her eight years to get her undergraduate degree.

My mother always gave me music boxes, for my birthday, for Christmas, music boxes with porcelain ballerinas spinning on the carved or lacquered tops. I wasn't graceful. I wasn't even musical. What was her agenda, anyway? What was the subtext?

My father kept pushing Bach. I found Bach impossible, autumnal in all the wrong ways. It was beyond retro. It was like a wire mesh of rain, a sort of monsoon that could cut you. It was like a math class you did with your fingers. My father listened on the periphery while I thought about gray stones and bridges across pewter rivers where everyone carried umbrellas and believed Jesus Christ was the light at the end of the tunnel. It was worse than square dancing. It was worse than quilting.

"It's so unequivocally traditional," I used to try to tell them. "You were a revolutionary. Dad burned his draft card. Can't you see this is reactionary?"

"Don't be puerile," my mother would answer, wearing the stopwatch around her neck. "There are patterns to civilization. And this is one of them."

The Peruvian flute music, on the other hand, is cool. In this music, they have not yet invented the industrial revolution that leads to excessive punctuality or the failed experiment they call the nuclear family. This is the music of elements, untarnished, unrehearsed. It's clouds resting against mountains above cocoa leaves and one red flower surrendering to rain as if it had been born for just that seduction.

My father would listen to my piano practice while he was doing something else, thinking about the stochastic nature of the universe and the value of a disciplined mind. Whenever I think of my father, I want a hallucinogen. It's a sudden craving. I see paisley everywhere, and I want to melt into it.

I close my eyes, carefully, so they don't fall out of their sockets. It's possible I'm going deaf. It could be a side effect of the flute music. Or living under the pier for six months, with all the garbage washing up in the tide, old hospital gauze, soft unrecognizable objects that might be body parts.

I think about changing my clothes, but I'm convinced there's an aviary in my closet. There are acres of butterflies inside, so many, so thick, they could be a bolt of fabric or a silk kimono tacked to the wall.

I've always thought objects have a life force, personalities and intentions. I've seen wall hangings more interesting than the people who own them.

———

Apparently it's a visit-your-neighbor's-cell day. Some anorexic woman with a bad perm, really the remnants of a malevolent hair curling experience, has walked without knocking into my room. She seems to be evaluating it on a serious level, like a real estate agent, sizing it up, weighing the possibilities, how it would look if you knocked down a wall, put in a sunken alcove, bay windows, a balcony. You'd be shocked what a little hand-painted tile can do, a few oak shelves. I am still refusing all hygiene products. I am still wearing my sunglasses and hospital pajamas.

"I'm Bonnie," she offers.

"Okay," I say. "If that works for you."

"What's your name?"

"Debby," I reply. "I'm leaving today."

"Where are you from?" Bonnie asks.

"Cincinnati," I say. "My father was Iranian. He committed suicide. He died alone, like a dog, on the floor. He turned blue."

"That's terrible," Bonnie says.

"He molested me and my brothers. It was for the best." I'm beginning to enjoy this visit. I bum a cigarette.

"Do you have any hobbies?" Bonnie wants to know.

"I collect rain in old jam jars, mostly," I tell her. "And coins. I have a penny collection. I also bake breads."

She's only asked three questions, but if this visit goes to twenty, I won't be able to endure it. I haven't asked her anything and I don't plan to. She doesn't seem to notice.

"What are you in for?" Bonnie inquires. She's leaned forward, vaguely conspiratorial.

"Please?" I read that phrase in a European novel and I like it. Asking for clarification, but subtle.

"Drugs? Alcohol? Did you snuff somebody?" Bonnie asks. That is question number five.

"Of course not. I'm happily married to an attorney. I have two sons in Little League."

Bonnie smokes another cigarette. She studies the wall as if planning to hang something cheery on it, maybe some Monet haystacks or lilies.

"You're full of it," she decides. "Everybody knows you're just a local junky. Everybody knows your pimp is dead."

"That's a lie," I say, my voice rising. I don't believe her. Sapphire is coming to spring me at any moment. I've never doubted that.

"He's the one dead as a dog. Washed up in front of the new Loew's Hotel. Belly up like a diseased seal. Something ate the edges. They had to identify him from his dental records." Bonnie smiles. She's got buck teeth and her hand is on the door. "Have a nice day," she says.

———

The person down the hall has switched to Gregorian chants. It makes me think that at the edge of the world there are walled courtyards where burlap-draped monks kneel at dawn to open their throats to the sky.

I suddenly remember being in Golden Gate Park in San Francisco with my mother. She was giving a lecture at Berkeley and we spent the afternoon in the gardens. It was late April and everything was blooming on cue. We walked through a recreation of a Biblical garden, each plant, flower, and herb something mentioned in the Old Testament. Then a garden where my mother bent down to smell each plant, the fragrant, the bitter, that which was like onion and lemon, and something like gin. My mother began to cry.

"I can feel the edge of my life," she said. "I've never felt that before. I was always moving. The vastness was incalculable. It was like the Pacific to someone in a canoe. I didn't think it had an end. But I have finally reached the border."

I looked up and saw the tops of trees, a domed building, something that might have been lilac or wisteria. My mother was talking about borders and I was looking for a guy with a machine gun in a guard tower.

"Now I know all city parks are the same. Hyde Park. The bluffs above Santa Monica. The Tuileries. Just paths beneath trees where people walk in varying states of heartbreak. Staggering between divorces and biopsies. And at the edge, one final row of lavender azaleas."

I couldn't think of anything to say. Her intensity was nauseating. It was like AA. There was nothing personal in it. It was late April. The wind seemed tinged with burlap and canvas and a sense of warm rain. When I looked at my mother, her lower lip was quivering.

"This is how you can see a heart as it breaks," my mother said, seemingly composed. "The eyes lie. And the voice. You can learn to control that. But watch the lips. That's where you can really chart it."

The Gregorian chant is playing still or again. It is essential that the song does not vary. It must sound as if ordained. It is the music you hear when lighting a candle, when you know it is a tiny captured sun you hold and the flame at the end is the first and last spark in the universe.

I do not believe Jimmy Sapphire is dead. I don't like the shape of my thoughts. I decide to think only in Spanish. It's a more fluid and fragrant language. The glare of the lamp is intrusive. I've been wanting to do this for days, pick it up and hurl it to the floor. The base is glass, and I walk back and forth through the shards. I don't feel a thing. Later I wrap my torn feet in a yellow pajama top I find folded in the closet, which is not filled with birds, not even a few stray sparrows. I look at the glass on the floor, the sudden splinters, the accidental precision of a randomly broken world, an anatomy you can actually grind your flesh into.

When my counselor points at my feet and asks what it means, I say, "It's a fashion statement."

———

It's apparently a day for group indoctrination. It's my turn to deal with the twelve-step do-gooders, the former pillheads and dopers who can't get the disease out of their system. It's a way of life for them. It's like golf. It gets them out of the house and gives them purpose. They say they're not a religious cult, but their whole program is about sin and redemption, God and prayer.

There are nineteen drug addicts of varying description in my group. We're supposed to be exploring our senses. Last week, while

I was still locked up, they all ate oranges and talked about the taste and what it meant to them. Today, they're smelling perfumes. There are dozens of bottles and vials in the center of the table, and people pass them around like joints, taking a whiff or two and handing the bottle on.

Some gray-haired woman who looks like you think your grand-mother should look before all the old women got face lifts and started playing tennis, is talking about what she calls female procedures and how she failed to learn them. She realized it occurred during her ado-lescence, but she had no friends then. Fragrance was something that came to her later in life, almost in middle age. She never under-stood what suited her so she just purchased what was popular and ex-pensive.

She holds up a bottle that contains the best-selling perfume of the year. She passes it around our circle and I take a deep breath. It smells like a corrupted vanilla, a genetically engineered vanilla, perhaps, laced with metallic properties. It is sharp, not like citrus, but rather like a harbor that's been mined. The oil is thick and seems to indicate what may be explosive properties. It's a vanilla like an unexpected tattoo, a fire burn, or what happens to a body when it's been two or three nights in ocean water.

There is nothing subtle about this scent. This is not a fragrance dis-tilled by tradition, one that asserts an ordered world where you know the names of your sons before they are born. This is insistent, almost strident, like the core of instinct.

Of course, this has nothing to do with me. The old-fashioned grandmother is saying women don't wear the suggestion of lilac any-more because implication is no longer enough. They demand neon scents now, mean and inescapable, like a heat missile.

When it is my turn to speak, I say, "I have no thoughts on this sub-ject."

"I see," the leader, some big-shouldered man who looks neutered, says.

"You don't see shit. You don't see a single thing. You aren't even blind," I tell him. Then I limp out of the room.

———

They take a photograph on your first family-visit day. They say you'll want to save it. They say it's indelible.

232 · Under the Influence

It's the end of July and all the blues have been used up. They have
been leached from the air. They have been temporarily removed. They
have faded. They are less than bruises. My boyfriend who took the
name of a jewel as his alias doesn't come to see me. He overdosed and
something chewed off his leg from the thigh down as he bobbed in the
light blue early morning surf. Something kissed his feet after all, kissed
and swallowed in an act of sublime love. It wasn't death but passion
such as must be common on distant worlds, or in other times or regions.
This knowledge is the fundamental basis of all rumor and nightmare.

My mother and father move slowly across the drying grass, through
the day that has separated into frames in two dimensions. It occurs to
me that they're moving slowly because they are weighted down by so
much integrity it's hard to get any momentum going. My father, the
draft-card burner and Bach fan. I've heard it all, the entire litany, how
he was shunned by his petit-bourgeois family, left to fend for himself
in Boston in winter. He was eighteen years old, without bus fare, hik-
ing through ice to his job selling shoes, walking to six years of manual
labor, roofing, plumbing, carrying boxes and bags on his back like a
pack animal while all his friends went to med school. My father, almost
dying twice in Massachusetts General Hospital from pneumonia.

We are all alone, the three of us, in a room with only one exit, and
they are standing in front of it. It's a temporary lobby of some sort,
with a piano, a bookcase, a Persian rug with mute flowers like petals
floating in a bay. They look like severed mouths. They look like the last
sound you make before you drown. No one asks me to play the piano.

"I always knew this would happen," my mother begins. "I knew
when you were twelve."

"Knew what?" I ask. I wear sunglasses. My feet are bandaged. The
day is composed of sheared glass. Agate morning. Amber noon. Petty
yellow everywhere. Stilted yellow. Stalled and soiled, urine and grease.
I'm not going to play any more waltzes or sonatinas. I'm not going back
to college.

"That you'd run off with some guy named for an insect or a reptile,"
my mother says. "Some lowlife called Spider or Scorpion or Snake."

I don't bother to correct her, to tell her I loved someone with the
facets of a jewel. He exposed the underbelly, he unzipped it and I entered into the nuances and I learned how to navigate them.

"Don't you want to know how I feel?" I ask.

"We know how you feel," my mother says. "You were a bored college girl. Then a guy with a dirty mouth took off your dress. Now you think you possess the secret of the universe."

Someone from the staff arrives, a boy with a dark blue crescent moon tattooed on his right hand. He serves tea in porcelain cups with rosebuds and gold rims. I wonder how the cup would look with its golden lip bitten off. Then the boy takes the photograph. It's a Polaroid. I get to keep it after my parents leave.

I stand in my room while the sun goes down. I hold the photograph, looking intently into the edges, the periphery. I am trying to hear what they are thinking. My father is white in this black-and-white picture. His features seem dug in, as if with a scalpel. There is an absence of sound. He is not mentally calculating square roots while hammering a roof in Boston. He is not thinking about mathematics or Bach while walking through a snowdrift to a job that humiliates him. He has come to the end of equations, the final plaza where there are no bells, no cathedrals, no statues of poets, no view of the harbor. There is gray and gray only, and there will never be anything other than this moment when they carve a mouth for you with a razor. It is the concept of a mouth, an illusion, a sort of cartoon. It's a jagged hole and that's okay because it is the end of words.

I don't have to look at my mother's face. She has realized that at the end of her world is a row of lavender azaleas and one other structure she never noticed before. Beyond this hedge of indifferent vegetation, there is a room where they keep her only daughter locked.

There is a palm tree on the absolute periphery, outside the wrought iron grated balcony. There is a bench below on the lawn, and a paler area of shadow. I do not look at my mother's face. I don't have to. She is thinking she was wrong, with the stopwatch, with Chopin. There is no civilization. There are no patterns. There is nothing worth remembering, not orally, not with musical notation. You roof a house. You make a stand. Floating things eat your feet. Strangers violate your children. There is a scent of putrid vanilla rising from the plaza. It is mixed in with the blood and rags. It is the fragrance of some violent aftermath. It is a perfume for women who choose to live in a blackout, in a region where forgiveness has either been rendered obsolete or not yet invented. Prophecy. Superstition. The third planet from the sun is now and has always been a world of barbarians.

I know, from the feel of the photograph, from some essence in the fiber of the moist glossy paper, from some subtle interplay of light and shadow that travels through the neurons of my fingers, that my mother's lip is permanently quivering.

HOLY HUNGER: A MEMOIR OF DESIRE

Margaret Bullitt-Jonas

1998

The daughter of privileged though emotionally withholding parents, Margaret Bullitt-Jonas learned as a child to numb her overwhelming sense of confusion and despair by overeating. Though she did not particularly enjoy the food she consumed, Bullitt-Jonas used her frequent secret binges as a coping mechanism that carried her well into adulthood. Finally, while enrolled at Harvard, she began the arduous task of stopping her lethal habit. In this excerpt from Holy Hunger: A Memoir of Desire, *Bullitt-Jonas recounts the role that Overeaters Anonymous played in her recovery from food addiction.*

Many years after I stopped eating compulsively, long after I walked into my first meeting of Overeaters Anonymous, at once anxious and hopeful, wary and eager, with my eyes downcast, my heart pounding with anxiety, and my coat wrapped tightly around my bulging body (having gained twenty pounds in the past six weeks), I happened to see a clip from *Sesame Street* that made me burst out laughing. As I remember the sequence, Ernie is clutching his beloved rubber duckie when he comes upon a jazz band. Suddenly there's nothing that Ernie wants to do more than to play jazz too. He wants to join in, catch the rhythm and carry the beat, add his own distinctive voice to the cascading play of sound. He wants to pick up the saxophone and let his spirit soar. But there's just one little problem: His hands are already full. He can't play the saxophone if he's clinging to his duck. What should he do? Ernie is worried and confused, torn between conflicting desires.

At last, an unlikely assortment of advisers steps forward to release him from his dilemma. To the brisk and jazzy beat of the band, this improbable collection of newscasters, actors, musicians, and performers—including, among others, Harry Reasoner, Barbara Walters, Itzhak Perlman, Paul Simon, Ralph Nader, and some of the stars of *Taxi* and *Upstairs, Downstairs*—repeats one after the other the same, very simple advice: "Put down the duckie. Put down the duckie. You've got to put down the duckie if you want to play the saxophone." Their voices are sometimes chiding and sometimes kind, sometimes coaxing and sometimes stern, sometimes melodic and sometimes tuneless, but their message is always the same: If you want to make music, you have to let go of the duck.

Why did I laugh? Because it's so obvious: No one can play the saxophone and hold a rubber duck at the same time. Because I saw myself in Ernie: like him, I longed, when I came in to OA, to join with life, to let loose, to let my spirit fly free. And because, like him, I was afraid. I needed encouragement to do what was so obvious and yet so terrifyingly difficult, so simple and yet so terribly hard: to put down the food and live.

My early weeks and months in OA revolved around one simple message, one basic refrain that began to pulse through my mind with the regularity of a heartbeat: Don't eat, no matter what. No matter what, don't eat.

In the lexicon of OA, the verb "to eat," when it stands alone without a direct object, is shorthand for "compulsive overeating." To refuse "to eat" means to refuse the first compulsive bite, to refuse to binge. If I wanted to have a life, if I wanted to find out who I was and why I was here on this earth, if I wanted to learn how to love and how to let love in, if I wanted to be happy and at peace with myself, if I wanted my existence to have any sense of meaning or purpose, if I wanted nothing more noble or ambitious than simply to stop being so miserable and so filled with self-hatred—if I wanted *any* of these things, I'd have to stop eating compulsively. I'd have to put the food down. It was as stark, as simple, and as scary as that.

Addiction is now widely considered to be a threefold illness, at once physical, emotional, and spiritual. To some degree, our healing takes place on all three levels at once, but in the early stages of recovery, the addict must focus all her energy and attention on physical recovery.

The enormous challenge in my first weeks of OA was unambiguous and unequivocal: not to overeat, no matter what. As far as physical recovery is concerned, it makes no difference what you're feeling. It doesn't matter if you're angry with your mother and don't know what to say. It doesn't matter if your boyfriend has left you, if your cat has died, or if you've just bounced your rent check. It doesn't matter if you think nobody loves you, if there's half an hour to kill before the plane takes off and you're worried about the flight, if you've blown or aced the exam, if your boss just chewed you out or handed you a bonus. It doesn't matter if you just found out you're pregnant, or if you just found out you're not. It doesn't matter if you're stressed out, bored, or lonely; if you're angry or ecstatic, sorrowful or joyful, excited or exhausted. In fact, it doesn't matter *what* you're feeling, or what's going on, or not going on, in your life. In any case, in every case, the same principle holds true: you don't eat, no matter what. No matter what, you don't eat.

Physical recovery isn't about nuances of feelings or insights into why you overeat. It's simply about behavior, about what a person does or doesn't do. Did the hand reach for the fork, the spoon, the extra food, or not? Was the lid screwed back on the jar of peanut butter, or not? Was the cereal box closed after one serving was taken, or not? Was the piece of cake refused, or not? For someone like me, long accustomed to handling every problem, challenge, and feeling by eating over it, this was a radical reorientation indeed. Day after day, the OA program asked me to accept the fact that although excessive food had once served me as lover and friend, companion and confidante, those days were over. For good. A line had been crossed. An activity that had once given me some measure of solace and satisfaction now brought nothing but misery. Food was no longer the answer. The answer was not in the food. Like every other addict, I had to put the rubber duckie down if I wanted to make any music with my life.

I needed to hear this message over and over again. In the first months of recovery, I needed to hear it every day, and many times a day, because it so easily slipped out of awareness. Left to my own devices, I could easily fall back into the familiar cacophony of voices that always preceded a binge. What was one little bite after all? How bad could one little slip be? What was the big deal? Who would care, who would know, if I just helped myself to a few extra slices of bread, had just another spoonful or two of peanut butter? How bad could a few bites be? I could always go back to OA the next day and begin again—right?

I remember having lunch with an OA friend just one week after I'd come into OA, one week after I'd begun eating with moderation and care. I remember casually remarking that I was thinking about going on a binge that night. My friend lunged across the table, grabbed my elbows, and looked me squarely in the eye.

"Focus!" she cried. "Focus! You need to make two phone calls. You need to get to another meeting today." And then came the refrain that had slipped my mind, the refrain that cut through all the wheedling, seductive voices spinning webs of confusion within my head: "Just don't eat. Whatever else you do today, just don't eat. A good day is a day in which you don't eat compulsively. Even if you accomplish nothing else today—even if you don't do a stitch of work, even if you're a bitch all day, even if you lie around all day in your pajamas—if you don't eat, it's a good day. Just get through today without eating. That's all you have to do. Eat tomorrow, if you have to. But don't eat today."

My friend's fervor shocked me to my senses. I was startled that somebody cared so much about whether or not I self-destructed with food. Jarred awake by her clarity, I remembered who I was: a compulsive eater trying to recover, one day at a time. And I remembered, too, the insidious nature of an eating disorder: an extra bite here or there might not matter in itself, but before long an extra bite could swell into an extra serving, and then, like a sleepwalker wandering through her own private nightmare, within a few days I could be polishing off all the food in the house. In the wink of an eye I could find myself sliding back down into the chaos that so recently had been killing me.

So I did what she told me, what I now knew I *must* do if I wanted to save my life. I got myself to another meeting. I made two phone calls. I put together another day of abstinence.

It is friends like that, support like that, that empowers the powerless. It is friends like that, support like that, that carries each recovering person through another day of sobriety or another day of abstinence, until the days gradually become weeks, and the weeks, years. That incident over lunch was just one critical moment among many when my OA friends prodded me to pay attention and stay awake, giving me the strength to listen and stay faithful to my own deep desire for healing.

On the days when I lost my desire to stay well, when I could find no motivation not to overeat and plenty of reasons why I should, my OA friends encouraged me to stay abstinent anyway, until I could again claim for myself the longing to be whole and to be set free. In the meantime, until that moment came, they would carry my heart's desire for me. Physical recovery came first, even if desire and insight lagged temporarily behind.

Just as my life had once revolved around food, so too did the early stages of recovery revolve around abstinence. Eating in moderation—what OA calls abstinence—had to become the central focus of each day, for it was the task that made any other task possible. Every morning I had to ask myself: What do I need to do today in order to maintain my abstinence? What must I do to keep food in its rightful place?

I remember being taken aback, in my early days in the program, by an insistent and solemn refrain that played through our meetings like a recurring motif: "Abstinence is the most important thing in my life without exception."

"Jeepers," I sputtered to myself. "What about your spouse, your family, your friends? What about world peace? Or social justice? What about God?"

Only after some experience with the program did I come to see that for a compulsive overeater, maintaining abstinence is like focusing a camera: If the image in the center is clear, the whole picture comes into focus. Only if my food is clear am I free to love self, family, and friends. Only if I'm abstinent am I free to give myself to larger goals, or to God.

In order to help keep that clarity at the center, the OA program offers a variety of tools. In order to maintain my abstinence, I learned I must use them all. For instance, I learned to go to meetings. In the first months of recovery, I went to at least one meeting a day. In church basements and hospital cafeterias, in classrooms and meeting rooms, in corridors and halls, I met with strangers from all walks of life who were somehow just like me in the ways that mattered—people whose struggles and conflicts, shames and fears, desires and hopes, I could recognize as variations of my own. Here was a resting place for me, a place to find welcome and acceptance, a place to tell the truth. Here was a place to gain inspiration and hope, a community in whose company I could begin the slow process of healing, even though in the early days I felt too shy to speak and could do nothing more than watch and listen.

In meetings I found a world quite distinct from the world of my family—a world in which I could take my first faltering steps toward telling the truth, making my pain explicit, taking responsibility for my choices, and slowly setting aside blame. I didn't know it then, but the more I saturated myself in twelve-step meetings, the more I was learning a whole new way of life, one that empowered me not only to stop eating compulsively, but also to find new ways of relating to myself and to my family. Twelve-step meetings can change you. When you reenter your family, step back into the fray, you're no longer the same person.

I learned to use another tool of the twelve-step program: I found a sponsor, a person who had more experience in recovery than I did and was willing to offer me personal guidance as I groped my way toward wholeness.

I learned to commit myself to a daily food plan. I learned to avoid binge foods and sugar. I learned to take time to plan and to fix in writing what I intended to eat each day.

I learned to "turn over" my food to my sponsor, to "give my food plan away." For all my embarrassment at sharing such an intimate part of my life with somebody else, I learned to call my sponsor every morning and tell her what I planned to eat.

I learned to make other phone calls too. Addiction is rightly considered a disease of isolation. When loneliness closed in, when I felt anxious or overwhelmed, agitated or upset, I learned to pick up the phone instead of diving into the food. I learned to ask for help. I learned to carry a little notebook with me, which I slowly filled with OA members' phone numbers and first names. I learned, despite my shame and anxiety, that it was in fact possible to call someone I barely knew, possible to ask for a few minutes of someone's time, possible to talk about what was "eating" me until the urge to eat had passed.

I learned that it was possible to be abstinent if I took each day one by one; if I chose to live, as the program puts it, "one day at a time." The thought of giving up sugar forever was intolerable. The thought of a lifetime without Halloween candy, Thanksgiving pie, Christmas cookies, Valentine's Day chocolate, or cake and ice cream on my birthday, was more than I could bear. Just thinking about this loss was enough to evoke such anxiety and self-pity that I was tempted to plunge head-long into a binge. So I learned not to dwell on words like "never," "always," and "forever." Maybe one day I would eat sugar again, I told myself, but just for today I needed to protect my abstinence. I learned to focus on what I must do to stay abstinent just for now, just for today. If a twenty-four-hour stretch of abstinence seemed too long to endure, I focused on what I must do to stay abstinent for the next hour, or the next five minutes.

At various points during my recovery, I brought my own food with me to wedding receptions and on airplane flights. I weighed and measured my food, both alone at home and with others in restaurants. Sometimes I ate with chopsticks. Their awkwardness made me eat more slowly, tasting every bite. In the intense first weeks of the program, when my body was enduring some analogue of a drunk's going through detox, my mind topsy-turvy with the stress of withdrawal, I needed to simplify my life—to cancel unnecessary appointments, refuse dinner engagements, turn down projects—so that I could focus all my energy on the challenge before me: to eat with awareness, to eat with care.

For a long time, "working the program" meant being willing to look weird. I remember a friend of mine watching with bemusement as we prepared lunch one day at my house shortly after I joined OA. She wasn't one of my handful of "eating friends." She was one of the friends who thought I was fairly normal around food, someone who hardly gave my eating habits a second thought. In her presence, I'd always eaten sensibly, waiting until I was alone before pulling out all the stops and gorging on whatever I could find. I'd already planned what I would say if she or anyone else ever commented about my having gained some weight. I'd shrug and look perplexed, as if she had presented me with a mystery that I myself didn't understand, as if I had no idea how it could have happened, it must have been something in the air I breathed.

Now that I was abstinent, I handled food in public the same way that I handled it in private. A day at a time, the ancient deadly split between my secret self and the self I showed the world was being mended. I was done with lying about food. So in front of my astonished friend I did exactly what I did when I prepared an abstinent meal alone. I pulled out a measuring cup. I stuffed as much cooked broccoli into the cup as it could hold. I pressed the broccoli down. I mashed it into a shapeless pulp. I squeezed in every bit of green bud and fiber, until the measuring cup was packed to the brim. Then I took a knife and slid it carefully across the top.

My friend raised her eyebrows quizzically. "Is this what recovery is all about?" she asked.

How fussy this was, she seemed to imply, how patently greedy. Of course she was right. And I was stricken with shame. (Now she knows how greedy I really am! How strange I am around food!) Yet even in those early weeks in OA, I knew that I had been given the tools—the map, the compass—that could lead me out of the woods. But only if I was willing to use them and put up with looking like a fool. Only if I could face my shame and not let it stop me.

I explained my new routine to my friend. I'm sure I was defensive. I couldn't help but be embarrassed, but there it was; this was what I needed to do, if I was going to save my life. I'd "committed" my food for the day, I told her. I'd promised my sponsor I'd eat a cup of broccoli as part of my lunch, and so one cup I'd have, no more and no less. I was entitled to a full cup of broccoli, and I didn't want to feel deprived. When it came to food, I told my friend, I needed total clarity. For now, at least, I couldn't trust my eyes to tell me what "one serving" of broccoli might be. For me, eating "one serving" of anything meant eating the whole thing, entire, all at once. Something external and objective— a measuring cup, a teaspoon, a portable scale—could let me know where the limits lay. Then I'd be free to taste and to enjoy my food. I'd know that it was safe, that it wasn't more than my body needed, that it wouldn't lead me to binge.

Was all of this rigid? Without a doubt. Was it obsessive? Certainly. Was it necessary? I'm convinced of it. Like a house whose foundation has eroded and whose walls are toppling, I needed to be braced by an external scaffolding that could hold and contain me while the basic repairs were being made. All the insights and good intentions in the world weren't enough to stop my addictive behavior. Food had a way of slipping into my mouth even before I'd made any sort of conscious choice. Somehow the spoon was licked clean, the extra helpings were grabbed, the hand was already in motion toward the mouth, before I knew it or clearly intended it. I needed a structure outside me to help me stop—guidelines to follow, a path to walk, a net to catch me when I slipped.

More than fifteen years have passed since I came into OA, and how I work the program has changed radically. I no longer need a scaffolding to surround me so closely. There's room now for some flexibility and spontaneity when it comes to food, although I still never touch sugar. I figure it's best to let sleeping dogs lie. No more battles with Cerberus at the gates of hell. I never want to tackle that beast again.

I no longer go to many meetings, no longer follow the guidance of a sponsor or turn over a daily food plan. I no longer weigh and measure food before it goes into my mouth or travel with a measuring cup and scale. And no, I don't mash my broccoli into a pulp anymore. I eat three moderate meals a day and keep second helpings and snacks to a minimum.

Do I have to stay alert with food? Absolutely. Am I still a compulsive overeater? Yes, although a day at a time I live in balance, in grateful recovery. Am I anxious about food, worried about my weight, absorbed in the struggle to make peace with what I do or do not eat? No. The tools of OA have done their good work. The house is standing. Its windows are open wide to the world. Its doors are able to open and close. The walls of the self are durable again: there are clearer boundaries to me now, an outside and an inside, the capacity to say yes and the capacity to say no. I can eat with pleasure when I'm hungry and stop eating when I'm full.

And yet, although I don't use the OA tools as I once did, I still know they're nearby whenever I need them. If the roof springs a leak or a wall begins to sag, if food begins to call me again with its siren song, to lure me with its phony promises and deceptive deals, I know what to do and where to go. I pick up the tools at once. I get on the phone and talk with an OA friend. Recommit myself to abstinence. Pray. Write. Ask for help. If need be, I go to a meeting.

But the first step in the long process of recovery, and the foundation of a food addict's subsequent well-being, is putting down the fork, putting down the food, one day at a time. No insight into self, however subtle; no analysis of the dynamics of addiction, however accurate; no understanding of the nature of desire, however sophisticated or enlightening—none of these fine things can substitute for action. The healing of addiction depends, first and foremost, not on what we know, nor on what we feel, but on what we do—a fact that remains as stubbornly true for "old-timers" as it does for newcomers.

After spending a certain amount of time in twelve-step meetings, almost anyone can master the language. We may learn to speak eloquently about the value of "surrender to a Higher Power." We may be able to rattle off glibly the tools of the program and explain their use. We may grasp the fine points of the Big Book of Alcoholics Anonymous, the basic text of all twelve-step programs. And yet if we take no action, if we don't use the tools about which we speak, if we don't put into practice the principles that we espouse, full recovery will remain elusive.

When it comes to addiction, it's easy to kid ourselves and to settle for talk. That's why I learned in OA to mistrust so-called fat serenity, the pipe dream of being spiritually healthy and at peace, even though we continue to overeat as compulsively and chaotically as ever. OA taught me that physical recovery must come first. Action gives birth to insight. It's only when we put the food down that a deeper level of healing can arise; only when we stop our restless, random, greedy munching that we can begin to listen to the desire of our heart and to learn anything about what serenity might really be.

FROM

DOUBLE DOWN:
REFLECTIONS ON GAMBLING
AND LOSS

Frederick and Steven Barthelme

1999

A few weeks before Thanksgiving 1996, Frederick and Steven Barthelme were escorted away from the blackjack tables at a Mississippi casino. Within a year, the brothers faced criminal charges for allegedly cheating with the help of the dealer. Though the Barthelmes were both respected authors and college professors, they suddenly found themselves reeling from the consequences of their shared addiction to gambling. The brothers were eventually cleared of the charges and restored their reputations, but they never regained the $250,000 they lost over a three-year period. In their memoir, Double Down, *the Barthelmes describe their descent into the gripping world of slot machines and blackjack tables.*

We had heard about gambling and addiction, about people who had lost their jobs, their houses, their cars, their families, their lives. We'd heard about people who got crosswise with a bookie or other unconventional lender. We had seen the gambling movies, Karel Reisz's *The Gambler*, Robert Altman's *California Split*. We had read Dostoyevsky's novella. We had read *Under the Volcano*, seen *The Lost Weekend* and *Days of Wine and Roses*. We wondered if that was us. Decided that it was.

We discussed addiction on those long drives down Highway 49. We were analytical about it, examined it in excruciating detail. We knew that your average psychologist would have said we were addicts in a minute. We knew the threatening jargon, that we were "enabling" each other, that we were a codependency case, and in the normal course of things, had we seen ourselves flying to the coast every four or five days for eighteen hours of blackjack and slot machines, we might have said we were addicts. But in the car headed down there this characterization seemed insufficient.

There was a catch: So what? Being an addict didn't mean anything. One of the virtues of having gambling as your vice—as opposed to sex, drugs, or alcohol—was that the disadvantages were felt only at the bank. As long as you had the bankroll, these disadvantages were only superficial wounds. At worst, we were in an early stage of addiction, before the wounds amounted to much, and the customary assumption (which all of the movies, books, and hand-wringing newspaper articles made) that the later, catastrophic stages were inevitable was something we didn't buy. We doubted it. We had been trained to doubt the omnipotent sway of psychology.

Ours was not a family brought up on psychology. In our father's view, the great seething life of feelings could be a damn nuisance. Father had more than a teaspoon of the Frank Bunker Gilbreth about him. Although the family did recognize the psychological dimension, pragmatism—some kind of physical pragmatism—superseded psychology when explanations or remedies were wanted.

Being good sons of our father, we rode to the coast night after night, streaming through the sweltering Mississippi heat, clouds of grasshoppers popping off the highway like a plague of sparks, humidity as thick as gravy, and when we said to each other that we were addicts, when we talked about being addicts, it was a joke—a joke with a nasty twist, but still a joke. Later, after we became accused felons, we would call each other Lyle and Erik, with the idea that a joke needs a Menendezian edge.

You're a gambling addict, so what? Have you got money in the bank? Yes? Go on being an addict. A part of the pleasure was being able to go over the top, way over the top, without any of the mess or travail associated with doing drugs or becoming alcoholics or cheating on our wives, which is not to say the wives approved. They did not. But neither did they react the way they might have had we become enmeshed in other vices.

Sometimes, at first, they went with us. Later, not. But even then, during our long gambling nights, we would call in, advise our spouses how we were doing, how far ahead or behind we were, tell them that we loved them. And we did love them, somehow more fiercely when we were at the coast, when we were free to go to the coast. Something about the intensity of the experience of gambling, of risking the money, of risking loss, made the security and solidity of the home front much more important, much more sweet. More than that, it was a detachment, the anesthetic clarity with which you sometimes saw things in the middle of a drunk. Once Rick stood at the bank of telephones downstairs at the Grand, leaning his forehead against the chrome surface of a wall phone, standing there after hanging up from a conversation with Rie. They had exchanged I love yous and suddenly, after the call, he felt that love with crippling intensity.

An addict is someone who "surrenders" to something, the dictionary will tell you, "habitually or obsessively." Most people are at least a little addicted to something—work, food, exercise, sex, watching sports on television, cooking, reading, the stock market. Some people are addicted to washing their hands. Some people trim their hedges from dawn to dusk. Some people play too much golf. Almost anything can be the object of addiction.

Whatever his pleasure, an addict usually knows he is, or may be, an addict, but inside the warmth of his addiction, the label seems secondary, does not signify, as we like to say over at the college. It's like telling a horse he's a horse. Take President Clinton, for example. When he was involved in certain activities, he must have known he was addicted to something; he just didn't care. We felt just like the president. We didn't care. We supposed, in our conversations, both in Hattiesburg and en route to the coast, that when the time came we would bail. We knew that push would come to shove at some point, and at that point we would get out of the game.

Steve, wisely but very late in all of this, bought a house with some of his inheritance. Made a down payment, got a low mortgage, *invested* in a home. Buying houses didn't come easy to us, in part because the house in which we had grown up was as much a cultural declaration as a dwelling, embodying ideas about design always to be defended against Philistines. Since we had left that house, we had lived in more or less ordinary houses for many years, but we had always rented. Buying an undistinguished house seemed like giving in, disloyalty. There were other reasons, of course. We had led unstable lives, so the idea of settling in the same place for thirty years had seemed laughable. Until Steve started teaching, and for some time afterward, he had never had the steady income to envision buying a house. Buying a house seemed rash when half one's worldly goods were in cardboard boxes awaiting the next move.

We admitted having "addictive personalities," but we *liked* our addiction, the object of our addiction. It wasn't so different from all the other things, large and small, that we had intense attachments to— Diet Coke and Russian writers, springer spaniels and computers, box wrenches and movies. From childhood we had been taught that the object of an addiction was secondary. It was the way in which you cared about something, the quality of your interest rather than its object, that mattered. The first measure of the quality of an interest was its intensity, its thoroughgoingness. Best was to surrender oneself to something habitually or obsessively. We had done that all our lives.

Now the important thing was gambling. The care and feeding of our addiction, the pleasure of our addiction. Gambling was a very cerebral, almost slow-motion activity, which made it easy to savor. It was markedly more satisfying because we were doing it together. As brothers, we shared all the surprise and exhilaration of a new and consuming interest, like any new hobby—skydiving, methamphetamine. Codependency has its good side. Both doing it, we were each part performer and part audience. Every gambling session wrote its own swift, strange story, filled with highs and lows, finely calibrated details ("she flipped another five . . .") and compelling nuances ("and I thought, 'Fuck, ace, next one's an ace,' and then, sure as shit . . ."). Gamblers want to talk. For us, there was always someone to tell, someone who knew in his blood what you were talking about. After a trip, our conversations went on for days, full of lurid, taunting laughter. The kind that revealed just how completely we were hooked on risk, on gambling.

We weren't measuring ourselves against the real daredevils of the culture; we were measuring ourselves against other normal people, middle-class people, good solid stock, people with jobs, families, houses, cars, and responsibilities that they dispatched in a workmanlike way. People like us. We told ourselves that betting a thousand dollars on a hand of blackjack might be stupid, but it wasn't as stupid as shooting yourself full of heroin or, as various members of our family had done for years, drinking yourself into oblivion by five o'clock in the afternoon—or better yet, doing it by noon, waking up at three and doing it again by five, having dinner and doing it again by nine. Maybe we were just looking for a way to keep up with the rest of the family, members of which had had their troubles with various forms of conspicuous consumption, of obsession, of, well, for lack of a better word, addiction. Yes, it ran in the family. From our father on down, maybe even from *his* father on down.

The only time you really think of yourself as an addict is when you want to stop. When it's time to stop. When you're in so much trouble that stopping is the only thing left. But we never got there. We could afford it. It was fun. It was a way to blow off steam. It took us out of ourselves in a way that we hadn't been taken out of ourselves by anything else.

We had had good luck with addictions in the past. Both of us had been drinkers and smokers. Rick had been a drunk in his early twenties, but had stopped dead after he moved to New York and discovered that getting drunk and waking up at four A.M. on a Lower East Side street was not healthy. Steve had long since given up heavy drinking for steady drinking, three drinks a day, give or take a couple, for the past thirty years. Both of us had had smoking habits—two or three packs a day—and while we'd tried to curb them, following the path of declining tar and nicotine, going from regular cigarettes to pretend cigarettes like True and Carlton, we'd had no intention of quitting until, as mentioned, our two older brothers were diagnosed with throat cancer, one within a month of the other.

We quit smoking.

But gambling wasn't producing a downside for us. Gambling was only producing the release, the euphoria, and the opportunity to behave bizarrely, just like—we imagined—ordinary, everyday people. We didn't think we were wild and crazy; we thought gambling made us regular guys.

It was an aesthetic thing too. Everywhere around us were writers and artists and professors, hard at work at what Ishmael Reed describes as "all wearing the same funny hat." It had long seemed obvious that

the best course was the other direction. Neither of us had the customary late-twentieth-century middle-class phobia for people who were
deemed ordinary. In fact, ordinary was what we both liked best.

What we didn't like about the academy was the falseness: conservative people presenting themselves in Che Guevara suits, digging hard
for career advantage while settling hearty congratulations all around
for assigning radical authors to their students to read, thus threatening
the established order. Soon they would take their SUVs into the mountains.

This put a little extra heat under the affection we had for the ordinary people we imagined existed somewhere and for whom we felt a
special kinship. It was ordinariness that we were extending with our
gambling, by being addicted to it, by doing it to excess, by risking more
money than made any sense at all, by telling ourselves that we were
going to win, or that we might win, when we knew as surely as anybody else that the likelihood of that was slim. Still, you'd be surprised
at how much positive thinking goes on on the highway at midnight.

You'd be surprised by how dearly the heart holds the idea that
tonight you might actually win, that this two thousand dollars, the last
two thousand you have in your bank account, will be the basis of your
big comeback. Even in the heat of battle, down five or fifteen thousand
in a night, the not particularly well heeled but still liquid blackjack
loser can imagine winning it all back in a flash.

And he would not imagine it had he not already done it once or
twice or maybe more. Had he not experienced that thrill of the cards
having run against him all night, run against him for five consecutive
hours and having in that time lost an enormous amount of money,
gone to the cashier's cage again and again, new resources, the thrill that
comes when the cards turn, when they become your cards, when they
became his cards, not the casino's, when in the space of forty-five minutes you recognize that you're going to win whatever you bet. And if
you recognize it soon enough, and if you're secure enough in the
recognition, you can turn around the whole night, turn around five
thousand dollars in twenty minutes. You can turn around fifteen thousand dollars in an hour.

It's a rare, even amazing experience. It almost makes gambling
worthwhile. Everything you touch turns to gold. You bet five hundred
dollars and you bet a thousand. You double down and you win. Your

stacks of chips grow. Pretty soon they are paying you in hundreds, then five hundreds—the purple chips. You've got a stack of those in front of you. Then, if the going is really good, they start paying you in orange—the thousand-dollar chips. The thousand-dollar chips are slightly larger, a sixteenth of an inch larger in diameter than all the other chips. You stack them separately.

Your stack grows, and maybe you bet one of them or two of them on a hand. Or you play two hands. And still you win. Sure, this isn't Monte Carlo, you're not some duke or some heiress, and so you're not betting hundreds of thousands of dollars a hand, but that fact makes your betting and your winning just that much sweeter, because you have no business in the world betting a thousand dollars on a hand of blackjack, and you know it. You have no business in the world betting five thousand dollars on a hand of blackjack, and you know it. So when you do, and when the cards are coming your way, and when your five thousand turns to ten, your ten to twenty, it's mesmerizing. Suddenly that business they always say about feeling like you'll live forever becomes a little bit true, because you've crossed over some line, gone into some other territory, become somebody else.

You're part of the table, part of the machine that plays blackjack, part of the casino, part of the system. Only you're not the part that gives your money to them anymore, you're not the part you usually play: the mark, the bozo. You've skidded out onto the ice in the middle of the Olympics in a huge stadium filled with cheering people and swaying, lime-colored spotlights and, suddenly, inexplicably, you can skate like an angel.

Sleeping with Alcohol

Donna Steiner

2000

The poet and essayist Donna Steiner was in her mid-thirties when she first met a woman who would become her lover for six years. As their life together unfolded, her lover's drinking increasingly stole from their relationship. In her essay "Sleeping with Alcohol," Steiner writes: "She drinks. Meaning life is sometimes difficult in ways that it would not be difficult minus alcohol. . . . But there's another fact, the one that says she is incrementally, methodically destroying herself, and destroying us. For every night's consumption of alcohol, something of value is lost, and although each individual loss may appear subtle, they accumulate." Steiner was awarded the Annie Dillard Award for the essay, which was later nominated for a Pushcart Prize.

Start small. The bottle cap. Silver on the underside, green and black on the top. It's fluted around the edge, like a pie crust, and dented in the middle, like a felt hat. The green is the green of grass; beer companies like to associate their products with nature. When I poke the cap with my finger it skitters across the desktop, making a sound that isn't unpleasant. It's a sound I'm accustomed to, for she will often toss the caps onto the kitchen floor—they make great cat toys. We know an artist who creates beautiful, expensive murals using nothing but bottle tops and flip tabs. The murals look like aquariums, all gleam and fluidity, like daydreams of cold liquid.

I study one amber-hued beer bottle. It's slender, nine inches high, and seductive in the way that bottles often are. This one looks to me like a human torso, and my instinct is to hold it, covet it. I don't drink, but I want to experience what the serious drinker experiences. With no one to witness my foolishness, I surrender to the process. Lifting the bottle to my mouth is a small turn-on. The lips fit perfectly around the opening. I feel a charge, a subtle electricity. My throat feels as though it's vibrating: a little air, a little liquid, a little moisture left on the lips. One kisses a bottle mouth—she taught me that.

There's a pretty picture on the label: snowcapped mountains overlooking a green lake. She loves to hike in the woods; I can picture her sitting on a rock overlooking the tranquil lake. There's a list of states in which the bottle can be returned for a five-cent rebate. (Exchange fifty-two bottles and earn enough for a six-pack. Or: nine nights of drinking will earn her one night's free supply.) CONSUMPTION OF ALCOHOLIC BEVERAGES IMPAIRS YOUR ABILITY TO DRIVE A CAR OR OPERATE MACHINERY, AND MAY CAUSE HEALTH PROBLEMS. The alcohol content isn't listed, and "may cause health problems" means this stuff can kill you.

There's something contemplative about drinking. One drinks, pauses, places the bottle on the table, pauses again. A drink, like a cigarette or a pair of eyeglasses, can make you look thoughtful—it can make you *feel* thoughtful. The bottle, resting in the curve of your palm, becomes the focus of the mind's wandering. The drinker savors the up and down, the choreography of drinking: the bottle comes up, the head tilts back and the eyes briefly close, the liquid goes down, and as the bottle is set down the eyes open. It's a pleasurable rhythm, the arm as a lever, a delicious exercise, a drawn-out, self-imposed tease. The bottle is turned in the hand, admired, held up to the light. Its arc, its smooth lines and sensuous curves, and especially its soon-to-be-delivered promise all conspire to make the drinker slowly less sober. Thoughts become sinuous, like a river, hazy like morning fog. The tongue turns funny in the mouth, and the first bottle becomes the second, the third. Each stands in for the one before, all identical, making it easy to lose count. Few things make the mouth happier and the soul, ultimately, more lonely.

———

She refers to herself as a drunk.

When I think about her I don't think: *drunk*. I think: *runner*. I think: *artist*. I see her dancing around our apartment, mouthing the words to

Motown songs but miming disco moves. I consider how her voice deepens when she wants to talk about something serious, how she has no tolerance for indirect conversation or ambiguous language. I remember how my hands trembled when I met her. She has the most resilient body—cigarettes, alcohol, it doesn't seem to matter. After not training for a year she can go out and run five miles easily, ten or more with a little effort. She wakes up in the morning in the middle of a conversation, asking "What's the difference between a barnacle and a crustacean?" I've learned to feign grogginess, to mutter "I'm not sure" as I reach for a reference book. She has a long list of wacky endearments for me, including "my fresh coat of paint" and "my little prize-winning chicken." And she's in the very small group of people who think I'm fun—even when she's sober.

———

Okay. (*Say it!*) Sometimes I think: *drunk*.

———

Summer, 1998. A typical night. She arrives home from work, carrying a book bag, a lunch bag, and a plastic grocery bag. The latter holds her nightly six-pack. She sets the beer in the refrigerator before changing into running clothes. We drive to the track, discussing our respective days. She puts in her miles, covering the distance with a posture I'd recognize anywhere—shoulders slightly tense, her eyes focused on something far away, jaw set. As she accumulates laps I walk around the oval and watch the light change the appearance of the mountains, seeming to flatten them. When she's through, we walk a half-mile together, then leave. We stop for fast food, then return home and catch the end of an NBA game, a thriller, with Utah pulling off the win in Chicago. She drinks a beer or two during the game, then retreats to the porch to polish off the other four. During the third or fourth bottle I join her outside. By eleven I'm sleepy and say good night.

At two-thirty I awaken; the bed beside me is empty. This is not common, but neither is it unexpected. Sometimes she's walking to or just returning from the corner store with a follow-up six-pack. At times like that I don't fall back asleep. (*She'd make an easy target...*) I listen for her, or I go outside, scan the street for her slender, huddled figure. Tonight I hear the bathroom faucet and know she's home. She makes her way toward our bedroom. Her shoulder hits the door frame, but she finds the bed and is asleep within seconds.

I get up. I check the door, make sure it's locked. There's a receipt on the table, which we'll use for scrap paper. Nine bottles are neatly lined up on the kitchen counter, like bud vases or bowling pins. She drinks in multiples of six, which means the other three are elsewhere. Sometimes the caps are stacked up, collected in a little tower, and when I drop them into the trash they sound like tambourines as they rattle down.

The only unusual part of this night: the fast food. Usually we eat at home. The rest—the track, the lateness of the hour, my casual, late-night surveillance—is routine. This is how we live. She drinks, I observe. You would never suspect that we're into threesomes. But if you could see in the dark you'd see me, my lover, and alcohol. Mostly I think I sleep with her. But sometimes, in moments of exceptional despair, I think: *I am sleeping with alcohol.*

———

I tell her I'm thinking of writing this essay and ask if she'd be okay about it. She says sure. I'd like to conduct an interview, and one night we sit down for about thirty minutes, side by side. I have a notebook and a pen, she has a bottle. She's drunk from start to finish, drinking as we talk—therefore, more drunk toward the end than the beginning. When we're through she says, "Let's do it again, same questions, when I'm sober." I agree, but I'm not sure my writing schedule and her drinking schedule will allow for that possibility.

I hadn't planned the questions in advance, so again, I start small.

How much does a six-pack of beer cost?

Cheap beer is $2.49 plus tax, which comes to $2.61. Better beer, on sale, is $4.99 plus tax. Really good beer is around $6.00, but I never buy that. Too expensive.

Do you remember your first drink?

Yes. When we were little my parents would let my brother and me have wine mixed with water on holidays. I was eight or nine.

Did you like it?

I loved it.

I remember my first sip of beer, too. My grandfather lived with us in the summertime, and he always had projects. He'd work really hard, and at the end of the day he would have one beer and a cigar. That was it—one beer. He'd give me a sip. I must have been around seven.

He'd drink real slow. I remember once a wasp flew into the beer can. When he sipped, it stung him on the mouth.

Why do you drink beer, as opposed to wine or anything else?

Beer tastes the best. (pause) Wine takes too much effort. The whole picking-out-the-wine thing—it's like learning an art. Wine would be like getting into Baroque art. Too much effort.

What's your favorite?

Saranac, or Black Dog. Black Dog is very good, although I like the Saranac, too. I like a small brewery that does a lot of different brews and has specialties.

How many beers does it take to get drunk?

Whoa. Tough question. (pause)

What do you mean, "drunk"? (pause)

It depends on the brew. Microbrews are much stronger than regular brews, and light beers are like drinking soda to a real drinker. They're like drinking nothing.

So, say a six-pack of Black Dog?

That can make you drunk. (pause) It's a pretty darn strong beer. (pause) You know, there's nothing listed on the side of the bottle to tell you what you're drinking . . . A lot depends on expectation. I read this the other day—if you expect to get really drunk, you will. It's a pretty well-documented study, totally scientific. And I have felt that to be true—if you think you're going to get drunk, you will.

Has anyone ever asked you to quit?

Yeah.

Did you quit?

Not at the time she asked. Probably about two years later.

How long did you quit for?

Seven or eight years.

What's the worst thing that ever happened to you while you were drunk?

(She laughs.) Well, I got raped, I broke my foot. (She's counting on her fingers.) I don't know. I got kicked out of college, I had a car accident, I lost my driver's license.

(long pause)

That's all.

What do you think of AA?

I think it's a really great thing—camaraderie and all that. I did attempt once to do it, you know, like they ask—to go to ninety meetings in ninety days. I was very diligent, but I just couldn't quite accept the idea that we were gonna be drunks for life. It didn't seem plausible to me.

Why?

It was the same problem I had in rehab, and it just seemed logical that plenty of people quit with no support system and it was over and done with. Boom. (pause) The whole notion of AA is so mired in God stuff. You know, I really—for a person not prone to being brainwashed—I actually went to church. I'd sort of bought the God thing. I went to the church and sat there for a while—but it still didn't make any sense to me.

What would be the best incentive for quitting?

Love. (No hesitation. Although I am totally into my role as the detached interviewer, my eyes fill with tears.) (long pause) But that's never enough.

How come?

(long pause) I think because drinking sometimes makes you feel ... like you're somehow filling your time in a productive way, you know, without it you feel a little at sea, like you wouldn't know what to do with your time. Of course, you're also thinking, "Well, I'm only sitting here drinking." But when you're *not* drinking you sit there thinking, "I'm not *doing* anything." Even if you are doing something, it feels like nothing.

I felt like I wasn't doing anything if I wasn't drinking ... Time *flows* when you're drinking.

All this is just during the transition period ... that I'd feel so lost ... once you're through it, you're fine. During, it's like ... God, what am I gonna do next, how am I gonna fill the time?

I read that Marguerite Duras, in the midst of her alcoholism, had thought of killing herself but what stopped her was the thought that "once you're dead you won't be able to drink any more ..."

(She laughs.)

When I'm not drinking I'm perfectly happy. It's nice to go to work clear-headed and enjoy people. Like last week when I wasn't drinking— I didn't *want* to drink. But that is the ultimate quandary: why the hell do I do this?

What's the best thing about drinking?

(long pause) I don't know. (sigh) Zoning away from most things. Being able to just ... sometimes you have time sort of *stop*. You just kind of sit outside and look at the same star for a long time and think about it. It's different from other drugs in that you're still there, you can control your dosage, you know how drunk you're gonna be. It's a control freak's drug, in a lot of ways.

Do you think you'll ever quit drinking?

No. (long silence)

I'm sorry I'm so hard to live with.

You're very easy to live with, for the most part.

Yeah, but for that last part I'm a real pain in the ass.

———

The night before we'd sat on the porch, late, 1 A.M., then 2, close to 3. Early in the evening I'd spotted a falling star. It had blazed, perfectly vertical, with a long, bright tail, then was gone. She saw it, too. As the night wore on I saw several more, until I'd counted four. She was finishing her sixth beer. Strange, complicated math.

———

Even in the middle of winter, on the East Coast, she'd bundle up and sit outside, snow falling, late into the night as the temperature dropped below zero. I'd fear she'd fall asleep, that I'd find her in the morning, dead of exposure. The partner of the alcoholic fears many things; some fears are realized and some aren't.

A friend's father fell on New Year's Eve. At the top of the staircase he was drunk. At the bottom he was dead. Five minutes before midnight, five minutes after. Ten stairs.

We have stairs. Our home has hard edges and sharp corners, surfaces that could break a bone or blind an eye. She stumbled into bed the other night. The lights were on. I watched her try to remove her clothes—once, twice, she lost her balance. A painting she'd completed was propped against the wall. I heard the canvas *ping* each time her ankle struck it. Finally she sat down, wrestling off her pants. You make a choice to live with the fear, or you leave.

I have no intentions of leaving. I walk around our apartment, continuing as reporter, looking for evidence. Not evidence of alcohol— that would be easy. If I moved this chair I'd find seven or eight cat-batted bottle caps. There's probably a stray bottle or two under her drawing table. So what? I want evidence of something else, proof of why I stay. Her jacket's tossed on a chair, and one of the cats is curled upon it. I lean in and smell the jacket, and the cat's warm fur. The phone number of our favorite pizza place is stuck on the refrigerator, along with the first card she gave me: a picture of a map. Written inside: *Let's go every-where.* Her guitar rests against the wall, and her bike leans against mine. Hers is covered with dried, splattered mud; mine is covered with dust. Piles of books, art supplies, the painting of Kitchen Mesa, New Mexico. She'd wanted to sell the painting when she finished it; I'd begged her to keep it. A few of her books, field guides—*North American Wildflowers, Eastern Forests, Western Birds, Eastern Birds.* Above the shelf, the first photograph taken of us. I look deliriously happy; she needs a haircut. The other day she said that my scalp smelled great. I asked, "What does it smell like?" and she replied, "Outdoors and olives, and tiny toasted nuts." When I remind her of this answer it makes her laugh, but she doesn't remember saying it.

———

She drinks. Meaning life is sometimes difficult in ways that it would not be difficult minus alcohol. A statement of fact, 100 percent accurate. But there's another fact, the one that says she is incrementally, methodically destroying herself, and destroying us. For every night's consumption of alcohol, something of value is lost, and although each individual loss may appear subtle, they accumulate. Coordination, so important to an athlete, is affected. She cuts her fingertips with carving knives, burns her palms while cooking. Communication is damaged. She can become increasingly remote, or arbitrarily contentious. Drunk enough, she will contradict or repeat herself, habits that would disgust her sober, eloquent self. Other times she is witty, adept at theorizing or storytelling, charming. She can be amorous or silly or suddenly vulnerable, and is often irresistible, even as I smell the alcohol, which seems, at times, to emanate from her pores. Someday I will regret turning quietly away from the brushes with disaster, I'll regret the rationalizations, and I'll regret my gratefulness for *now*—*now* she is here, *now* she is intelligent and beautiful and now there is health—or the illusion of health. The greatest fear: that I'll regret it all.

———

I'm lying in bed and she is asleep beside me. Her hand rests on my chest, right above my heart, and at first it feels warm and light, precious beyond words. But soon I can think of nothing but its weight, as though my heart is being pressed upon, quietly smothered. It is an image for how alcohol works, one of the ways in which it corrupts good lives. It steadily, insidiously shifts the focus—away from intimacy, toward despair.

———

I tell her I'm using the interview in the essay. "Do I sound like an idiot?" she asks. I say no. "Oh good. God forbid I should sound like an idiot *and* a drunk."

———

It's almost impossible to grow up in the United States without a degree of experimentation with alcohol, and since I wasn't a complete outcast as a kid, I had a few encounters. I think the first was at a friend's house, seventh grade, or sixth. It may have been whiskey, although I still can't tell the difference between one form of hard liquor and the next. Blindfolded, I'd know to say "beer" as opposed to "wine," but that's about as sophisticated as I can be. A bunch of neighborhood kids each took a sip, and then we went outside to wait. We thought we'd get drunk and were a bit disappointed, but mostly relieved, when we didn't.

I drank, just a little, in my twenties. "Just a little" is literal. I've consumed less than thirty bottles of beer in my life, perhaps ten glasses of wine, a few sips of champagne. I may have been slightly intoxicated on one or two occasions, but the taste of alcohol is a deterrent—I hate it. I realized fairly early that I wasn't going to be the hard-drinking, hard-loving writer. I'd have to settle for half. Little did I know that someday the one I waited my whole life to find would turn out to be the other half.

———

Living with an alcoholic you learn the extreme fragility of good intentions. "I'm going to quit drinking" mutates into "I'd *like* to" and "I *wish* I could," then to "Maybe I can cut down," and finally, to "I want to quit, someday, really . . ." You learn the meaning of patience. You learn how tough you can be, and how complicit. You think you learn how to love someone unconditionally. But you wonder, always, if she loves the bottle more than she'll ever love you.

And you learn the code. It took me a while to learn, but once I did it became routine to accept it, to collaborate on and refine the code. The pretense is very simple. If she doesn't bring home beer after work, at some point in the evening she'll say, "I'm going out for cigarettes/milk/the newspaper." It doesn't matter what the noun is, because they all translate the same way: beer. When she implements the code, my proper response is "Okay." Or I'll say, "Pick me up some Gatorade." The code is totally unremarkable, and occasionally humorous. I'll ask, "Are you going out for REAL cigarettes or for EUPHEMISTIC cigarettes?" and we'll laugh. Once in a while I'll prompt a variation of the code. I'll say, innocently, "If you're stopping at the store after work, could you bring home some _____," knowing the "if" is ridiculous. Of course she will stop. I hardly ever need to go to the store.

———

It's all so predictable and mundane, and it's not a pattern that enhances our lives in any meaningful way. And yet I wonder why relationships involving alcohol are seen as shabbier, more pathetic than those in which both parties are sober. Most of our friends are coupled; we are no more and no less complicated in our relationship than they are. But I sometimes sense their pity, a degree of noncomprehension: *how can you live like that?* I wonder what they see, or think they see. Her alcoholism doesn't feel like a choice, but neither, frankly, does it feel like an illness. It feels like some murky combination of the two that we've chosen to call a fact. The most accurate, although exceedingly dull, description would be "problem." We contend with a problem, which happens to be alcohol. We are unexceptional.

———

But there are markers in the lives of any couple in which alcohol is the third party, events that sober couples don't experience. In the early months of our relationship she rarely *appeared* intoxicated, and I was slow to learn the signs. Even now, unless I'm counting bottles, I often can't tell if she's drunk. There's some lag time before the full effects of the alcohol register. She doesn't begin to slur, for example, until around the seventh or eighth beer, and may begin to weave or stumble shortly thereafter.

I remember the first time I helped her to bed, the first time I saw her trip over nothing at all. I remember the first time she stumbled and took me down with her, my back and thigh absorbing most of the impact as we fell into a bookcase. I remember the first time we had sex while she was drunk. I don't remember the second time, or third, or fourth. Eventually I stopped counting. And I remember, most sharply, the sadness and shock I felt upon waking one morning, when I realized that my lover had appeared drunk *in my dream.*

We live, for the most part, as though nothing is wrong, as if nothing is out of the ordinary. We live as though we are brave, persevering, mature. We try to live as though there's no shame, no stigma, no pressure to change. We try, but it's all there, part of the background, like an ugly piece of furniture we throw a sheet over.

We live as though the alcohol is temporary and we are permanent.

———

"No." That's what she said, remember, in response to my question "Do you think you'll ever quit?" *But she was drunk when she said it.*

———

I like broken things, torn things, tired things. I have a small collection of bone and shell pieces, fragments and hinges that are more attractive, to me, than intact ones. I like old sheets and worn towels. A towel is perfect when you can see through the fabric. Sheets seem to smell better as they age; the older they get, the more they smell like fresh air or clean closets. It's related to my affection for the smell of skin, my desire to just move in close to a body and breathe deeply—my idea of intoxication. My favorite sheets aren't yet worn enough to be considered perfect, but I know they will *become* worn—the anticipation is slightly thrilling in itself. The sheets are blue and gold striped, with black and beige for accents. I loved them so much that I bought two sets. They were too stiff when purchased, rough and scratchy, and it's possible to burn tender body parts on new sheets—especially in the early months of a love affair. But I've washed them so often that now, four years later, they've become less dangerous, more familiar.

The one who sleeps beside me has become less dangerous and more familiar, too. I didn't know, when I met her, that alcohol was an ongoing chapter in her history. If I'd known from the start, I would not have proceeded differently. I approached the problem from a position of naïve compassion, but I've grown self-protective. I'm frequently harsh, as she is, on both of us. At times I see her as self-involved, self-indulgent, and see myself as misguided and desperate. That's what alcohol does. It tempers hope, alters perception. It lets the heart roam a little less widely, as though possibilities have become fewer, the world itself somehow *less.* It forces you to assess, a day at a time, risks versus benefits. The effort wears you out in ways that cannot be judged at-tractive.

———

If I could drink one of her bottles each night, then over the course of a year her alcohol intake would be reduced by . . . Yeah, a strange and complicated math.

———

What is the cost, the toll alcohol will take? I can feel our couplehood eroding, as though we are standing on a bank that's becoming satu-rated, our footing steadily becoming less stable. I wonder if we're past the point or not yet at the point when I can look into her eyes and say "Stop; this is killing you." Marguerite Duras: "We live in a world para-lyzed with principles. We just let other people die." Regardless of any principle, or plea, or ultimatum—or regardless of their absence—I believe my lover cannot stop drinking. (. . . *letting* her die!)

Is the bottle half empty or half full? The question is dramatically beside the point. Always, eventually, it ends up empty.

———

3 A.M. Moonlight seeps in around the window shades. She's just com-ing to bed, but she overshoots her mark and ends up near the closet, in a corner of the room. She can't see; it's dark and she's already removed her glasses. But of course that's only part of the problem. She's unable to crack the maze of the dark room. Her brain can't hear me silently rooting for her, *Just turn around; a simple ninety-degree turn will do it.* It's like watching one of those battery-powered kids' trucks that can't back up so it just spins its wheels. I hear her bumping gently against a wall-mounted mirror. All she has to do is turn, but the smooth glass and her faintly perceived reflection confound her, like a bird persisting against a window. Her white T-shirt catches the little light of the night. Beautiful.

Beautiful, and drunk. I get out of bed, and I take her hand.

FROM

LOVE SICK:
ONE WOMAN'S JOURNEY
THROUGH SEXUAL ADDICTION

Sue William Silverman

2001

The day before entering a twenty-eight-day rehab for sexual addic-
tion, Sue William Silverman met her lover, Rick, at a nearby hotel.
She had already entered therapy in an attempt to curb her extra-
marital affairs. Still, she was unable to forgo one last encounter—
regardless of the pain it would eventually inflict upon her and her
husband, Andrew. In her memoir Love Sick, *Silverman explores*
the origins of her sexual addiction and the lessons she must learn
before reclaiming her life.

Every Thursday at noon I have sex with Rick in room #213 of the
Rainbow Motel. Today, even though I promised my therapist I wouldn't
come here again, I pull into the lot and park beside Rick's black Ford
Bronco. I cut the engine and air conditioner and listen to stillness, to
nothing, to heat. Sun-rays splinter the windshield. Heat from the pavement rises, stifling, around the car, around me. No insects flutter in the
brittle grass next to the lot. Trees don't rustle with bird wings. A neon
rainbow, mute and colorless by day, arcs over a sign switched to
VACANCY. Only the little girl from India, daughter of the motel owner,
invigorates the stasis. Holding a string tied to a green balloon, she races
down the diving board and leaps into the swimming pool. With the
windows closed, I can't hear the splash. If she laughs, I can't hear this,

either. For a moment she disappears. The balloon gaily sways above the water. The girl pops to the surface. She begins the game again.

The girl's energy exhausts me—as much as the stagnation of neon, air, time. I close my eyes. Still, I sense no darkness, no cool shadows, no relief from the scorching Georgia heat. Rather, a harsh light, white as a sheet, penetrates my lids as if I am caught in an unforgiving glare.

I worry the girl by the pool will see me. She's too young to know what I do here in the Rainbow Motel.

I should leave. I should leave here now. I should drive home and rinse pink gloss from my lips, wipe mascara from my lashes, change out of my too-short skirt and too-tight black lace blouse. I should cook a nourishing dinner for my husband. I should grasp the balloon and let it waft me across the sky, far from my implacable need for men. Dangerous men. Not physically dangerous. Emotionally dangerous. These men see me just as an object, a body. They are men incapable of love—even though I endlessly, addictively, try to convince myself that sex at noon for an hour with a married man *has* to be the real thing, must be love.

So I can't leave here. I need Rick. One last time. One last high. One last fix.

I should drive to the rehab unit and find my therapist right now.

———

Pausing outside the door of room #213, I hear the television: a car crash, urgent voices. I turn the knob and lock it behind me. Rick lies on the sheet smoking a cigarette, the remote beside him. He inhales. Exhales. Smoke swirls. I watch it disperse. An ash drifts onto the pillowcase. He doesn't notice. He hasn't stopped watching me since I entered.

He leans over and stubs out the cigarette. He clicks off the television and beckons me closer. A gold necklace nestles in his blond hair, a rich glitter of gold on gold as if chain mail emblazons his chest. Lying beside him, I curl short strands of his hair around my finger as if, in all this incandescence, we radiate love. His Eau Sauvage cologne is the only scent in the world I will ever need or want. I close my eyes, drenched in it. In him. I must feel Rick's touch, a drug surging through veins, trancing me as I urgently swallow oblivion and ether. Sex, a sweet amnesiac. The elixir drains through my body, thin as a flame. I crave this,

need him—or You, Man, whoever You are—until I'm blissfully sati-
ated. . . .

Is this bliss?

I open my eyes. He's leaning over me, his palm on the pillow beside
my head. I can hear the second hand of his watch ticking beside my
ear. His breath numbs the hollow at the base of my neck. Sweat gath-
ers on his temples. The necklace taps my chin as he fucks me. A gift
from his wife? I wonder. He kisses me. Strokes me. But this is just a
repetition of all the other times with Rick. Nothing unusual. Just the
basics. Routine sex. He doesn't even bother to try to impress me with
fancy positions like Crushing Spices. Flower in Bloom. Dear to Cupid.
Just the missionary position. Sometimes sixty-nine—but all Rick wants
is to get the job done. Quickly.

Not that I mind. *I don't do this for pleasure. I do this for love.*

Except I feel a damp chill between my shoulder blades—thinking
of all the times my spine has creased this mattress—so many mattresses. The second hand ticks. He pushes up on his elbows, his head
above mine. He glances down, focusing more on my torso than on me.
I hug him tighter. Feel *me*. See *me*. I touch his throat with the tip of my
tongue. His skin tastes like salt water and indigo. My limbs feel weighted
with leaden male gravity. Smothered. I feel as if I sink below water, far
beneath a night sea.

Can't I understand that this, what we do here, has only, ever, been
numbed emotions of familiar strangers, fucking? Why can't I accept
the difference between this and love? How can love be two bodies
wrapped in a sheet that's singed by careless cigarettes, here, in a room
with plastic curtains, tin ashtrays, base metal, stained carpet, bad al-
chemy, artificial air, and a television promoting the same pornographic
movies every hour on the hour? Here in a room when, by one o'clock,
Rick looks depleted, the blue of his eyes seeming to have bled beneath
the skin.

———

Rick retrieves a Polaroid camera from a small gym bag. He aims it at
me, still lying in bed, my head propped on the pillow. He jokes: "Smile."
I stare straight into the lens. In the flash I am dazed, as if I've imploded.

I know he needs this photo like a stash, a memento, in order to remember while I'm gone.

Tomorrow morning I am to enter an inpatient treatment facility where I must remain sexually sober for twenty-eight long days. I don't want to go. But if I don't, I'll remain addicted to sex, to men, to dangerous men. My therapist, whom I've been seeing for almost a year, says I must go. For out here, loose in the world, I haven't been able to stop on my own.

Rick goes to shower.

Pieces of my body surface in the Polaroid. My neck down to my knees. I want to be pleased. For only when my body is desired do I feel beautiful, powerful, loved. Except I *don't* feel powerful, loved, or whole now. I feel shy, embarrassed, exhausted. Less. Yes, as if I am less than a body. For right now my body seems to exist only in this Polaroid.

—

For months, like a mantra, my therapist has told me, "These men are killing you." I don't know if he means emotionally, spiritually, or physically. I don't ask. He explains that I confuse sex with love, compulsively repeating this destructive pattern with one man after another. I do this because as a girl I learned that sex is love from my father, the first dangerous man who sexually misloved me.

"I thought the intensity with Rick *must* be love," I say.

"The intensity is an addict's 'high,'" my therapist says. "Not love." To numb the shame and fear associated both with the past and with my current sexual behavior, I medicate, paradoxically, by using sex, he explains. "But sometimes that 'high' stops working. Usually after a scary binge."

Like last Thursday at Rick's house.

Rick and I didn't meet at the Rainbow Motel. His son was home from school with the flu, and Rick took the day off from work to stay with him. Rick and I undressed in the bedroom he shares with his wife, while his son slept in his room down the hall. The house was hushed. The door to the bedroom locked. But then I heard a small sound: his son crying.

Rick heard him, too. I expected Rick to rush to him. We wouldn't have sex. Instead, we would read his son a story. *I* wanted to read his son a story. Give him a glass of water. *I* wanted to give him a glass of water. Press a washcloth to his cheeks. I paused, sure I felt his son's fever, damp and urgent. He needed his father.

His father didn't need him.

Rick's hands tugged at belts and zippers: hurry. We *will* do this . . .

even though his son might get out of bed, knock on the door, see me leave his parents' bedroom. What I then forced myself to know was that *this*, this one careless act of sex, was more important to Rick than his son. And because I, too, couldn't say no, because I feared Rick would leave me if I refused him sex, I began to know, had to accept, that sex was more important to me, too. In a moment of clarity I realized that, while the sober part of me wanted to attend his son, a tangled, humid, inescapable part stopped me. Time stalled: with Rick's hands forever on his belt buckle; with my fingers always on the zipper of my skirt.

And a moment later, I no longer heard his son crying.

The next therapy session I told my therapist, Ted, about Rick's son. More: I confessed that I'd been secretly meeting Rick for weeks without telling him, Ted. I couldn't stop. Before I'd left Ted's office, he called the inpatient unit where he worked and scheduled my admittance. He told me it wasn't possible for him to work with clients who showed up for a session "drunk" or "hungover." He could no longer see me as an outpatient; he could only help me in the rehab unit. "To have *real* feelings, you have to be sexually sober," he said. "Not numbed out." Afraid to be abandoned by Ted, beginning to accept the emotional destructiveness of my behavior, I agreed to go.

Now, as I cross the motel parking lot, dingy afternoon light fuses my blouse to my sweaty back. All I want is to sleep it off. My footsteps sound hollow. My mouth tastes contaminated, metallic. The little girl and her green balloon are gone. Without her energy, the pool is a flat, glassy sheen. Driving from the lot, I pass the neon sign, silently spelling RAINBOW MOTEL.

I should never return here; yet I can't imagine not meeting Rick every Thursday at noon. For what I do in room #213 is the only reason, I believe, a man would love me . . . *what my father taught me was love.*

———

That evening my husband and I eat a silent dinner at the kitchen table. Andrew sits erect, solid, focused on a Braves baseball game on the portable television, while I hunch over my plate. Andrew takes angry bites of an overdone hamburger, the third one I fixed this week, and canned string beans, all I managed to prepare after returning from the motel. I nibble at an edge of hamburger and spear one bean onto my fork. I put it down without eating. Looking at all the food, I think I might be sick. Fumes from the motel seem to rise from the hem of my skirt. My body feels sticky and smudged. It feels unhealthy. Andrew seems not to see, pretends not to notice, this mess that is me. Or, yes, he notices. But he never asks questions. He is too afraid of the answers.

"Sorry about the dinner," I say.

He isn't angry about the affairs; he doesn't know about them. He's angry about my emotional disarray. He wants me to be industrious and smiling. Normal. I worry, even with therapy, I won't learn how to love him the way I should, won't learn how to act like a wife.

"I was wondering," I say, during a television commercial break, "maybe you could drive me over there tomorrow and help me get settled."

"I can't just not teach my classes." His fingers grip the fork.

I want to touch his hand, loosen the grip, warm our fingers.

"I need to finish grading papers." He pushes back his chair. "Remember to call your parents, tell them where you're going," he says. His six-foot body fills the doorway. "I wouldn't know what to say if they call here looking for you."

I scrape my uneaten hamburger and beans into the garbage. Nothing to clean from Andrew's plate, only a smear of ketchup, a few bread crumbs. I squeeze Ivory liquid soap onto the sponge and wash several days' worth of dishes. With a Brillo pad I scour the long-encrusted broiler pan. I sprinkle Comet in the stained sink. I set Andrew's blue cereal bowl on the counter next to his coffee mug, ready for his breakfast in the morning. I want to do more: mop linoleum, polish hardwood floors. I *want* to try harder to please Andrew. I never can. There's always a distraction, always a Rick, or someone. Now, tonight, I feel the burden of calling my parents, the burden of going to the hospital, press against my back. I feel as if I've lost all my muscles.

I turn on the lamp in the living room and sit on our Victorian couch. I pick up the telephone and dial my parents' number. My mother answers on the second ring. Even though my parents know I'm in therapy, I've never said the word *incest* aloud in their presence. Whenever I visit, once or twice a year, we still eat dinner on pretty Wedgwood plates the way we always did. We are silently confused with each other, or else we speak as if no one heard my father turn the doorknob on all my childhood bedrooms . . . never heard the door click shut all those nights.

Now I say to my mother that I have something important to tell her. There is a pause before she answers, "Sure, honey," then places her hand over the receiver. She calls to my father, who picks up the extension. "Hi, precious," he says to me.

I tell them there's nothing to worry about. I've just been depressed and need to go away for about a month. "I'll be at this treatment facility where my therapist works."

"I don't understand," my mother says. "I thought you said you've been doing so much better."

I have told them this lie. They are paying for my therapy sessions, and I want them to think they're getting their money's worth. Ironically, they want me to feel better even as they never ask why I need therapy in the first place.

"How do you know this therapist knows what he's doing?" my father says. "He doesn't know anything about you."

This therapist knows my life is out of control, I want to say. He knows I'm afraid to eat, can't feed my body. He knows I fuck men because it's what *you* taught me is love.

Father, this therapist knows *everything*. About you.

The back of my neck is sweaty, and I coil my hair around my fist. Quizzle, my cat, jumps on the couch and curls beside me.

I barely hear my voice. "He knows I don't know how to love right," I say.

"What kind of people would be in a place like that?" he says.

The more he speaks, the more weightless my head feels, the more sluggish my body. My stomach cramps: with hunger, with fear. I don't know if I can do this.

"People like *me*," I whisper.

"I won't hear about this," he says.

"Dad, wait. My therapist said he'll want to schedule a family session. I mean, I know you can't come down here, but we'll do it on the phone. Like a conference call."

"If he wants a meeting, tell him to send me an agenda."

"That's not exactly how it's done."

"Then how can I know what we're going to talk about?"

What do you think we're going to talk about?

The phone clicks.

I know we'll never have a family session, even on the phone.

"Mom?"

"I'm still here."

"You think he's really angry?"

"Can't you call him from the hospital *without* these therapists?"

My therapist has told me I'm to have no unsupervised contact with my father while in the hospital. No contact with Rick, either.

"How about I'll send you flowers?" she adds.

I don't want flowers. I don't want presents. All you give are presents. You gave *me* as a present. To your husband. By feigning illness and staying in bed, your eyes shut, the door closed, you could pretend not to notice how you made me available to your husband—a gift—a little-girl wife.

"Mother, I don't want flowers, I want . . ."

"What?"

The impossible: a real father; a mother who saw what she saw, knew what she knew. Even though the last time my father touched me sexually was when I left home for college some twenty-five years ago, it feels as if I've never left that home at all.

"Just to get better, I guess," I answer.

"Well, be sure to pack a warm robe and slippers," my mother says. "Bring plenty of vitamin C. You know how cold they keep those places." I am about to hang up when she adds, "Oh, and call your sister. She's doing so well in her new job."

I put down the phone and sink back into the velvet cushion on the couch. I grew up in pretty houses decorated with art objects my father bought on his many travels; how easily our family hid its secrets behind carved wood masks from Samoa, straw fans from Guam. How successful we seemed, with elegant tea sets from Japan, silk curtains from Hong Kong. Now Andrew and I have nice antiques, an Oriental rug, watercolor paintings. *Things.* I was raised to believe that if a family appears perfect, it must *be* perfect. I have tried to keep up appearances.

———

I open the door to Andrew's study. He doesn't look up. He is an English professor, and he sits at his desk grading student papers. I lean over his shoulder and wrap my arms around his chest. I tell him I called my parents, that my father hung up, that my mother worries I'll catch cold. He sighs, and doesn't put down his pencil.

I straighten and lean against his desk. Bookcases jammed with volumes by James Joyce, Thomas Pynchon, Tolstoy, Cervantes, Jane Austen, Derrida, Riffaterre, Kant, line the walls like thick insulation. He is writing a book of his own, evolved from his dissertation. I have typed the manuscript several times for him, several revisions. I have proofread it twice. Yet I only have a vague understanding of what it's about.

Even though I married Andrew for his cool distant silence—so different from my father's needy raging—now, this moment, I want to get his attention. I want to say: Look at me! I want to crack the silence of our marriage and reveal to him the *complete* reason my therapist says I must enter the hospital now: to be sequestered, quarantined, from men. But I can't tell Andrew. For I believe if he sees the real me, he'll leave me. All he knows for sure is that I'm entering treatment because what happened to me as a child caused an eating disorder and I hate food.

I turn, about to close the door to his study. "I'm sorry," is all I'm able to say. "You know?"

"Look, I'm sure it'll be fine," he says. "Call me when you get there. Let me know you made it okay."

Later I lie awake, where I sleep by myself, in a small second-story bedroom. The attic fan whooshes air from the basement up through the house and out the windows, out the vents in the gable. The house feels vacant. Andrew sleeps directly below me in a king-sized bed. I roll onto my stomach in my narrow bed and press my fingertips against the wood floor. I want to feel a quiet vibration from his breath. I want to tiptoe down the stairs and slip beneath the covers beside him. I want the scent of his freshly laundered sheets on my own body, his clean, strong hand to hold mine. I want to feel a reassuring, constant presence of this man labeled "husband." I don't know how. Ordinary married life is too tame and mild. I want to hold on to him, but Andrew, as well as our ten-year marriage, only skims the periphery of my senses.

Initially I moved in with Andrew because he asked me. I was searching for love, even though I was married to someone else at the time. But bored with my first marriage, I thought all I needed to be happy was to switch partners. After a divorce and living together about a year, Andrew and I decided to marry. The morning of our wedding, however, I awoke with a headache, my muscles stiff with the responsi-

Love Sick · 273

bility of maintaining a relationship: yes, too ordinary, committed, boring. Not as intense or exciting—not as short-lived—as a one-night stand or an affair. Scant weeks before the wedding I'd even come close to having sex with the president of a company where I was doing "temp" work for $4.50 an hour. I'm not sure why I said no to that president, except maybe this time I really wanted to make a stab at marriage.

I'd ordered my "wedding dress" out of a catalogue. It was a red cotton floral outfit, marked down to nineteen dollars.

Andrew urged me to buy something nicer. I couldn't.

How could I tell him I bought the dress because *I* felt marked down? How could I wear white or cream or tan when red is my true color?

———

Three-thirty in the morning. The silence of our house, our marriage, wells up around me. Night is a thick humid wall. I need a way out. I push back the sheet and retrieve a lavender wood box I've hidden for years in my closet. I sit on the floor. Inside the box is my stash—stuff hoarded for when I need a fix—these mementos of men almost as good as a real man. Letters, photos, jewelry, books, pressed flowers. A maroon cashmere scarf that an older married man gave me when I was a college student in Boston. I drape the scarf around my neck.

From my dresser I remove khaki shorts, underwear, socks, a few wrinkled T-shirts, a pair of gray sweats, and place them in my canvas suitcase. I slide my fingers along metal hangers in the closet. Short skirts. Silk and lacy blouses. Rainbow Motel blouses. I also own blazers and oxford shirts, professional clothes, from various past jobs, even though I am currently unemployed. Size-four dresses to clothe my anorexic body. Size-eight for when I'm eating. But little in this closet is appropriate for a hospital. On a shelf in the back I find an oversized white T-shirt with the stenciled message: STRANDED ON THE STRAND. It is so old the seams are splitting, the print fading. I bought it in Galveston, where I once lived, in an area called the Strand. I always read the message literally: I have felt stranded. Everywhere. I decide to wear it tomorrow.

I tuck the maroon scarf between the shirts in my suitcase.

Next to my bedroom is the bath. I collect deodorant, toothbrush, toothpaste, comb. No makeup. Not even lipstick for this new sober self

I will try to create tomorrow. In the medicine cabinet is my supply of Gillette single-edged razor blades. Why not? The metal feels cool, comforting. The blades are to slice small cuts in my skin. How peaceful, whenever I drift into a trance of silver razors, obsessed with watching slivers of blood trail down my thighs. Small hurts always distract me from the larger hurts. Blood, starvation, promiscuity, are *managed* pain, meant to relieve larger, *un*manageable pain.

I slip a razor blade under the bar of Dove soap in my pink plastic soap dish and put it in my suitcase.

CONFESSIONS OF A
MIDDLE-AGED ECSTASY EATER

Anonymous

2001

As teenagers across America were discovering the vibrant high of Ecstasy, a middle-aged man embarked on his own odyssey with the popular club drug. In "Confessions of a Middle-Aged Ecstasy Eater," originally published in Granta, *a father's sudden hunger for escape is fueled by the breakup of his marriage as well as his drug-dealing, teenage son's frightening brushes with suicide and skirmishes with the law. Reminiscent of Thomas De Quincey's* Confessions of an English Opium-Eater, *this selection portrays the moral quandaries of a man who is driven headlong into the throes of addiction.*

But who are they [this whole class of opium eaters]? Reader, I am sorry to say, a very numerous class indeed . . . I do not readily believe that any man, having once tasted the divine luxuries of opium, will afterwards descend to the gross and mortal enjoyments of alcohol. I take it for granted:

> That those eat now, who never ate before
> And those who always ate, now eat more.

—THOMAS DE QUINCEY,
CONFESSIONS OF AN ENGLISH OPIUM-EATER,
THE LONDON MAGAZINE, 1821

To the reader. I hereby present you with a record, of sorts, of a remarkable period in my life. According to my application of it, I trust, as I likewise hope, that it may prove not merely interesting, but, to a considerable degree, useful and instructive. It is in that hope that I have troubled myself to draw it up, even as I feel compelled in advance to apologize for breaching that delicate and honourable reserve which, until quite recently—when certain publishers became aware that there was for the marketing of such breaching an apparently limitless audience, that is, one ripe to be r(e)aped—has restrained me from the public exposure of my own errors and infirmities.

Which makes me no less reluctant to do so, for while there are many whom it would please loudly to dispute it—they do not know me well enough, or know all too well but that certain part of me—I am, at heart, an abashed man. Indeed so alive am I to the professional reproach and public humiliation that such exposure necessarily would arouse that I have for months resisted the prodding of certain parties to permit any part of my narrative to come before the public. And it is not without enormous anxiety, nor an absence of insomniac nights, that I have, at last, reached the decision to do so however constrained I am to remain anonymous in the doing.

This is not, understand, owing to my self-accusation constituting a confession of guilt, any more than it does an expression of hubris. I feel no guilt, none at all. I know this to be true for I am as susceptible to guilt (and shame and self-loathing) as to self-aggrandizement, and in this instance I feel of either, as I do of both, neither tweak nor discernible twinge. As pertains to what follows, such feelings are utterly beside the point.

That said, I am not, thank God, Thomas De Quincey (or Coleridge, Baudelaire, Cocteau, Huxley, Paul Bowles, Carlos Castenada, William Burroughs, Ken Kesey or Hunter S. Thompson, to name but the more usual of the usual suspects), and the irreparable harm that revealing my identity inevitably would inflict, not only upon my professional reputation but upon those whom I love and care deeply for, simply is not commensurate with the benefits liable to redound to me in so doing. Perhaps some day, one day when we all of us are more—what?— grown up? Grown up enough, at least, to be less hysterical and apocalyptic about the subject at hand. But for now, more's the pity, no. If I do not court censure, neither do I curry accolade, and so for the time being am, as I must be, content to skulk behind the craven's mask.

I am fast—I am tempted to say far too fast, save that it never ceases to strike me as the unlikeliest of miracles—approaching my fiftieth year, and most of my adult life has been lived comfortably upon the right side of the law, first as a journalist, then as a novelist, prose-poet and essayist. I am at present, or so I gather, what I so long ago explicitly aspired to become—a man of letters.

From my birth I was as it seems to me now an intellectual creature first—I emerged from the womb (if one is to believe my mother, and how dare I do otherwise) brow furrowed, face knit in an expression of the most singular concentration and perplexity: "Where the hell am I and why am I here, what precisely is going on and what, pray tell, if there be one, which seems increasingly unlikely, is the point?" and I do not wonder, for those questions I grapple with still, as still without adequate answers. And so intellectual in the highest sense my pursuits and pleasures have always been, even from my schoolboy days.

I know little for an immanent certainty, but this I immanently, most certainly do (one needn't be Stephen Hawking to appreciate such evident truth)—nothing surpasses the life of the mind, that same mind, as William Gass has rightly observed, that is the "only claw man has." And so, if eating Ecstasy be chiefly a sensual, and so a mindless pleasure, and if, as I confess, I have indulged in it to excess, no less true is that I have struggled to understand my habit, if not yet with the religious zeal required properly to get shed of it.

But then, perhaps I do not wish to get shed of it, not really, or not nearly enough. And this is but one of the many lessons, insofar as one may be disposed to receive them, that Ecstasy is wont to impart: that first principles—of life, love, God, beauty—fly apart, and it is not incumbent upon us to puzzle them through that we might piece them together again, but merely do as we might to hold on for dear life, to ride out the storm and, as we may manage it, gather unto ourselves some little enjoyment in the doing. Anything else not only is an utter waste of time, but an exercise in self-deception, deceit and the grossest, most overweening vanity. Ecstasy—and not merely the drug—never was intended to be intellectualized.

Order, even creatively ordered order, perhaps especially creatively ordered order—that which it pleases intellectuals such as myself to anoint Art (and oh, how we do insist in the solemnity of our self-congratulation upon the capitalization of that A)—is powerless against the chaos, because that chaos resides not only out there, in the "real" world, but inside each one of us. It is hewn to the double helix, the anarchic state of our collective soul, and its only counter, its only effective antidote, is death. Against which, I fear, no vaccine—at least, not yet. (Though if science can design for us Ecstasy, can immortality be far behind?)

I have occasionally been asked how I first came to it, that is, how I became a regular Ecstasy eater, the assumption being, I presume, that I was seeking a cheap (I have paid as little as ten dollars a pill when buying "in bulk," seldom more than twenty-five dollars) and ephemeral thrill, pursuing a temporary state of pleasurable, if wholly artificial excitement, the craic of that High, the visceral flow of its fix, the ultimate *roll*. And perhaps, at first, I was. I was aware of its reputation as the "Love Drug," had heard it described—I can no longer recall just where—as a "four-hour, full-body orgasm," had read Sean Elder's seminal 1986 article, "On Ecstasy," and all of this I found—what?— intriguing, appealing, alluring? Well, I found it worthy of further investigation.

Which is odd, because ordinarily I would not have condescended to pay it the slightest heed. Even at university, the high times of those heady years—in my case 1969 to 1976—I was not a user, chronic, casual or otherwise. Despite an environment in which experimentation with illegal substances was culturally certified as little more than an alternative form of recreation, indeed in which smoking grass and dropping acid (if not yet snorting coke or shooting smack), was not only benignly accepted, but benevolently smiled upon, I deliberately chose not to indulge. (OK, once. I did some speed. I had fallen behind in a course and was facing an all-nighter. I swallowed the pill, whole— something called a "white cross" as I for no earthly reason recall—and was up, each of my senses on red alert, my heart a snare drum in my ears, my eyes seeming literally to sweat, the world standing newel-post straight at full attention for the ensuing forty-eight hours. I saw tigers everywhere and heard the incessant wailing of sirens. I learned later I ought to have ingested only half. I never did it again.) And this, one ought not with a measure of humility hesitate to aver, required no fair amount of self-discipline, as it did a right gathering of will. The dope was everywhere, it seemed at times to be in the very drinking water, in the air itself, and everyone—including my friends (my closest was a jazz musician, imagine), more than a few girlfriends, and most of my professors, as they were content enough to broadcast—was doing it.

Except me. I wasn't. And this had nothing to do with feelings of superiority or intolerance (however consistently I may have refused to suffer hedonists gladly), or the bucking of countercultural convention, as it did less with morality or politics or religion. (I was in those days, right down to the black of my beret, an existentialist on the first count, a raving anarchist of the Malatesta school on the second, a crypto-Kierkegaardian on the third—or so I recollect fancying myself.) It had to do solely with fear. Not only was I afraid of "fucking with my mind," I was petrified of irreparably fucking it up. I took myself seriously, far too seriously—those were serious times for those of us who took them seriously, as seriously as did I—and I steadfastly refused to buy into the druggie/head trip/stoner agitprop of the day. Reading *The Electric Kool-Aid Acid Test* or *Fear and Loathing in Las Vegas,* listening to Hendrix or the Doors, Cream or the Airplane was more than enough for me. I was possessed of no itch to experience the psychedelics of that "trip" first-hand, as I felt no exigency about making God's more intimate acquaintance.

Not that I was, despite my Midwestern Calvinist upbringing, narrow-minded or uncurious, nor was I unhip. If I was far from some paragon of Mailer's White Negro, well, even the Negroes I knew—I hung out a lot in jazz clubs—were not paragons of Mailer's White Negro. (Indeed, over time, I have come to surmise that only Mailer himself—and perhaps Mick Jagger—ever was.) Simply, I was scared. Small wonder, then, how often those select few with knowledge of my current habit have remarked—less appalled, perhaps, than incredulous—upon my being the "least likely person in the world" to have fallen prey to it.

Well, yes. And likewise, no. For while I cannot swear with spot-on certainty, I believe that my coming to Ecstasy—or it to me—goes further than mere thrill-seeking. I believe it goes to the centre of my life at the time, a life that, to employ a colloquially turned phrase, was a mess. I was headed south, a south sunless, unlovely and cold.

This is difficult, even now, to talk about. We all have our war stories. Mine is but one more heaped among the remains of the rest. I do not presume to claim for it some vaunted or exalted status. I have no desire to extol what merits no extolling (much less to aestheticize it). If ecstasy is not meant to be intellectualized, neither is suffering intended to be phenomenalized, particularly where it is of no higher order than anyone else's. If it is special, somehow different, that is only because it is mine and mine alone. It was a period of personal devastation. Such periods eventually are visited upon us all. We all encounter those dark fires through which we must walk or perforce self-immolate, and no one who lives his life as it is meant to be lived ought to expect to emerge from them unscathed. One's scars are not chevrons; they are not meant to be brandished like stigmata.

It began with my only child, a son—he was then my best friend, from time to time still is—and I did not see it coming (not that I was looking; I was sitting on a fast ball, not the curve I was eventually served), and it culminated in Ecstasy, and to that I see no end. He was beautiful and sensitive—perhaps too sensitive, more than I knew or he had a right to be, this permeable membrane—and extraordinarily talented, talented enough that at thirteen his poetry had won the notice of university professors and New York book editors alike; the budding Rimbaud. So when he undertook to destroy himself, he took his mother and father with him. That was not, nor is it, his fault. He was thirteen and had neither the capacity nor context to grasp what he was doing. He was then being held hostage to problems of his own, problems he could no more articulate than dogs do long division, trees turn somersaults or thunder parse sentences, and which he would have roundly denied if he could. And if he had been capable of knowing the pain and heartache his behaviour was causing the two people he loved most in the world, he would not have cared. He was not, then, possessed of the wherewithal.

One always can be more specific, describe more, one always can concretize experience. The only issue is how detailed, how concrete, how descriptively specific one wishes to be. So: he attempted suicide. (The details are unimportant; the very devil is in them.) He ran away, serially. He purchased a handgun from a school friend. He stole, sometimes from stores, more often from his parents, typically in the middle of the night. He was arrested for stealing. He was sentenced to community service. He committed various, not particularly imaginative acts of vandalism. He taunted and cussed at strangers on the street. He got drunk—beer, wine, liquor, whatever he could lay his hands on—and when he got drunk, he got violent. He verbally and physically abused his mother. He attempted, using a pair of candles, to set her hair on fire. The second time he used gasoline. He dismantled furniture, broke china, smashed crystal and, unprovoked, punched out windows and kicked in walls. He shredded his wardrobe with scissors, every stitch of his clothing, and when he had finished, started in on his mother's. He trashed his bedroom down to lathings, shims and cinder block. He graffitied what remained with every racial and sexual epithet imaginable. He slept on the floor amid rotting food, curdled milk, the mouse droppings that appeared in their wake and a rubble of plaster, drywall and broken glass. He refused to bathe. He defecated in the yard and urinated in Coke cans which he deployed about his bedroom in pentagrams, these red metal voodoo dolls. He carved his arms with the filed-down ends of paper clips. He discovered marijuana, then cocaine. Then PCP. Then Special K (an animal tranquillizer, which he called "catfood"). He fought with friends. One scrape involved a spot of knife play culminating in a facial slash requiring a ten-stitch repair. The few that remained he manipulated and abused, this adolescent Svengali. He was flung through a plate-glass window by a schoolmate, a football player, escaping serious injury, according to the principal, "only by divine intervention." He was expelled from high school. He impregnated a girl. There was an abortion. He disappeared for days at a time, often into New York City where he slept in storefronts and abandoned buildings and on park benches; at least twice he was shaken down at knifepoint. He sold or bartered his personal belongings, many of them Christmas and birthday presents—guitars, stereo equipment, CD collections, wristwatches, leather jackets—to raise money to buy drugs. He contracted one sexually transmitted disease, then another. He was under age, so when he drove his friends' cars he did so illegally. High on cocaine, he eventually rolled one on the Interstate while going in excess of eighty mph. That he and his two passengers, one his girlfriend, were not killed outright—the car came to rest on its roof in a creek bed; they climbed out bruised and bloodied through its open trunk—was in the by-now familiar words of the State Trooper, "only a matter of divine intervention." He escaped incarceration at the state juvenile detention facility only because the court was inexplicably merciful. He dropped out of a second, "alternative" school. He worked sporadically, a succession of menial, part-time jobs, none of which lasted more than a few weeks: window washer, hod carrier, gas jockey, bellhop. Eventually he was removed from his home and consigned—exiled, really—first to lockdown in a private psychiatric ward, then to a special school out of state. He was counselled. He was diagnosed with a variety of acronyms: AD, ADD, ODD, ICD, possible BP. He was prescribed medication: Zoloft, Depakote, Paxil, Wellbutrin. When that school and that counsel and that medication did not "take," he was given different medication and more counselling and sent to yet another school out of state, a private high school with an annual tuition fee of $40,000. While there, during an off-campus weekend, he was arrested and jailed overnight for possession and sentenced to community service. He briefly participated in a scam to pass counterfeit money. He took his exam and got his driver's licence. Two months later he had accumulated thirteen points. His licence was suspended. He kept driving anyway. He was now dealing as well as using drugs and the wheels were essential to what he called his "livelihood," as they were conducive to his lifestyle, a lifestyle redolent of a vampire's, for he lived upside down, sleeping all day, drugging all night. Eventually, in the course of one five-day spree, he totalled two automobiles, one his father's, pulverizing his ankle so badly in the process that it required twenty-six staples, ten screws and two stainless-steel plates to reconstruct. I would not swear to the precise chronology of any of this—even now it remains a blur—but to this I would: he strewed wreckage everywhere. His was another kind of reality, an unreality perhaps, an anti-reality, and those drawn into the chaos of its orbit, those who found themselves cobbed in its web inevitably suffered damage.

In the meantime his parents' marriage, all twenty years of it, was collapsing. My wife was and remains a beautiful, caring, generous, gifted woman. She is the oldest soul I know, the blithest spirit, and I would not hesitate to give my life for her, and though we no longer live together, have not lived together for years, I admire and, on some level, love her still, as I know I always shall. But sometimes that is not enough. Sometimes nothing is enough, as sometimes everything isn't. The marriage had its long-standing problems, its rifts and fractures and shoals, and when it came under siege and then assault, when our son began the process of so thoroughly, as we took to referring to it, "flushing himself," the stress was too much. We lost our way, then ran aground, and then, at last, we broke.

We tried over and over again to address the issues, patch the problems, spackle them, caulk them, span them, fill them, whatever it is one does when one senses imminent demolition and doesn't know quite why and is floundering as one flails and hasn't a clue what to do. We tried because we once had had something valuable, because we shared an intimate history of mutual investment, because we once had cherished the sound of one another's laughter, because not trying seemed to us grotesque. We tried because we loved one another and because we loved our son, in the face of whose own self-demolition neither of us could have survived intact. If that sounds melodramatic, it should. It was a melodramatic time.

So we broke, and I left. Oh, not straight away—the break was anything but clean; it was tortured, as it became Byzantine—and I never went far. A basement apartment across the street, a rodent-infested one the next town over. I was in and out, out and in, back in and back out for years. I was at a loss as to how I could properly leave and unsure I wished to find out. But then, I wasn't sure of much, not any more, and that disconcerted almost as much as it depressed me, because being dead certain, even when I was dead wrong, was a quality I had typically hung my hat on. The quintessential male facade, and one behind which I was quaking.

I couldn't seem to stop quaking.

Eventually I found a place just bleak enough to mirror the way I felt, and I felt dreadful, wretched, unsalvageable, I felt vile and violated, and I felt lost. And solitary. And wrong. All of me, wrong. I stopped shaving, bathing, sleeping. In time I stopped eating. (Over one three-month period I shed forty pounds.) I no longer recognized the aesthetics of myself. There are any number of poetic words that lend themselves to the state to which I had descended, but a single, six-letter one seems best: bereft—"void of; taken away, removed, quite gone." Somehow I had become radioactive, the world a wilderness of asperity, and I was left to maunder it untethered and mapless, self-menaced and heartsore and seared.

The place was a single, windowless room scarce larger than a tool shed, a root cellar space attached to the back of an abandoned garage, and I wallowed in it, in its cobwebs and scum-scrim and filth—I hadn't, naturally, the wherewithal to clean up after myself—alone. And so it was alone that I began to disintegrate. I continued to write, frantically, incessantly, desperately, because writing was the only way I knew to stay afloat, though looking back I cannot say whether I was writing myself out of what I sensed was an approaching madness, or writing myself more deeply into it.

The nightmares arrived on cue. Not images of hell and its hounds—those I might have withstood—but waterfalls and rivers of words. No images, no meanings, just words, disconnected, decontextualized, foaming, alone. Words as onrushing water, whirlpools and eddies and swirls. I was afflicted by freshets and torrents, marooned in the froth of their flow. Cascades, cataracts, outpours, an unending, recurring cadence that streamed forth in syntactical arabesques. I was haemorrhaging rhymes and the metre of verbs, and each morning, 4 A.M., 5 A.M., morning after morning for months, I awoke unbuoyed and drenched to the bone.

And I wondered, as I wonder still, which of us is possessed of the temerity to suggest that we are not drowning? To gainsay that we are not being dragged under, again and again, and forever?

Somehow, I no longer recall just how and prefer even now not to, I completed the 500-page draft of a novel about, of all things, Lizzie Borden, but when I submitted it to my agent he deemed it "one of the most brilliant pieces of insanity" he had ever read, declared it utterly unmarketable, and declined to take it on. (He was, I see now, as I was incapable of seeing then, perfectly correct to do so. Brilliant it may have been, insane it decidedly remains.) We parted company, upon the heels of which my editor quit his job at a prominent New York publishing house. My marriage was dead—though I still insisted upon thinking of it as merely semi-comatose—my son still very much alive, I was agentless, editorless, apparently unpublishable, was living like a tramp and a recluse, my income close to nil, and slowly, and then not so slowly, I was, I had convinced myself, going mad. Having cast myself out—of home-and-hearth, as from all human contact—I had become in every way imaginable an outcast. Dostoevsky's subterranean man. The ex that prefixes exist.

There is, it bears mention, suicide in my family—my mother's brother (at thirteen, with a .22, to the head)—and while such history, or its spectre, has a way of haunting one's more susceptible moments, I never contemplated cashing myself in. I had peeked at the desolation behind that door years before only to decide at the last possible moment—at such times it always is the last possible moment and one lives in its present perpetually—not to see it through. It simply was not in me. Suicide, permit me to suggest, is an act of vanity, the penulti-mate gesture of the born narcissist, and while I had, and have, a surplus of the stuff, it is also—let no one tell you differently—an occasion of infernal courage, a gesture of brute bravery. I wanted the mettle, as I hadn't the nerve.

So for the first time in my life I sought help. My therapist was a wise, caring, gentle man, and while he tried—when I scraped fiscal bottom he carried me gratis for months—a year later he had failed to solve me. I continued to dream in words, only now I did so wide awake, this perambulatory radio of the mind, and I powerless to switch it off. I didn't hear voices, no intonation, inflection, insinuation—what I was hearing was characterless, qualityless, robotic, disembodied—I simply heard words, braids and imbrications, interlacings and overleafings, plaited webs and thatched rafts of words, and the organic pacings and tempos of their architecture. Every day deeper into this deep blue sea, its rip tides and undertows. Every day further out, beyond the crest of the next crashing wave, the slough of its swell—bluer, bluing, more blued.

So—isn't it obvious?—I began visiting bowling alleys, dozens of them, month after month. Something about the explosion of the ball and the collision of caroming pins, a sound distinct to my childhood, the only one I could imagine might mute the ones inside my head. I never bowled myself, just sat hunched to whatever bar top I found my-self bellied to, nursing a beer and moving my lips to such poetry as I had at hand: Rimbaud and Rilke, Leonard Cohen and Jim Carroll, Heaney and Ashbery and Charles Olson. And Paul Metcalf, with whom I had recently begun a lively and regular correspondence. I read Metcalf—Herman Melville's great-grandson—above all. (A few months later he was dead of a heart attack at the age of eighty-one and I felt not only aggrieved, but oddly accountable.) But eventually it proved too dispiriting. The bowlers began to appear too alien, their displays of team triumph and defeat only underscored my own lack of affect, and at last I ran clean out of bowling alleys. And now I could sense it, the lurking of something hard, and dark as it was cold. It had been decades since I had read, much less thought about Fitzgerald's "The Crack-up," but now I began to suspect that this might be something much like that: the pending implosion. Something was inside, something outsized and other, and it was stronger than I was, and more potent, and it meant me only ill. My life—this is precisely what it felt like—had cornered me at last.

Perhaps certain questions suggest themselves: what about religion, for example, or sex, their consolation and refuge, the salvation to be had of their purchase. Although I had once had the former in spadefuls—in my early twenties I had been awarded a scholarship to Vanderbilt Divinity School, one that at the eleventh hour I had chosen not to pursue—in time I had come to travel a different path. I became a journalist, a newspaper reporter, and in the process lost what little faith I once had possessed. I was engaged in "real" life in those days, the quotidian issues driving the lives of others, and by the time I threw over my thriving career several years later I had seen far too much of it for it to engage me further. Not that I experienced my loss of faith in any active or meaningful way. God simply, gradually, imperceptibly became as incidental and finally irrelevant to my life as our lives, I am convinced, are to Him. Those who have faith, those who somehow have succeeded in finding the depth and fortitude of character to keep it, doubtless will deem such a declaration exceedingly sad. I do not. The point is, that particular option was closed to me. The despair I was feeling not even Christ might assuage.

As for sex, despite protracted periods of acquiescent celibacy inside my marriage, I had always liked it, the little I had had, and now I missed it, terribly, became, in fact, abstracted by its absence. Sex tends, I think—deplorably—to be taken for granted when one has easy and routine access to it, but when one finds oneself deprived of that access, well, one yearns. All day, every day. At least I do. Did. Unfortunately, while I have always adored women—to a greater extent than I feel kinship with men—I am constitutionally incapable of one-night stands, casual affairs or even what might these days be considered an acceptable level of discreet larking about. Not that I haven't had my opportunities, but I have never failed, save once, to take a rain check. Infidelity, philandering, debauchery, promiscuity, profligacy, skirt-chasing—call it what one will—none were among the reasons my marriage unravelled, though the meagre quantity and quality of the sex certainly was. And my reticence, if that is what it was, had very little to do with epidemiology—with AIDS and its lesser cousins—as it had nothing whatever to do with morality. Indeed, what it had to do with, God knows. The point is, that option was not open to me either.

So: suicide, religion, sex. Three strikes, as is said, and you are out. Quite gone. Void of. Bereft. Thrice over.

And then the unthinkable happened, or rather, two things happened. I met someone, a woman, and while I in my recalcitrant fashion followed up on that meeting so that she might eventually save me (as save me she eventually did), my son was becoming—with a vengeance, which is his own fashion, the only fashion he knows, headlong as headstrong in all things—what is called in the parlance, a "raver." And he seemed for the first time in years—he was seventeen by then—happy. Not giddy or euphoric, but content, at peace with himself, within himself. I do not mean to invoke images of Zen and Buddha—my son is roughly as Zen-like as Eminem—but the transformation was as striking as it was palpable, this sea change. Indeed it seemed so definitive that I could not help asking him about it, and when I did, he smiled— I shall always remember that smile, he has the most incandescent smile in the world—and said simply, "Uh-huh. I am." And when I asked him why, what had happened, what accounted, he smiled again and said, "Aw, you wouldn't understand. But it's my whole life now. I know why I'm alive."

I remember my response. And perhaps had I responded in some other way or simply not responded at all, what was about to happen would never have happened. Or perhaps it would have. Perhaps it would have happened anyway. Perhaps it had to happen, and no matter what I said or left unsaid it was going to happen, because that is the way these things happen. What I said was, "Congratulations. I'm happy for you. Really. I wish I did." Because despite everything, my son and I have never withheld, not from one another. He confides, as do I. He tells me things no child ought ever tell a parent, things no parent wants to hear, disgusting things often, morally reprehensible things, nauseatingly cruel things, things that are so appallingly beyond the pale, so rife with risk, rank with recklessness, so absent all human feeling and judgement that I am left, as I seldom am, quite speechless. For one cannot speak when one's teeth are set so on edge, and one is tectonically grinding them.

And so he turned to me and said, "Seriously?" And when I answered

288 · Under the Influence

not only in the affirmative, but the declarative, he told me a story and made me an offer, and so was hatched yet another aspect of our relationship, an aspect that is as wholly illicit as it is morally unsavoury, and one that continues to this day.

We both know it is wrong, this part of it, the arrangement, the dilemma it poses, wrong in the most intimate and unholy of ways, as we both know that neither of us care enough about the fact to do anything about it. Why should we? We have disappointed one another so often in the past that it seems to matter less than not at all. It is a shared shame now, something the two of us have that no one else has, and it has become, like the abiding commonness of our blood, a large and integral part of what bonds us—father and son, parent and child. Perhaps no truth is more momentous, as none more difficult to face, than the blackest, most abject one about oneself. My son supplies me with drugs, with Ecstasy, and if I am to be consigned to perdition, if I am to roast in hell, this, it seems to me, is first among the reasons that I shall do so. And it seems to me, further, that it is one damn fine good reason, because reckoned objectively, it is a horror, it is a latter-day horror story, save that it is not a story, it is not fiction, it is about as far from fiction as one can conceivably get. It is as real and true as it is unthinkable, and there are times when the obscenity of it takes my breath away and dizzies that benighted part of me steeped in self-disgust.

And so the first time I ate E—or X, or EX, or XTC, or MDMA (methylenedioxymethamphetamine) or ADAM—it was owing to my having given my son permission to sell it to me. I became his customer, a buyer, a reliable and steady client, the lowest link on the food chain of the multi-billion-dollar commerce that proceeds unabated every day, every hour, in every large city and small town in every state in this union, in what is called by those paid to "war" against them, as likewise those who traffic in them, "controlled substances."

You must pardon me—I do not mean to sound smug—but I find it funny. I find it ironic. It tickles and entertains and amuses me. Because I cannot think of a single commodity in our country—one that, meretricious as it may sound, I love dearly, know well and for which my father and his father fought and sacrificed much—that is less controlled than are such substances, nor a single "war" that is as pathetically futile, vaingloriously chimeric and long-ago-lost as is this one. It is not that I am unsympathetic to those who, after all, are only doing their jobs (often at grave risk to their lives)—however much I might suggest that such frontline foot soldiers would do better to find another line of work—but I am nothing but unrepentedly hostile towards policies and laws (or rather, the sort of tortured, twisted, two-penny logic that produced and continues to pursue them) that, however well-intentioned, are so indefensibly stupid, monstrously ill-conceived, implicitly dishonest, and, in the impracticability and inequity of their application, as unjust as they are dumb.

I went, only last week, to see the movie *Traffic*. Fine film, if not nearly so fine as the critics seem to think, but then the critics, as they so often do, miss the point. *Traffic* is not a movie about the evil of drugs and inhumanity of the drug trade, it is a movie about the idiocy of our drug policy and the evils it not only fosters, but ensures will continue to flower.

Why is this so difficult to apprehend? What prevents us from possessing the humility of character to embrace the lessons hard won of our defeat? Why do we pretend? Is it really necessary to cite statistics or solicit the rhetoric, fatuous as it is fatigued, of "experts"? We know better, or ought: the handwriting is on the wall, the toothpaste has vacated the tube, Rome is long since burned to the ground, the Emperor is wearing no clothes, and our folly has returned home to roost. You can fight City Hall, but wrestle as you will, you cannot reform or arrest human appetite any more than you can with a wave of the wand make a gay person straight or summon the voice of God that He might shed the ecumenical light of His omniscience upon the subject.

Ecstasy was made a Schedule One illegal drug—for which we can all thank that cynosure of intellect, Texas Senator Lloyd Bentsen—in June of 1985. Which, at present, makes it as illegal as heroin. This, in its preposterous disproportion, is just the sort of run-amok governmental lunacy guaranteed to ensure that those like myself—and more importantly, our children—will write off that same government and those who enforce its drug laws as out of touch, coercive, morally bankrupt and, yes—wake up guys! wake up and smell the poppies!—un-American. Because America is not, or did not use to be, about throwing sixteen-year-old kids in jail for—all in the spirit of free-market capitalism and entrepreneurial enterprise—home-growing a little cannabis, even as the rest of us chain-smoke our Camels, sip our Absoluts with a twist, and devour our Prozac.

Visit a rehab centre sometime. You will learn two things inside that first hour. One, that there are people in this world—some quite admirable, others ostensibly less so—who are more prey to addiction than others; there always have been, always will be, addicts. And two, that the "gateway" argument is as simplistic as it is spurious. We are not losing our kids to drugs. We have lost our kids because we haven't the time, inclination, strength of character or political will to do the right thing in their name: to eliminate the black market that so mercilessly exploits them—and the runaway violence it spawns—by legalizing, taxing and regulating the trade.

"Controlled" substances? That, regrettably, is but a misnomer meriting our laughter, as it ought to occasion our tears. There is no control. There is a bureaucracy, and a so-called policy, and some laws, and the lot is a sham and a smokescreen that increasingly deceives no one. There is but a single way to "lick the scourge and eliminate the blight," to win, that is, the so-called war on drugs—to win it so that it might have some chance, however slim, of staying won—and that way consists of two words, words that are more American than any two of which I can conceive (save, perhaps, "Uncle Sam"): Wall Street.

But then, who cares what I think? Anybody can think anything about everything, as everybody inevitably does. I pretend to no monopoly of wisdom upon the subject. But I know something of Ecstasy, perhaps I even know a lot, or more than most, and certainly more than most of a certain age, which is to say, a comparable, middling one. And what I know I know because I have eaten and continue to eat so much of it. I am an experienced, seasoned, veteran eater of E—I would not hazard a guess as to the exact quantity, though it is fair to say a lot—and it is a fact of which I am neither proud nor mortified.

So here, in a word, a most sober, solemn, even a sombre word, is what I know: *yum.*

Ecstasy is delicious. Or, put it another way, Ecstasy is delicious and I recommend highly, loudly and long that everyone whose health—physical *and* psychological—does not contraindicate or preclude its ingestion, ought to ingest it. Young/old, man/woman, rich/poor, gay/straight, black/white, saint/sinner, genius/dolt, Christian and Jew and Muslim, Democrat, Republican and Independent, lawmaker and lawbreaker, heartbreaker and soulshaker, the sexually degenerate and

sexually celibate, the whole damn Rainbow Coalition. (Am I being deliberately provocative? Of course. As I am being entirely serious.)

Go out, I admonish you, all of you, hie thyselves thither, hit the
streets or collar that neighbourhood kid, drum up a contact, do a deal,
repair thyselves home, soften the lights, put on some music—the best
stuff—pour yourself a pitcher of ice water, perhaps two, keep a tin of
Altoids handy, as well as a tube of Vicks Inhalant and a couple of packs
of mineral ice, make yourself comfortable, lay back and . . . swallow.

Swallow that pill, let it slide, feel the glide, and relax. Quiet your
mind. Calm your soul. An hour from now, perhaps somewhat less, you
are going to experience something you have never experienced before.
You are going to experience something you will never forget. You are
going to experience something that shall forever change such time as
remains to you on this earth. You are going to experience something
that will halve your life into before and after: BE/AE. You are going
to experience something that is, every second of it, delicious—
deliciously, positively, unprecedentedly w-o-n-d-e-r-f-u-l.

It is your self-anointing, and I envy you it. I envy you that first time.
So relish it, savour, languish in, treasure. Consecrate it, that sacred four
hours. You have just swallowed wonder, ambrosia and mead, you have
partaken of lustre and grace.

Just make certain that before you swallow you know that the pill is
authentic, genuine, the real deal, the goods, and not some innocuous
rip-off or inimical knock-off. Do that, and the rest, as they say, is a
piece of cake, a piece of cake that, in this instance, is like no other you
have ever tasted. Think of the best day of your life, or recall the sweet-
est, purest, most special thing along the way—person, place, moment,
memory, sentiment, experience, accomplishment. Got it? Now multi-
ply that tenfold. That does not begin to describe how impossibly delicious E is.

I am not unaware of how redolent this is of Timothy Leary's often
loopy proselytizing for LSD, and I know how out of step is the sort of
ethos he once so widely touted—turn on, tune in, drop out—but this
has nothing to do with that. Ecstasy is a clarifier. That, ultimately, is its
value. That it enables one to see, feel and think, if not more deeply,
then certainly more clearly. That it clears the deck of all that is un-
clear that one might more clearly—and immediately—experience

that clarity. And not just in the moment. The high, as all highs do, sub-sides, but the clarity, the lucidity lingers. The residue of the *roll*.

In that sense, not to mention in its chemical composition, it is quite the opposite of LSD, which at the peak of its use came cauled—for all I know, still does; I never have used LSD and am possessed of no in-clination to do so—in all sorts of religious accoutrements and conno-tations. (One does not, by the way, hallucinate on E, not even mildly, at least I never have. Nor does one become or perceive oneself as having become someone or something else. One remains indubitably oneself, just vastly, profoundly more so.) Ecstasy has nothing to do with reli-gion, save to make clear to its user that such religion—the questing after something more or higher, the meaning of God and existence, the miracle of faith, call it what you will—while understandable (a whole lot is understandable on E, a lot more than is understandable off of it), is mainly nonsense. There is no need to quest, not any more, for what is being quested after is right here, right now—the birth of a state of better being.

Ecstasy is a clarifier, but it is a personal clarifier. It is not—despite all the peace/love/unity/respect hype surrounding it—a universal one. Its lessons may be universal in their implications, but they are in-tended to be applied to oneself, not to be shared with one's neighbour, friends, colleagues or community. Which is not to say that the drug does not have its social dimensions or that one ought not do E in the company of others. Indeed I would not find it congenial to do, nor have I ever done it, alone. (As close as I ever came was on an unpeo-pled, night-time side street in downtown London, and it was raining, and it was one of the memorable experiences of my life—neon, glis-tening, menthol, veneered in layer after thickening layer of thick honey. Lovely streets, London, and lovely, so lovely, its rain.)

But better by far to do it with those one loves, and best of all with one's one-and-only lover. The point is, one must do it oneself to truly "get it." Listening to the stories and anecdotes of others or such les-sons as they may have drawn from the experience, reading an arti-cle such as this one certainly does no harm, but everyone takes from E something different, something as uniquely, idiosyncratically private as the person taking it. And if what one takes in the broadest sense is all about human connection and empathy—E has proven highly effec-tive in certain kinds of couples therapy—it is all the more about connecting with and feeling empathy for oneself. It is, contrary to its image as the current drug of choice among teenagers and the prevalence of its use at their bacchanalian, all-night, tribal dance rites—their "raves"—the most intimate of drugs.

I did it my first time with the woman I mentioned earlier, the one who saved me. It was her first time as well. Neither of us used or so much as experimented with illegal drugs—we typically limited ourselves to wine, beer and cigarettes, and those in moderation—and we were, as zero hour approached, visibly apprehensive, an attitude, I think, that is healthy, as it is only sane. Perhaps—who knows?—it even exaggerated the impact of what was about to occur.

It was, in our case, a pair of Calvin Kleins. EX comes in a variety of shapes, sizes, colours and brand names—Nikes, Mitsubishis, Motorolas, Versaces, Rolling Stones, etc.—thousands of types, each with their subtle distinctions with respect to the quality and length of the *roll*. I recall their being round, perhaps oblong, about the size of a Tylenol, smaller, and of some somehow comforting amber hue. As I say, I was too apprehensive to register all of the details. My heart, its thumpeting, was in the way.

We had cleared our schedules ahead of time, switched off the phones, and we were in her home, just the two of us, in our bathrobes, in the living room, on the couch—a couch, it is fit to say, with which we were by that time well acquainted. Van was on the stereo, *Astral Weeks, Moondance, Common One, The Best of: Volume One.* A fire was roaring in the fireplace and we were feeding it. The lamp on the end table was turned way down low. It was mid-evening, and we had ready, as my son had taken care to instruct us, our pair of tumblers and pitchers of iced-down spring water. E increases body temperature and heart rate and elevates blood pressure, so drinking water—not beer, not liquor—is pro forma as one rolls along. And one wishes to drink, because E causes dehydration—one of its most immediate side effects is dry mouth. (Interesting, because what it does to one's emotions is precisely the opposite. It lubricates them, emulsifies, one's feelings as gels and butters and lotions.)

With much mutually nervous, serio-comic, ceremonial chit-chat, then, we each popped our pill, swallowed, waited, and—nothing.

We locked eyes. We still were alive. I think we were only half amazed. I know we were relieved. Van was still belting as only Van can.

If I was dying I knew that this was how I wanted to do it; I can think of worse voices to hear with one's dying breath than that of the Belfast Cowboy's wailing, "It's too late to stop now!" as indeed at that moment it was. (The young are partial to other ways: techno, electronica, trance, jungle, house, hardcore, gabba, drum and bass, and they are not, I might suggest to those of another, older generation, to my generation, without their merits. Indeed, they constitute the very aural-assault, awash-in-the-sonics brand of music tailor-made to maximize the benefits of a certain kind of more, shall we say, kinetic experience. To each their own.)

Typically, it takes a while for Ecstasy to kick in. Thirty-five minutes is precipitous, that twice over dilatory. It depends—on the pill, mainly, but also on the contents of one's stomach (empty is better than full), on one's mood (up is better than down), on one's physical/mental state (alert is better than exhausted). So, that first time, you sit and wonder, precisely because you have the time to do so, if what is going to happen really is going to happen, and if it does, just when it may occur, and how you will know. And then it does, the *roll* begins—the world around you billows open like an eye—and you stop wondering those things. You stop on a dime and you go, or rather, are lifted and taken—coronaed, crowned, coroneted, spangled and lantern-lit, your smiling face flambeaued as a thousand chandeliers.

One of the most discernible early effects—it happened that first time, though often it does not, being a function of the chemical composition of the pill—is what I have heard described as "fluttery" vision, but which I prefer to describe as "staggered" or "ratcheted" or "toggled." This phenomenon is as close to an hallucinatory quality as E produces, and it is so mild—and weirdly pleasant—that to label it as such is frankly inaccurate. When it happened to us we knew it immediately—that is, we knew something was going on, something . . . extra—and we looked at one another, smiled, and virtually in unison commented upon it. As I recall—we are both fifty years old, remember—we thought it "cool."

It is a little difficult to describe. One's vision does not blur, nor do images get darker or lighter, pulse, expand or contract, fragment or disintegrate, or change colour, but they do get a little, I suppose *choppy* is the word, choppy but not chopped up. That is, they remain intact and stationary—a lamp's a lamp, a window's a window, a fire's a fire—

they just move a little, as if jagged were a verb, within the texture of their own lines. These striations. Very unthreatening, and very, well, cool. (Rad. Phat. Whatever.) There is bound to be a medical explanation for it, perhaps there is even a name, but I remain ignorant of such and so intend to remain.

And then suddenly Van was singing waaaaay over there, and then waaaaay inside here, right inside, ground zero, the very epicentre, the pith of my brain, pathing through, yet way outside and up above and down below and all around as well, vaulting in dips, convolving in loops, volplaning, vanplaning, brimming up, pouring forth, washing over and enveloping the room even as he filled and spanned and embraced in the spread of the swoon of his voice, the wings of its swanning, every corner and corridor and cubbyhole of the house inside my head. This capacious passing through of each and every note of his music, not only as sound, but as resonant space—particle, wave—and as I have learned since, time. And that also was. Cool.

What happened next was that everything and all at once, while clearly remaining itself, its old self, at the same time not became, but *was* its altered self, transfigured, transmogrified, a new self, a simultaneously deeper and higher, older and newer self, and so a better self— everything smoother and softer and rounder, every edge bull-nosed, every surface sanded. And warmer. Which was curious. Because it didn't feel warmer, it just looked warmer. But as much as the surroundings . . . bloomed, it was in myself that the blossoming burgeoned, surged, swelled, an harmonic wind of well-being, cognate and congruent, and in its passage, home—the world as nest, and as womb.

In any event, the world was suddenly guilt- and worry- and wrinkle-free, palpably, beautifully buoyant—visually, texturally, aurally— transcendently right and renewed, arresting and exquisite and sublime and glorious and divine (sometimes words are paltry things, such puny things), more of any and all of those things than I had ever thought possible. Or perhaps I had thought them possible, and perhaps that is part of the point: that whatever beautiful thing one can imagine or has ever imagined, it is that much more beautiful on E. I cannot prove this theory, and it would mean that those with more active or fecund or developed imaginations are likely to have better, more maximally beautiful experiences. Or perhaps it is simply that they are more acutely attuned to the beauty of those experiences. As I say, I cannot prove this, and I can conceive of no plausible way of doing so. (It is similar to the old conundrum about whether the more well-endowed man has the more intense orgasm. But how to measure such a thing? There is not, nor can there ever be a basis for comparison.) All the same, the proposition feels right to me.

And so we looked at one another and felt one another, with our fingers and our lips and our tongues, indeed with the whole of our new-found faces, this plumbing of the new map of our bodies—new softer hair, new smoother flesh, new pinker, fresher, more fragrant, shimmering, altogether fluffier genitalia (fluffier is precisely the word)—and we smelled and tasted one another—she smelled of burst peaches and tasted as the recent salts of pearls—because one's sense of smell and taste is no less augmented and intensified, honed and heightened than are the other senses. That is, we bathed in one another, each of our five senses, the ten in all, because that commingling is what had taken place, its rhapsody, and humanity, and caress. And as the world includes oneself, and as at that moment it included my lover, we looked to one another exactly as we felt and smelled and tasted: rapturous, heavenly, transcendent, numinous, aglow. She a resplendent, bejewelled goddess, I a radiant god. "Their eyes came open into the soul of the other," Don DeLillo once wrote of a kindred experience, the "flow of time." That, in so many words, is, to a very serif, how it was.

Later, if still in midstream, I got up, walked to the bathroom—walking on E is no more difficult than walking on water or floating on air—and looked in the mirror. I wanted to see what I looked like—I am just vain enough that the thought occurred to me even in the midst of the *roll*—though I already had seen reflected in my lover's eyes that I looked sufficiently, there is no other word, gorgeous. (If I looked half as gorgeous as she did to me I reckoned I was in for a treat.) And the person I saw looking back at me was, gorgeous, but gorgeous in a way that floored almost as much as it thrilled me.

———

As I have mentioned, I am almost fifty years old, and here, now, as I stared grinning in astonishment, I looked twenty-eight. And not some fifty-year-old version of myself at twenty-eight, but me the way I was back then, back when, when I was twenty-eight. I moved closer, peered harder. I could scarcely believe it. I had recaptured myself. Dorian Gray. Fountain of Youth. Foods of the Gods. Spontaneous regeneration. Metempsychosis. Somehow I had been restored, and I felt what I can only describe as an all-consuming nostalgia for the present.

And then, after helping each other off with our bathrobes, our old, nubby, cotton-twill bathrobes—suddenly spun of the finest cashmere and angelica, these clouds of talcum and down—we embraced, and kissed, and more, we got down, as is said, and as used to be said, to business, and she whispered in my ear: "We've found fucking gold."

It distinctly was not an out-of-the-body experience, as it was not a mind-expanding one.

It distinctly was a further-into-the-body experience, and a mind-clarifying one. An impenetrably penetrating experience. An excavation of the self. An exhumation of the other. Because that is how one finds gold—one exhumes it, excavates, one digs for it, deep, and deeper.

And so we did. We dug. For four hours we dug, sinking further into each other, as likewise into ourselves, and eventually, after four hours of digging, digging that was in its every decline mutually synchronized, after four hours that felt exactly like forty minutes—for on E, unlike, say, on grass, time flies, sails by, condensed, abbreviated, attenuated and tremendously foreshortened—we found it. Only it wasn't gold. It was something far better. It was sex, the very EX in sex—and the climb and climax of sex—as revelation. And as soul.

So I take it back. Maybe Ecstasy does have something to do with religion, although the word spirit seems to me a more felicitous fit, because the peace one feels, and the insights one gains—epiphanies may be a better word—are no less than oceanic. They are tidal, as they are catholic. You know, afterwards, that you contain oceans, oceans you previously had but the faintest inkling existed, and that those oceans are filled with beauty and grace and light and love—more words, bankrupt words—and that they are yours, yours to share as it may please and delight you.

And this, I might argue, is not a bad thing. Indeed it is so much the opposite of a bad thing that I believe it is worth the cost of that which one must pay to purchase it. Because there is a cost, that cost is high, it is as expensive as it is extravagant, and much like the experience itself, it is one which varies with each occasion as it fluctuates with each person who encounters that dark piper.

The simple truth is, when you eat Ecstasy, you are deliberately messing with your mind, or more accurately your brain, or more accurately still your brain chemistry. You are releasing, in a rush, as a deluge or monsoon—and that rush is unnatural, unnatural in the sense that had God intended you to experience it it would not require a flock of white-coated "cookers" in a clandestine laboratory someplace in Holland or Israel or France to design and customize a pill for you to do so, nor would the delivery and distribution of those pills so lavishly profit the Mob—you are, as I say, triggering a veritable tsunami of serotonin, the human body's pleasure juice, that in turn floods in the most sensory, sentient way your consciousness, which in turn turns everything "gold," or rather, golden. (Again, there is available—there always is—an exact, physiological explanation of the phenomenon and the anatomical circuitry and neural pathways involved, and again I have no interest in pursuing it. Why demystify what is in its sum, if not its parts, so mystical?) And in the wake of that rush—not the day after perhaps, when you are still basking, deliciously exhausted in its afterglow (albeit that a deep, submuscular, burning neck, shoulder and back discomfort often compromise it), but the day after that, or the next, or the next, what I have heard described as "Black Tuesday"— you run the risk not only of emotionally crashing, but of feeling so rawly depleted (because your tank of serotonin is running on no more than fumes), that you are tempted to pledge, "I have never felt this awful in my life, as empty, hollowed, flat, so soulless and lost to myself, so amputated and abscised, so emotionally exsanguinated, and I shall never, not ever, do this again." And also, "Whatever was I thinking?"

My advice, for what it is worth: wait a minimum of four weeks, the time purportedly required for one's serotonin to refill its reservoir and your thoughts and feelings to sort themselves through and get up and running again, before repeating the performance. Do it more often than that, get too greedy, and the upshot is "E-tardism"—a trimming down, clipping-off and curbing of the drug's effects, not to mention possible long-term damage to the serotonergic nerve grid of the brain, damage of the sort that may leave you so addled, you will find it not only a full-time challenge to control your own drool, but to recall that words are composed of letters and that each represents an actual sound, one intended to be pronounced aloud. So: moderation in all things, even things that are excessively restorative, for on occasion, cures do kill.

But here is the Catch-22 with which one inevitably must grapple, or at least I did, and still do: what one thinks—if one stops to think about it—is precisely this: "What is a mind, if not something to be messed with? What is consciousness, if not a state to be altered?" I mean this quite seriously, quite literally, and if it helps to substitute for the phrase "messed with" the word "clarified" or "purified" or "al-chemized" or "beautified" or "beatified" then perhaps my meaning is taken. A mind is a terrible thing to waste, and there is much being wasted when one deliberately chooses not to explore the ecstasy of its deeper horizons.

"Everyone is doing the best he can to keep the dark/from climbing over his back," Charlie Smith writes in his brilliant new collection of poems, *Heroin*. "Life should be ecstasy," Allen Ginsberg told an interviewer before his death. They are right. In our way, we are all doing our best to dodge the dark while clearing a space where a little ecstasy might be permitted to bloom. I am only suggesting that our best can be still better, and that there exists this way of making it so, and that it is ours for the literal taking.

Perhaps there are those who feel no need to do so, to experience such ecstasy, that they are blessed with a sufficiency of it in their daily lives. Perhaps there are those who feel that such ecstasy, because it is "unnatural," induced artificially, chemically, "under the influence," cannot possibly be "existentially authentic," and must therefore be false, a fraud and a lie, and that it cannot possibly be sustained. Perhaps there are those who suspect that the disparity is too great, that having experienced such ecstasy, they will find it too daunting to endure the rigours and asperities of a mundane, largely prosaic, often overwhelm-ingly corrupt and ugly world. Perhaps there are those who feel that such ecstasy cannot be reconciled with their religious, political, philo-sophical or domestic agendas, that it threatens or violates the very essence of that in which they are so wholly invested. Perhaps there are those who are reluctant to risk engaging in what our culture defines as socially unacceptable, even legally transgressive behaviour. Perhaps there are those who are afraid of footing the physical and emotional toll, or of becoming psychologically addicted. And perhaps there are those who simply, unapologetically, are flat-out scared. Scared of beauty. And of bliss.

There are such people, and they are most people, almost all people, and they have every right to their feelings and beliefs, values and convictions. They are, after all, but the sum of having lived lives that are unimaginable to any of us but those who have honourably lived them. I know, because I was, for most of my own, one of them.

I am not any more, one of them. I am not one of anything. I am, trite as it may sound, simply me, and here lately, that is more than enough. It is plenty. And there is something else, a secret: there are times, once a month, sometimes more or less, when the truth of that makes me, well, ecstatic.

My son? He is nineteen now, and in his spare time—having some months ago kicked the Ecstasy habit himself—he spins mixes at raves, and this fall he is entering college, quite a reputable college, as a Psychology major. And he is writing poetry again. Brilliant stuff, more brilliant than ever. This righting of his ship, and the compass of its course.

Minor triumphs perhaps. Still, it does make one wonder. Would he have made it back intact without E? Would he have arrived at that which all of us deserve and so few manage to find, his chance for happiness? And it makes one wonder, too, you know, about what they say: Better living through chemistry.

Notes About the Contributors

FREDERICK BARTHELME is a short-story writer, novelist, and memoirist. He is the author of numerous works, including *Moon Deluxe* (1983), *Bob the Gambler* (1997), *Double Down* (1999), and *The Law of Averages: New and Selected Stories* (2000).

STEVEN BARTHELME is a short-story writer and memoirist. His works include *And He Tells the Little Horse the Whole Story* (1987) and *Double Down* (1999).

KATE BRAVERMAN is a poet, short-story writer, and novelist. Her works include *Lithium for Medea* (first published in 1979 and reissued in 2002), *Lullaby for Sinners* (1980), *Palm Latitudes* (1989), *Squandering the Blue* (1990), *Wonders of the West* (1997), *Small Craft Warnings* (1998), and *The Incantation of Frida K* (2002). She lives in rural western New York.

MARGARET BULLITT-JONAS is a writer and an Episcopal priest. She is the author of *Holy Hunger: A Memoir of Desire* (1998) and is also the associate rector of All Saints Parish in Brookline, Massachusetts.

WILLIAM S. BURROUGHS (1914–97) was an American novelist and essayist who lived as an expatriate in Paris. His works include *Junkie* (1953), *Naked Lunch* (1959), *Exterminator!* (1960), *The Wild Boys* (1971), *Port of Saints* (1980), *Cities of the Red Night* (1981), *Queer* (1985), *The Adding Machine* (1986), and *Interzone* (1989).

JOHN CHEEVER (1912–82) was a short-story writer and novelist. His works include *The Way Some People Live* (1943), *The Wapshot Chronicle* (1957), *The Housebreaker of Shady Hill* (1958), *Some People, Places and Things That Will Not Appear in My Next Novel* (1961), *The Brigadier and the Golf Widow* (1964), *Bullet Park* (1969), and *Falconer* (1977).

THOMAS DE QUINCEY (1785–1859) was a widely published English essayist. He is the author of *Confessions of an English Opium-Eater* (1821) and *Autobiographic Sketches* (1853).

VIRGIL G. EATON (1850–1917) a prominent nineteenth-century newspaperman, was editor in chief of the *Bangor News* in Bangor, Maine, and also wrote articles for *The Boston Globe* and *The New York Sun.*

SIGMUND FREUD (1856–1939) was an Austrian neurologist. Best known as the founder of psychoanalysis, he is the coauthor of *Studies in Hysteria* (1895) and the author of *The Cocaine Papers* (1884), *The Interpretation of Dreams* (1900), *Three Essays on the Theory of Sexuality* (1905), *Introductory Lectures on Psychoanalysis* (1917), *The Ego and the Id* (1923), and *Civilization and Its Discontents* (1930), among other works.

MARGARITA SPALDING GERRY (1870–1939) was an American playwright, short-story writer, and biographer. She is the author of *The Toy Shop: A Story of Abraham Lincoln* (1908).

O. HENRY (1862–1910) is the pseudonym of William Sydney Porter. A newspaper columnist and master short-story writer, he is the author of *The Four Million* (1906), which includes "The Gift of the Magi," *Heart of the West* (1907), *The Voice of the City* (1908), *Roads of Destiny* (1909), *Whirligigs* (1910), *Sixes and Sevens* (1911), *Rolling Stones* (1912), *Waifs and Strays* (1917), and *Postscripts* (1923).

WILLIAM LEE HOWARD (1860–1918) was an American physician. In the early 1900s he published numerous articles on child-rearing.

ALDOUS HUXLEY (1894–1963) was an English novelist and essayist. Best known for his satirical novel *Brave New World* (1932), he is also the author of *Antic Hay* (1923), *Point Counter Point* (1928), *Eyeless in Gaza* (1936), and *The Doors of Perception* (1954), among other works.

JACK LONDON (1876–1916) was an American short-story writer, novelist, and memoirist. His works include *The Call of the Wild* (1903), *White Fang* (1906), *Love of Life* (1907), *Martin Eden* (1909), *South Sea Tales* (1911), and *John Barleycorn* (1913).

DOROTHY PARKER (1893–1967) was a critic, poet, playwright, and short-story writer. Her works include *Enough Rope* (1926), *Sunset Gun* (1928), *Death and Taxes* (1931), *After Such Pleasures* (1933), and *Here Lies* (1939).

EDGAR ALLAN POE (1809–49) was an American poet, short-story writer, and critic. Widely considered the father of the modern detective story, he is the author of "The Fall of the House of Usher" (1839), "The Tell-Tale Heart" (1843), "The Murders in the Rue Morgue" (1841), and "The Purloined Letter" (1844), among other works.

SUE WILLIAM SILVERMAN is a memoirist. She is the author of *Because I Remember Terror, Father, I Remember You* (1999), and *Love Sick: One Woman's Journey Through Sexual Addiction* (2001).

TERRY SOUTHERN (1924–2000) was a screenwriter, novelist, and short-story writer. His works include the novels *Candy* (1958), *The Magic Christian* (1959), and *Texas Summer* (1991).

DONNA STEINER is a poet and essayist. Her work has appeared in the *Bellingham Review* and *Utne Reader*. She teaches creative writing, composition, and literature at Pima Community College in Tucson, Arizona.

LEO TOLSTOY (1828–1910) was a Russian novelist and philosopher. He is the author of *War and Peace* (1869), *Anna Karenina* (1877), *The Death of Ivan Ilyich* (1886), and *Resurrection* (1899), among other works.

ABRAHAM VERGHESE is a physician and writer. He is the author of numerous short stories as well as *My Own Country: A Doctor's Story* (1994), an account of his experiences treating AIDS patients.

LINDA YABLONSKY is a critic and novelist. She is the author of *The Story of Junk* (1997).

PERMISSION CREDITS

REBECCA SHANNONHOUSE is a freelance writer and the editor of *Out of Her Mind: Women Writing on Madness* (now available as a Modern Library trade paperback). Her writing has appeared in *The New York Times,* the *San Francisco Chronicle, USA Today,* and other publications. She lives in Greenwich, Connecticut.

A Note on the Type

The principal text of this Modern Library edition
was set in a digitized version of Janson, a typeface that
dates from about 1690 and was cut by Nicholas Kis,
a Hungarian working in Amsterdam. The original matrices have
survived and are held by the Stempel foundry in Germany.
Hermann Zapf redesigned some of the weights and sizes for
Stempel, basing his revisions on the original design.

MODERN LIBRARY IS ONLINE AT
WWW.MODERNLIBRARY.COM

MODERN LIBRARY ONLINE IS YOUR GUIDE TO CLASSIC LITERATURE ON THE WEB

THE MODERN LIBRARY E-NEWSLETTER

Our free e-mail newsletter is sent to subscribers, and features sample chapters, interviews with and essays by our authors, upcoming books, special promotions, announcements, and news.

To subscribe to the Modern Library e-newsletter, send a blank e-mail to: **join-modernlibrary@list.randomhouse.com** or visit **www.modernlibrary.com**

THE MODERN LIBRARY WEBSITE

Check out the Modern Library website at
www.modernlibrary.com for:

• The Modern Library e-newsletter
• A list of our current and upcoming titles and series
• Reading Group Guides and exclusive author spotlights
• Special features with information on the classics and other paperback series
• Excerpts from new releases and other titles
• A list of our e-books and information on where to buy them
• The Modern Library Editorial Board's 100 Best Novels and 100 Best Nonfiction Books of the Twentieth Century written in the English language
• News and announcements

Questions? E-mail us at **modernlibrary@randomhouse.com**
For questions about examination or desk copies, please visit
the Random House Academic Resources site at
www.randomhouse.com/academic